ANTICHRIST
in Seventeenth-Century
England

UNIVERSITY OF
NEWCASTLE UPON TYNE
PUBLICATIONS

ANTICHRIST
in Seventeenth-Century England

———

The Riddell Memorial Lectures
Forty-first Series
delivered at the
University of Newcastle upon Tyne
on 3, 4, and 5 November 1969

BY

CHRISTOPHER HILL

Master of Balliol College
Oxford

LONDON
OXFORD UNIVERSITY PRESS
NEW YORK   TORONTO
1971

Oxford University Press, Ely House, London W. 1

GLASGOW   NEW YORK   TORONTO   MELBOURNE   WELLINGTON
CAPE TOWN   SALISBURY   IBADAN   NAIROBI   DAR ES SALAAM   LUSAKA   ADDIS ABABA
BOMBAY   CALCUTTA   MADRAS   KARACHI   LAHORE   DACCA
KUALA LUMPUR   SINGAPORE   HONG KONG   TOKYO

SBN 19 713911 6

PRINTED IN GREAT BRITAIN

PREFACE

I AM deeply grateful to the University of Newcastle upon Tyne, and the Riddell Memorial Lectures Committee, for the honour conferred on me by the invitation to deliver, in November 1969, the Riddell Memorial Lectures contained in this book. I have slightly expanded the text in an attempt to substantiate some points which could merely be asserted in lectures. I am also indebted to members of the Dean Kitchin Society of St. Catherine's College, Oxford, and of the History Society of the University of East Anglia, on whom I inflicted earlier versions of these lectures. The discussions which followed produced many helpful criticisms. I am particularly grateful to one member of my Norwich audience whom I have been unable to identify (see p. 167 below). The pioneering book of Mr. W. M. Lamont, *Godly Rule*, appeared after my text had been drafted, but I am indebted to this stimulating work for many ideas. So I am to Dr. Marjorie Reeves's *The Influence of Prophecy in the Later Middle Ages* (Oxford, 1969), which she generously allowed me to read before publication. My thanks are due to Mrs. P. Jayakar and Miss P. Lloyd for help with the typing, and to Lauren and Simon Adams, who undertook the tedious task of reading the proofs.

In quoting from seventeenth-century sources I have modernized spelling and capitalization, except in titles of books. Years are dated in the New Style. I sometimes cite a seventeenth-century source for matters like the beliefs of the Waldenses or the Huguenots, since for my purposes, what men thought about the past is even more important than what actually happened.

C.H.

Balliol College
January 1970

CONTENTS

ABBREVIATIONS

The following abbreviations have been used in the footnotes:

D.N.B.	*Dictionary of National Biography*
E.E.T.S.	Early English Text Society
O.E.D.	*Oxford English Dictionary*
P.M.L.A.	*Proceedings of the Modern Language Association*
P. and P.	*Past and Present*
T.R.H.S.	*Transactions of the Royal Historical Society*
V.C.H.	*Victoria County History*

The fourth ground of your hope is from the enemy with whom you have to deal, namely the Beast, the Dragon and the false Prophet, whose ruin the Lord of Hosts hath vowed and determined. It is a great advantage to know our enemies, but a greater encouragement to know that our enemies are God's enemies.

A[lexander] L[eighton], *Speculum Belli Sacri* (Amsterdam, 1624), pp. 304–5.

Judge Newdigate: What is Antichrist?

Boswell Middleton: He that practiseth and holdeth up those things which Jesus Christ witnesseth against is Antichrist.

Judge: What things are those?

B. M.: Such as are called of men masters, and go in long robes, and have the chief place in the assemblies, salutations in the market places, etc. Read to that in thy own conscience.

Judge: Thou art mad and talkest nonsense.

Examination of Boswell Middleton at York, 17 July 1654, in J. Besse, *An Abstract of the Sufferings of the People called Quakers*, i (1733), pp. 485–6.

I

BEFORE 1640:
THE ROMAN ANTICHRIST

Good and evil seem often to lie together flat upon the
world's surface. At other times they start up, like
armed men, and prepare for the last struggle.

BENJAMIN JOWETT, 'Excursus on the Man of
Sin', in *The Epistles of St. Paul to the Thessalonians,
Galatians, Romans* (2nd ed. 1859), i, p. 193.

I

My subject is one which meant a great deal to thinkers
of the sixteenth and early seventeenth centuries, but
which historians have tended to ignore: Antichrist, or
the Beast. So I must begin by defending it. The historian,
as Dean Inge said, is a natural snob. He tends to be on
the defensive about the past, *his* past: to cover up its
irrationalities except when these can be used to explain
failure. We stress the belief in the imminence of the end
of the world in Fifth Monarchists and others whom
historians arrogantly and wrongly label 'the lunatic
fringe'. We mention less often that John Milton, Sir
Henry Vane, and Sir Isaac Newton shared these beliefs.
Similarly with Antichrist, whose coming was to precede
the end of the world. His stock has slumped since the
seventeenth century. His very existence may now be
doubted. When R. H. Tawney wrote 'capitalism today

... is not so much un-Christian as anti-Christian',[1] the last adjective presumably meant 'hostile to Christianity', rather than 'pertaining to Antichrist' as it would have done in the seventeenth century. Nietzsche's *Der Antichrist* is more properly translated *The Antichristian* than *The Antichrist*.

But for many centuries Antichrist seemed an intensely real and very important person. Thomas Beard, Oliver Cromwell's schoolmaster and a best-seller in his day, said firmly: 'Next unto our Lord and Saviour Jesus Christ, there is nothing so necessary as the true and solid knowledge of Antichrist.'[2] The fact that in September 1638, at the height of the Scottish troubles, so eminent a person as Sir William Waller, future Parliamentarian general, was eagerly corresponding with Samuel Hartlib and John Dury about the number of the Beast[3] could perhaps be dismissed as the type of mild eccentricity permissible to generals in England. But when we find that John Pym, Oliver Cromwell, John Lilburne, Gerrard Winstanley, Henry Oldenburg, Secretary of the Royal Society, and the great Sir Isaac Newton himself were all interested in Antichrist, it is clear that there is something important here. The historian ignores at his peril a body of ideas which at one time aroused intense passion and controversy. He must try to explain what lies behind ideological concepts which have lost their significance for him. History is not an exclusively rational process.

[1] R. H. Tawney, 'A Note on Christianity and the Social Order', in *The Attack and Other Papers* (1953), p. 170.

[2] Thomas Beard, *Antichrist the Pope of Rome* (1625), preface.

[3] G. H. Turnbull, *Hartlib, Dury and Comenius* (Liverpool University Press, 1947), p. 197.

What seems to us a blind alley in human thought was for a hundred and fifty years after the Reformation— and for most of the fifteen hundred years before it, though this is not my concern here—full of life and significance. This indeed is natural. The Bible was generally believed to be an inspired book, containing divine truth on all matters; to be a guide to action in all spheres of life. That is why the medieval church had frowned on translation and study of the Bible by laymen. But the Reformation and the printing press changed all that in England. Bible commentators seemed to be precise—if unagreed—that many passages in the Old and New Testaments described the characteristics of Antichrist, whose overthrow was a necessary prelude to the coming of Christ's kingdom. Those who in the revolutionary crises of the sixteenth and early seventeenth centuries felt it their duty to hasten this historic process naturally wanted to know who the Antichrist was whose downfall was at hand. Was he the Pope? Bishops? The episcopal church generally? Any state church? Any political authority maintaining a state church? Or persecuting? Monarchy? Or was it just a term of abuse to be hurled at anybody one disliked? We shall come across all these interpretations and many more, since my object in these lectures is to consider the changing content of the Antichrist legend: as historian, not theologian.

The word Antichrist occurs in the Bible only in the Epistles of St. John, where it is applied to deceivers (in the plural) who deny that Jesus is the Messiah. Their existence is evidence that the last time is at hand. But Calvin and the Geneva translation of the Bible, which was used and pored over by three generations of English protestants before the Civil War, adopted a traditional identification of Antichrist with 'the Man of Sin', 'the son of perdition', who 'as God sitteth in the temple of God', of 2 Thessalonians 2: 3–9. Calvin and the marginal notes to the Geneva Bible further identified this 'adversary', 'the mystery of iniquity', with the Papacy. 'All men know who he is that saith he can shut up heaven and open it at his pleasure, and took upon him to be Lord and Master above all kings and princes, before whom kings and princes fall down and worship, honouring that Antichrist as a God.'[1] But the Pope was also taken to be prefigured by the second Beast in Revelation 13. In the Geneva notes the first Beast is defined as the Roman Empire. The second Beast has swallowed up all the authority of the first. 'The first empire Roman was as the pattern, and this second empire is but an image and shadow thereof.' Hobbes's famous phrase, calling the papacy the 'ghost of the deceased Roman Empire sitting crowned on the grave thereof',[2] puts into epigrammatic form what was for his protestant contemporaries the most obvious of platitudes, as Hobbes so often did.

So the second Beast in Revelation 13 and the Man of Sin in 2 Thessalonians 2 were traditionally identified with the Antichrist of John's Epistles, and all three with the Pope. The number of the Beast is 666: there are at least nine different ways in which the letters of the Pope's name or titles can be added up to that number.

---

[1] Note on 2 Thessalonians 2: 3–4. Cf. 1 Timothy 4: 1–4.

[2] T. Hobbes, *Leviathan* (Pelican ed.), p. 712. Cf. Milton: Rome 'endeavouring to keep up her old universal empire under a new name and mere shadow of a catholic religion' (*A Treatise of Civil Power in Ecclesiastical Causes* (1659), in *Works* (Columbia University Press, 1931–40), p. 19).

If you take the square root it gives the same result.[1] There are other entrancing mathematical problems in interpreting 'a time, times and half a time', which could mean anything from $3\frac{1}{2}$ days to 1,260 years. And once horned beasts are in question, there is a lot to be found in the prophecies of Daniel: though the Geneva Bible was more cautious than some commentators in identifying the Little Horn with the Pope.[2]

'Anti-', as Mr. Lucken points out,[3] means not only 'opposed to' but also 'equivalent to' or 'substitute for': this sense lends itself to a Manichean dualism, and helps to explain why 'true and solid knowledge of Antichrist' is the next most important thing to knowledge of Christ. In French the name is Antéchrist, before Christ: this sense is also to be borne in mind when Antichrist is associated with the last days.

Antichrist, the Beast, was not merely the Pope as a person, however, but the papacy as an institution which subsumed within itself all the evil, coercive, repressive aspects of the secular Empire: 'a most wicked and most insolent tyranny . . . usurped over the persons of men . . . and over their goods and actions'.[4] Antichrist therefore could stand for political repression in the name of religion, for the coercive organs associated therewith, and especially for the persecution of the righteous. 'This wicked Antichrist comprehendeth the whole succession

[1] Andreas Helvigius, *Antichristus Romanus* (Wittenberg, 1612), *passim*; F. Potter, *An Interpretation of the Number 666* (1642), chapter 12. See p. 28 below.

[2] Note on Daniel 7: 8. Chapters 7–12 are relevant.

[3] L. U. Lucken, *Antichrist and the Prophets of Antichrist in the Chester Cycle* (Washington, D.C., 1940), pp. 11–13. Cf. [Anon.], *Napiers Narration* (1641), sig. C^{v}–C2.

[4] Geneva Bible, note on Revelation 13: 16–17.

of the persecutors of the church.'[1] The Geneva Bible summarized the Apocalypse in the following words:

The lively description of Antichrist is set forth, whose time and power notwithstanding is limited, and albeit that he is permitted to ˋrage against the elect, yet his power stretcheth no further than to the hurt of their bodies. . . . For a season God will permit this Antichrist and strumpet under cover of fair speech and pleasant doctrine to deceive the world. . . . Read diligently, judge soberly, and call earnestly to God for the true understanding hereof.

The identification of the Pope with Antichrist had a long history. I hope I may be forgiven for passing lightly over the first fifteen hundred years of it. There are books on the subject.[2] But Antichrist did not figure only in scholarly and theological treatises in the Middle Ages. He appeared in the German *Play of Antichrist* (*c.* 1160), in the fourteenth-century Chester Miracle Plays, the Northumbrian *Cursor Mundi* and Langland's *Piers Plowman*, and in many other English, French, Italian, and German poems and plays, especially of the fourteenth century. In this popular literature he acquired many mythical, non-biblical characteristics, which it was one of the concerns of protestant scholarship to purge. By the end of the fourteenth century Matthew of Janov could say that Antichrist was so well known that when he appeared even small children

[1] Note on 2 Thessalonians 2: 3–4.

[2] E. Renan, *L'Antéchrist* (1873), esp. pp. 179–80, 415–17; W. Bousset, *The Antichrist Legend* (1896); E. Wadstein, *Die eschatologische Ideengruppe Antichrist-Weltsabbat-Weltende und Weltgericht* (Leipzig, 1896); E. Sacher, *Sibyllinische Texte und Forschungen* (Halle, 1898); H. Preuss, *Die Vorstellung vom Antichrist im späteren Mittelalter* (Leipzig, 1906); M. Reeves, *The Influence of Prophecy in the Later Middle Ages* (Oxford University Press, 1969), Part III, *passim*; *Puritans, the Millennium and the Future of Israel*, ed. P. Toon (Cambridge, 1970), pp. 12, 18, 26, and *passim*.

would recognize him.[1] A century and a quarter later Luther wished that his ancestors had inculcated the doctrine of Christ with as much diligence and zeal as they discussed Antichrist; Calvin too thought papists had talked far too much about Antichrist.[2]

The coming of Antichrist was associated with the last times. But the charge of being a forerunner of Antichrist, or Antichrist himself, was part of the normal vocabulary of abuse of medieval politicians, freely used by popes and emperors from the eleventh century onwards. Gregory VII was called Antichrist; Gregory IX thought Frederick II was a forerunner of Antichrist; but Frederick thought the Pope *was* Antichrist. When two rival popes existed, it was natural to think with Bernard of Clairvaux that 'the Beast of the Apocalypse' had 'seized the throne of Peter'.[3]

But those who most regularly and consistently equated the Pope or the papacy with Antichrist were the heretics—Joachim of Flora (*c.* 1135–1202), the Cathars, who thought Pope Sylvester I was Antichrist, the Albigensians, the Waldensians, the Spiritual Franciscans, the Fraticelli, Wyclif and the Lollards,

[1] Ed. J. Wright, *The Play of Antichrist* (Toronto, 1967), and references there cited; ed. Matthew, *The Chester Plays*, Part II (E.E.T.S., 1916); L. U. Lucken, *Antichrist and the Prophets of Antichrist in the Chester Cycle*; W. Langland, *The Vision of Piers Plowman*, Passus 23; S. F. Barrow and W. H. Hubner, *Antichrist and Adam* (Western Reserve University Bulletin, N.S., xxviii (1925), no. 8); Hippolytus, *De Christo ac Antichristo* and *De Consummatione mundi ac de Antichristo*, in J. P. Migne, *Patrologiae cursus completus, series Graeca*, x, cols. 725–88, 904–52; J. H. Newman, *The Patristical Idea of Antichrist* (Tract 83), in *Discussions and Arguments on Various Subjects* (1872), p. 67; R. Taylor, *The Political Prophecy in England* (Columbia University Press, 1911), pp. 26–39.

[2] Luther, *Commentary on Genesis, Opera latina*, xi, p. 261; Calvin, commentary on 1 John 2: 18 seq., both quoted by Preuss, op. cit., p. 41.

[3] Wadstein, op. cit., pp. 102–6.

Hus and the Hussites. If Antichrist had already appeared on earth, the last time must be at hand. Through the great heretical movements of these centuries this idea passed to the masses of the population. With it went another, in the long run even more subversive, idea—that not only the Pope but the whole Roman church was antichristian—its bishops, its clergy. Grosseteste expressed this in the decent obscurity of Latin: so did his admirer Wyclif.[1] But Lollards, Hus, and Taborites denounced the clergy as ministers of Antichrist *in the vernacular*.[2] The significance of this was vastly enhanced by the invention of printing. Luther, for instance, in 1528 published a *Commentary on the Apocalypse* by the Lollard Purvey in which the Pope was denounced as Antichrist; and others of the traditional sources on Antichrist were printed in the late fifteenth or sixteenth centuries.[3]

One aspect of this heretical tradition which will recur is the view that Antichrist is a holder of political power, who persecutes God's people.[4] Hussites denounced the Emperor Charles IV as Antichrist: not only bishops but also the nobility and the urban patriciate, the coercive civil power, represented this spirit of Antichrist. The Taborites indeed included the rich among Antichrist's hosts.[5]

[1] Ed. D. A. Callus, *Robert Grosseteste* (1955), pp. 180, 191.

[2] Sacher, op. cit., pp. 160, 224, 238; cf. Wadstein, op. cit., pp. 88, 105; J. Foxe, *Acts and Monuments* (ed. J. Pratt), iii, p. 63.

[3] Wadstein, op. cit., p. 118; Preuss, op. cit., p. 17; Sacher, op. cit., pp. 40–1.   [4] Wadstein, op. cit., pp. 5–6.

[5] J. Macek, *The Hussite Movement in Bohemia* (Prague, 1958), pp. 22, 33; P. Brock, *The Political and Social Doctrines of the Unity of Czech Brethren in the Fifteenth and Sixteenth Centuries* ('s Gravenhage, 1957), p. 90; Sacher, op. cit., pp. 90–1; N. Cohn, *The Pursuit of the Millennium* (1957), pp. 90–1, 228.

II

With Luther and the adoption of Lutheranism as a state religion in many countries, the doctrine that the Pope is Antichrist, hitherto mostly associated with disreputable lower-class heretics, acquired a new respectability. Luther wrote a pamphlet *Adversus execrabilis Antichristi bullam*, another *De Antichristo* (translated into English in 1529), referred to the Pope in his *Table Talk* as 'the right Antichrist', and held that 'the conviction that the Pope is Antichrist' is 'a life and death matter for the church'.[1] Calvin, as we have seen, identified the papacy with Antichrist. So did Melanchthon,[2] Bullinger,[3] Bucer,[4] Beza,[5] and indeed all the leading reformers, including radicals like Castellio and Servetus.[6] In England Cardinal Wolsey was denounced as 'Antichrist's chief member'.[7] The doctrine that the Pope is Antichrist was held by Robert Barnes, by John Frith

---

[1] *Dr. Martin Luthers Divine Discourses at his Table* (trans. Captain Henry Bell, 1652), pp. 299, 312, 325–6. This was the translation Laud was accused of trying to suppress. Cf. J. M. Headley, *Luther's View of Church History* (Yale University Press, 1963), esp. pp. 59, 151–5, 181–265.

[2] Garret Mattingly, *The Defeat of the Spanish Armada* (1959), p. 159.

[3] Ed. H. Robinson, *Original Letters relative to the English Reformation*, ii (Parker Soc., 1847), p. 743—Bullinger to Calvin, 1553; H. Bullinger, *A Hundred Sermons upon the Apocalypse* (English trans., 1573), *passim*.

[4] W. Pauck, *Das Reich Gottes auf Erden* (Berlin, 1928), pp. 65–6; C. Hopf, *Martin Bucer and the English Reformation* (Oxford, 1946), pp. 135, 253.

[5] A letter from Beza to Archbishop Grindal, quoted in [Anon.], *X Solid and Serious Queries Concerning the power of Church Discipline* (1646), p. 29; W. H. Frere and C. E. Douglas, *Puritan Manifestoes* (1907), p. 54.

[6] D. Cantimori, *Italienische Haeretike der Spätrenaissance* (Basel, 1949), p. 108; M. Reeves, op. cit., pp. 485–6.

[7] W. Roye and J. Barlowe, *Rede me and be not wrothe* (ed. E. Arber, 1871), p. 53.

who in 1529 translated Luther's *Revelation of Antichrist*, by heretics burnt in 1532,[2] and by Henry Brinklow (monks and nuns were 'imps of Antichrist').[3] The identification was also strongly urged by William Tyndale, who attacked 'the Pope, that very Antichrist'.[4] All the leading bishops of the reformed Church of England accepted the doctrine, starting with Archbishop Cranmer[5] and including Bale,[6] Coverdale[7] (who spoke of 'the intolerable wrongs done by the Antichrist of Rome' to King John), Ponet,[8] and the three martyrs Latimer,[9] Ridley,[10] and Hooper.[11] For Latimer the practice of canonization was evidence that the Pope was Antichrist: 'How can he know the saints?' For Hooper 'the only note and mark to know Antichrist'

[1] J. Foxe, op. cit. v, p. 585; cf. W. A. Clebsch, *England's Earliest Protestants, 1520–1535* (Yale University Press, 1964), pp. 65, 82, 85–8.

[2] Foxe, op. cit. iv, p. 705.

[3] H. Brinklow, *The Complaynt of Roderyck Mors* (E.E.T.S., 1874), p. 9. Cf. a letter from Satan to the Bishop of London, quoted by J. Fines, 'An Unnoticed Tract of the Tyndale–More Dispute?', *Bulletin of the Institute of Historical Research*, xlii, p. 228.

[4] W. Tyndale, *Doctrinal Treatises* (Parker Soc., 1848), pp. 185–6. See pp. 41–2 below.

[5] T. Cranmer, *Miscellaneous Writings and Letters* (Parker Soc., 1856), pp. 39, 167, 176; *On the Lord's Supper* (Parker Soc., 1844), p. 5.

[6] J. Bale, *Select Works* (Parker Soc., 1849), pp. 36, 420–42; cf. pp. 25, 251–2; ed. E. Creath, *Tudor Plays* (New York, 1966), pp. 121, 129: the church was 'a heap of udders of Antichrist' (*King John*).

[7] M. Coverdale, Epistle Dedicatory to Henry VIII of his translation of the Bible (1535); *Remains* (Parker Soc., 1844), pp. 8, 586–8.

[8] J. Ponnet [*sic*], *A Short Treatise of Politique Power* (1642), pp. 19, 65. Originally published in 1556. The date of the reprint of this pamphlet is interesting.

[9] H. Latimer, *Remains* (Parker Soc., 1845), pp. 345–6; *Sermons* (Parker Soc., 1844), p. 149.

[10] N. Ridley, *Works* (Parker Soc., 1841), pp. 53, 61–3, 414–15.

[11] J. Hooper, *Early Writings* (Parker Soc., 1843), p. 23; *Later Writings* (Parker Soc., 1852), pp. 44–5, 56, 512.

was that he deprived men of Christian liberty by commanding things indifferent.

Antichrist was 'discomfited' in 1549 and 1550.[1] But in Mary's reign 'Antichrist is come again', 'Antichrist wholly prevaileth', said the martyrs John Philpot and John Bradford.[2] The people serve Antichrist without knowing him, said a pamphlet addressed to the nobility of England in 1554.[3] At least three Marian martyrs not yet mentioned are said to have suffered for calling either the Pope or the Roman church Antichrist.[4] John Jewell in his anti-Catholic controversial writings made extensive use of the theme, which is elaborated in his *Exposition of Thessalonians*.[5] Among other Elizabethan bishops we may mention John Alymer,[6] Richard Cox,[7] Archbishop Sandys,[8] Richard Davies of St. Davids,[9] Bishop Anthony Rudd of the same diocese preaching before the Queen in 1596,[10] the anti-Puritan Young of Rochester,

---

[1] Robinson, *Original Letters relative to the English Reformation*, ii, pp. 395, 670–1. See also pp. 42–4 below.

[2] J. Philpot, *Examinations and Writings* (Parker Soc., 1842), p. 242; J. Bradford, *Sermons* (Parker Soc., 1842), pp. 160, 435, 441; *Letters* (Parker Soc., 1853), pp. 142, 146, 329.

[3] [Anon.], *A short description of Antichrist* (?1554), sig. A4–7.

[4] Andrew Willet, *Synopsis Papismi* (5th ed., 1634), p. 255. (First published 1594.) Prynne also quoted Bilney the Henrician martyr (*Canterburies Doome* (1644), pp. 277–8).

[5] J. Jewell, *Works*, ii (Parker Soc., 1847), pp. 915–33, 991, 1030–1; iv (Parker Soc., 1850), pp. 727–30.

[6] J. Aylmer, *An Harborowe for Faithful and trewe Subjects* (1559), sigs. B4, P4, R3.

[7] J. Strype, *Life of Whitgift* (1822), i, p. 185.

[8] E. Sandys, *Sermons* (Parker Soc., 1841), pp. 11–12, 388–9.

[9] R. Davies, *A Funeral Sermon* (1577) for the first Earl of Essex, quoted by H. A. Lloyd, *The Gentry of South-West Wales* (Cardiff, 1968), p. 178.

[10] Ed. H. Harrington and T. Park, *Nugae Antiquae* (1804), ii, pp. 215–17. The Queen's dislike of this sermon was due to the preacher's tactless allusion to her age, not to his doctrine.

who argued in 1579 that the Familist Henry Nicholas's doubts on the subject showed him to be a crypto-papist, for 'he might easily have showed that Rome is the seat of Antichrist'.[1] No less a person than John Whitgift himself proved the Pope to be Antichrist in his D.D. thesis, and repeated it in his lectures as Lady Margaret Professor of Divinity at Cambridge.[2] The more Puritan William Whitaker, Regius Professor of Divinity, did the same in a disputation of 1582,[3] and repeated it in his *Disputation on Holy Scripture* twenty-eight years later.[4] Marian exiles like Thomas Becon, who wrote a treatise on *The Acts of Christ and Antichrist* (1563),[5] William Turner, whose epitaph tells us that he 'fought to the bitter end as a soldier of Christ . . . against the Roman Antichrist',[6] and Bartholomew Traheron, who wrote *An Exposition of the 4 Chapter of . . . Revelation*,[7] can be listed side by side with Puritan conformists like William Fulke,[8] Henry Smith,[9] and William Perkins.[10] Bernard

[1] Strype, *Annals of the Reformation* (1824), II, ii, p. 274. Bishop Henry Jones added the name of Bishop Bilson, presumably on the strength of his anti-papal *True Difference between Christian Subjection, and Unchristian Rebellion* (1585) (Jones, *Sermon of Antichrist*, 1676, sig. B2^v). See pp. 153–4 below.

[2] Strype, *Life of Whitgift*, i, p. 15.

[3] Ibid., i, p. 459.

[4] Op. cit. (Parker Soc., 1849), pp. 20–3.

[5] Becon, *Prayers and Other Pieces* (Parker Soc., 1844), pp. 501–39.

[6] B. D. Jackson, *Life of William Turner* (1877), in W. Turner, *Libellus de Re Herbaria* (ed. W. T. Stearn, The Ray Soc., 1965), pp. 23–4. I owe this reference to the kindness of Mr. George Chapman, headmaster of Ashington County Grammar School.

[7] Op. cit. (1573), sig. A^v.

[8] W. Fulke, *Praelections upon the Sacred and Holy Revelation of St. John* (1573), esp. pp. 74–89 (trans. by George Giffard, with a fiery anti-papal dedication to the Earl of Warwick); *De Successione Ecclesiastica et Latente ab Antichristi Tyrannide Ecclesia* (1584), *passim*; *Answers to Stapleton, Martiall and Sanders* (Parker Soc., 1848), pp. 366–73, 392–3.

[9] H. Smith, *Sermons* (1631), i, pp. 67, 75; ii, sig. H4^v; v, pp. 85, 89–93.

[10] W. Perkins, *A Reformed Catholic* (1597), in *Works* (1616–18), i, pp. 555–634, esp. p. 617.

Gilpin believed that protestants could give no solid reason for leaving the Roman church except that the Pope was Antichrist.[1]

By the time of Elizabeth's accession the doctrine that the Pope was Antichrist had acquired a theoretical respectability which seemed to rescue it from the subversive dangers of medieval heresy and tie it safely to monarchy. This was mainly the work of Martin Bucer and John Foxe. Bucer's *De Regno Christi* (posthumously published in 1557) had been dedicated to Edward VI. For Bucer the Catholic church was the *regnum Antichristi*.[2] It was the duty of kings to reduce subjects to obedience to Christ, and they had a special duty to reform the clergy. God will prosper and protect kings against their enemies if they defend His cause.[3] This became a theoretical justification for the royal supremacy, on which Elizabethan bishops like Jewell, and James I himself, could draw. Foxe's great *Acts and Monuments*, given the widest possible circulation through its use as propaganda by the Elizabethan government, depicted Englishmen throughout the centuries battling against Antichrist, especially since the days of Wyclif.

[1] W. Gilpin, *The Life of Bernard Gilpin* (1753), pp. 21–3.

[2] Ed. H. Robinson, *Original Letters relative to the English Reformation* (Parker Soc., 1846–7), ii, pp. 539–41; W. Pauck, *Das Reich Gottes auf Erden* (Berlin, 1928), esp. pp. 65–6, 114; C. Hopf, *Martin Bucer and the English Reformation* (Oxford, 1946), pp. 135, 153–62, 253. Cf. H. Eells, *Martin Bucer* (Yale University Press, 1931), *passim*. The 'Epistle to the Reader' in the Geneva translation, *Du royaume de Jésus-Christ* (1558), makes explicit the contrast between Antichrist's kingdom and the kingdom of Christ.

[3] Bucer, *De Regno Christi*, esp. preface, Bk. I, ch. ii, Bk. II, ch. i, and last chapter; Bucer, *The Gratulation . . . unto the Churche of Englande for the restitution of Christes religion* (n.d.), sigs. a v–vi, k vii–viii. (Latin ed. 1548). I have benefited from discussing Bucer with Mr. K. R. M. Short.

In the sixteenth century, in the words of Bishop Cox, 'Antichrist and the Spaniard' were 'conspiring together against England'.[1] Foxe made his countrymen conscious of a long historical tradition, which in itself appeared to legitimate their views, and to confirm their conviction that the corruptions of the papacy were of long standing. This reinforced the belief that the latter days must be near. It was thanks to Elizabeth's 'true, natural and imperial crown', Foxe thought, that 'the brightness of God's word was set up again to confound the dark and false-vizored kingdom of Antichrist'.[2]

For men to be convinced that the Pope was Antichrist had clear propaganda uses for Tudor governments. This was true even before Foxe wrote. In 1548 Edward VI's government had justified the invasion of Scotland as a blow against Antichrist.[3] In the second half of the century, when Spain became England's main enemy, Sir Francis Drake proposed to stand for Queen and country against Antichrist and his members.[4] George Peele took the point up in *A Farewell to Sir John Norris and Sir Francis Drake*, urging them on to 'lofty Rome, / There to deface the pride of Antichrist'.[5] Already in 1584 Richard Hakluyt had written of the Spaniards as supporters of the great Antichrist of Rome.[6] The

[1] Strype, *Life of Whitgift*, i, p. 185.

[2] Foxe, op. cit. vii, p. 466; W. Haller, *Foxe's Book of Martyrs and the Elect Nation* (1963), *passim*; W. M. Lamont, *Godly Rule* (1969), pp. 23–4.

[3] W. Patten, *The Expedition into Scotland* (1548), in E. Arber, *An English Garner* (1895–7), iii, p. 68.

[4] A. L. Rowse, *The Expansion of Elizabethan England* (1955), p. 264; Garret Mattingly, *The Defeat of the Spanish Armada*, p. 92.

[5] G. Peele, *Works* (1888), ii, p. 239.

[6] R. Hakluyt, *Discourse of Western Planting*, in *The Original Writings and Correspondence of the two Richard Hakluyts* (ed. E. G. R. Taylor, Hakluyt Soc., 1935), ii, p. 315.

Italian financier Horatio Palavicino assured Walsingham in 1589 that he hoped to see the destruction of Antichrist's kingdom in the next year.[1] 'The antichristian fleet' was destroyed in 1588, said a later tract claiming to be by Napier.[2] Simon Harward spoke in 1592 of 'antichristian Catholics', meaning Spaniards,[3] and Henry Smith referred to the papist international as 'Antichrist and all his wicked confederates'.[4] Pamphleteers of 1646 and 1654 declared that God had preserved Queen Elizabeth 'from the rage and bloody plots of an antichristian brood'.[5] The Gunpowder plotters, Cornelius Burges told the House of Commons in November 1640, had been 'cursed instruments of Antichrist'.[6] Thomas Goodwin thought the defeat of the Spanish navy in English waters in 1639 (by the Dutch, alas!) a blow at Antichrist.[7] Barnabe Rich's *Short Survey of Ireland* (1609) had as its main point to establish that the Pope was Antichrist.[8] Unfortunately, as John Goodwin recalled in 1641, 'antichristian hornets' formed a majority of the Irish population.[9]

Translations of works by foreign protestants confirmed the identification of Pope and Antichrist.

[1] L. Stone, *An Elizabethan: Sir Horatio Palavicino* (Oxford, 1956), p. 12.   [2] [Anon.], *Napiers Narration* (1641), sig. B3.

[3] S. Harward, *The Solace for the Souldier and Saylor* (1592), sig. C2ᵛ. I owe this reference to Professor John Hale.

[4] H. Smith, *Sermons* (1631), p. 388; cf. A. Dent, *The Ruine of Rome* (1603), and T. Scott, *The Belgick Souldier* (Dort, 1624), p. 2.

[5] Elizabeth Warren, *The Old and Good Way Vindicated* (1646), pp. 30–1; George Smith, *Gods Unchangeableness* (1654), p. 14.

[6] C. Burges, *A Sermon preached to the Honourable House of Commons* (1641), p. 43; cf. *Another Sermon preached to the Honourable House of Commons* (5 Nov. 1641), p. 25.

[7] T. Goodwin, *Works* (Edinburgh, 1861–3), iii, p. 103.

[5] Op. cit., chs. ii–xxiv.

[9] [J. Goodwin], *Irelands Advocate* (1641), p. 27.

Examples are A. Marlorate's *Catholike Exposition upon the Revelation of St. Iohn,* translated by Arthur Golding in 1574,[1] and Duplessis-Mornay's *A Notable Treatise of the Church,* translated five years later by the Puritan John Field and dedicated to the Earl of Leicester, with a clarion call for leadership in an anti-Catholic crusade. Chapters IX and X of this treatise proved the Pope to be Antichrist, quoting among other authorities Petrarch.[2] In 1612 a 600-page folio by Duplessis-Mornay, devoted entirely to proving the Pope to be Antichrist, was translated into English by Samson Lennard, with dedications to Prince Henry, Archbishop Abbott, and Bishop King of London.[3] It long remained popular in England, being quoted in 1641 by Lord Brooke.[4] Pierre du Moulin's *The Accomplishment of the Prophecies* was another well-known French work.[5] There is in the Bodleian Library an unpublished treatise, *De Papatu Romano Antichristo,* by Alberico Gentili, dating from 1580–5.[6] Giacopo Brocardo's *Revelation of St. John Revealed* (English translation, 1582) was by an Italian refugee in Germany. From Heidelberg came a frequently quoted source, Francis Junius's *Apocalypsis, a Brief and Learned Commentarie upon the Revelation of St. John,*[7] Zacharias Ursinus's *The Summe of Christian*

[1] Op. cit., esp. sig. Aii. (French ed., 1564.)

[2] Philip of Mornay, Lord of Plessis Marlyn, *A Notable Treatise of the Church* (1579), sig. Uiiii.

[3] Philip Mornay, *The Mysterie of Iniquitie* (1612).

[4] Brooke, op. cit., in W. Haller, *Tracts on Liberty in the Puritan Revolution, 1638–1647* (Columbia University Press, 1933), ii, pp. 85, 103.

[5] Op. cit. (trans. J. Heath, 1613), esp. pp. 148 seqq.

[6] I owe this information to the kindness of Dr. D. Panizza of the University of Padua.

[7] Op. cit. (1592), esp. pp. 48–53. From 1599 onwards Junius's notes on Revelation were incorporated in some editions of the Geneva Bible.

Religion,[1] P. Boquinus's *Defence of the Olde and True profession of Christianitie,*[2] and various works by David Pareus[3] and J. H. Alsted.[4] *The Popish Kingdome, or reigne of Antichrist,* by the Hessian Thomas Kirchenmeyer (Naogeorgus), was translated by Barnabe Googe in 1570, with dedication to the Queen despite the poem's attack on bishops, church courts, and canon law. From the Netherlands, Sheltco a Geveren's *Of the Ende of the World and the Seconde Commyng of Christ* ran to five editions between 1577 and 1589.[5] The Hungarian, Bohemian, and Netherlands churches agreed that the Pope was Antichrist.[6]

So did the Scottish Kirk. John Knox referred to 'the generation of Antichrist, the pestilential prelates and their shavelings within Scotland'. All other churches keep 'some footsteps of Antichrist'; but the reformed

---

[1] Op. cit. (trans. H. Parry, 1601).

[2] Op. cit. (1581). Dedicated to Francis Russell, Earl of Bedford. (First published in Latin 1576.)

[3] D. Pareus, *Theologicall Miscellanies,* printed with the 1645 edition of Ursinus's *Summe of Christian Religion,* pp. 737–52; *Demonstratio Antichristi* (Heidelberg, 1617); *Opera Theologica Exegetica* (Frankfurt, 1647), esp. iv, pp. 389–90, 594, 709–44.   [4] See p. 29 below.

[5] Op. cit. (trans. T. Rogers, 1577), *passim.* I mention only books translated into English which seem to have been fairly influential in England. In 1610 in France Nicolas Vignier listed twenty-eight protestant authors from ten countries who had proclaimed the Pope to be Antichrist (N. Vignier, *Théâtre de l'Antéchrist,* sig. aa4). A twenty-ninth in an eleventh country, whom Vignier was too modest to mention in this 692-page volume, was himself (*L'Antéchrist romain opposé à l'Antéchrist juif du cardinal Bellarmine . . . et autres,* 1604). Among the 6,630 books left by Lazarus Seaman (*c.* 1608–76) were fifty on the subject of Antichrist published between 1570 and 1656, the majority in Latin. (*Catalogus . . . Librorum . . . Lazari Seaman,* 1676, *passim.* I am very grateful to Professor Ivan Roots for lending me his copy of this catalogue.) Seaman replaced John Cosin as Master of Peterhouse between 1644 and 1660.

[6] N. Bernard, *Certain Discourses* (1659), pp. 142–5; A. Willett, *Synopsis Papismi* (3rd ed., 1600), p. 220.

Kirk of Scotland retains nothing 'that ever flowed from that Man of Sin'.[1] In 1654 it was still recalled that when Edward VI offered Knox a bishopric in England he 'refused it, as having aliquid commune cum Antichristo'.[2] The identification of Pope and Antichrist was repeated in the *Second Book of Discipline* of 1577–8, and by James Durham, selected in 1650 by the General Assembly of the Kirk to attend Charles II.[3] In England Christopher Goodman[4] and Thomas Cartwright naturally shared the same position.[5] 'To prove the Pope Antichrist', John Field thought in 1581, was 'needless, considering how it is a beaten argument in every book'.[6] Henry Barrow was wholly orthodox on this point: 'the Papacy, being upholden and mixed with the Empire, and in the end swallowing it up, became the very throne of Antichrist.'[7] Robert Browne agreed: Rome as the seat of Antichrist must be burned.[8] Other Brownists and Barrowists agreed that the Pope was Antichrist. So did John Penry,[9] John Wilkinson,[10] Henry Ains-

---

[1] Quoted by J. Ridley, *John Knox* (Oxford University Press, 1968), p. 321; cf. pp. 56, 148, 151, 252, 367, 379, 406, 461, 465; Knox, *History of the Reformation in Scotland* (1950), ii, p. 3; T. McCrie, *Life of John Knox* (Edinburgh, 1818), ii. p. 150.

[2] John Tillinghast, *Generation-work*, Part III (1654), sig. b7.

[3] J. Durham, *A Commentarie Upon the Book of the Revelation* (1658), pp. 542–676.   [4] *D.N.B.*, *sub* Napier, John.

[5] Whitgift, *Works*, iii, pp. 399, 459.

[6] J. Field, *A Caveat for Parsons Howlet* (1581), sigs. Eiii, Eviii, Fii. Antichrist was, however, a company and estate of men rather than an individual. This tract was dedicated to the Earl of Leicester.

[7] Ed. L. H. Carlson, *The Writings of Henry Barrow, 1587–1590* (1962), p. 275.

[8] Ed. A. Peel and L. H. Carlson, *The Writings of Robert Harrison and Robert Browne* (1953), pp. 152, 524, and *passim*.

[9] C. Burrage, *Early English Dissenters* (1912), ii, p. 85.

[10] J. Wilkinson, *An Exposition of the 13 Chapter of the Revelation of Jesus Christ* (1619), pp. 4, 14, 18–19.

worth,[1] Robert Parker.[2] Such men showed their unortho-
doxy, as we shall see, by insisting that Antichrist was
not only the Pope.[3]

The identification was repeated by laymen too, as
diverse as the Edwardian merchants John and Otwell
Johnson,[4] Elizabeth's Lord Treasurer Burghley,[5] the
fourth Earl of Derby,[6] the financier Palavicino,[7] a
Puritan gentleman like Job Throckmorton,[8] a middle-
of-the-road man like Ralph Holinshed,[9] by poets like
Spenser, Donne, Phineas Fletcher, William Alabaster,
George Herbert, George Wither, and Milton, by poet-
asters like Barnabe Googe and George Goodwin.[10]

The years from the 1590s to the 1620s saw a great
number of publications on the subject, some of porten-
tous length. Three were published in 1599—Dean
Matthew Sutcliffe's *De Pontifico Romano*;[11] the *Disswasive*

[1] *The Trying Out of the Truth* (1615), esp. pp. 176–8, a controversy
between John and Henry Ainsworth; H. Ainsworth, *A Reply to a
Pretended Christian Plea for the Antichristian Church of Rome published by
Mr. Francis Iohnson* (1620), *passim*. Cf. S. Rutherford, *A Survey of the
Spirituall Antichrist* (1649), ii, p. 165, who quotes Henry Ainsworth with
approval.

[2] [Robert Parker], *A Scholasticall Discourse against Symbolizing with Antichrist in Ceremonies* (1607); *The Mystery of the Vialls opened* (1651), esp. p. 8.

[3] See pp. 52–60 below.

[4] B. Winchester, *Tudor Family Portrait* (1955), pp. 44–5.

[5] Burghley, *The Execution of Justice in England* (1581), in *Somers Tracts*
(1748–51), xiii, p. 20. The title of universal bishop was the prelude to an
antichristian church—an argument frequently used. Burghley also
thought that Babington's Plot in 1586 aimed 'to have erected the synagogue of Antichrist' (ed. J. Bruce, *Correspondence of Robert Dudley, Earl of
Leycester*, Camden Soc., 1844, p. 421).

[6] John Cauldwell, *A Sermon preached before the right honourable Earl of
Darbie* (1577), dedication.   [7] See p. 15 above.

[8] Sir J. E. Neale, *Elizabeth I and her Parliaments, 1584–1601* (1957),
p. 170.   [9] R. Holinshed, *Chronicle* (1577), quoted in *O.E.D.*

[10] See Appendix III below.

[11] Op. cit., esp. pp. 432–549. Cf. the same author's *An Answer to A*

from Poperie of Francis Dillingham, later one of the translators of the Authorized Version;[1] and George Giffard's *Sermons Upon the Whole Booke of the Revelation*. This last was published with a dedication to the Earl of Essex, urging him to put on white linen, mount a white horse, and take the field against the Beast, whom the King of Spain served.[2]

We may attribute this interest in part to the international threat from Habsburg power, still strong in the nineties and reviving with the outbreak of the Thirty Years War, in part to a consciousness that protestantism remained insecure in England, that the godly remnant was indeed small,[3] in part perhaps to anxieties roused by Bancroft's intrigues with English Catholics.[4] The literature comes mainly though not exclusively from the Calvinist wing in the Church of England, both Puritan and non-Puritan: it is not till well on in the twenties that dissenting voices are heard. First place among Jacobean foes of Antichrist must be given to King James himself. As early as 1588, fifteen years before succeeding to the English crown, James published *A Fruitfull Meditation . . . of the vii–x verses of the Second Chapter of the Revelation*, in which he argued that the Pope was Antichrist. He later said he would never recant this belief

---

Certaine Libel . . . to the slaunder of the Ecclesiasticall State (1592) and *An Abridgment Or Survey of Popery* (1606). This last work was dedicated to Prince Henry. Sutcliffe was later disgraced because of his opposition to James I's scheme for a Spanish marriage alliance.

[1] Op. cit., esp. sig. A4^v, pp. 1–10.

[2] Op. cit., esp. sig. A3^v–5^v, pp. 187–264. Giffard was later a nonconformist. Foxe's exposition of the Apocalypse was published posthumously in 1587.

[3] I owe this point to the unpublished Oxford D.Phil. thesis of Dr. N. Tyacke, 'Arminianism in England, in Religion and Politics, 1604 to 1640', p. 4.   [4] See p. 64 below.

'except they first renounce any meddling with princes in anything belonging to their temporal jurisdiction'.[1] In his *Apologie for the Oath of Allegiance* (1609), James established from Revelation that popery was antichristian. The Pope complained that the King 'called him Antichrist at every word' in his dinner-table conversation.[2]

Among Jacobean and Caroline bishops we may name George Abbott, who repeated his conviction that the Pope was Antichrist even in his will,[3] his brother Robert Abbott, Master of Balliol and Bishop of Salisbury, whose *Antichristi Demonstratio* was published in 1603, the same year as Bishop George Downame's *Treatise Concerning Antichrist*, dedicated to James I.[4] Robert Abbott also wrote *A Hand of Fellowship, to Helpe Keepe out Sinne and Antichrist* (1623). *The Ruine of Rome* by Arthur Dent also appeared in 1603—a stirring patriotic anti-Spanish diatribe, dedicated to Robert, Lord Rich.[5] Bishop Lewis Bayly of Bangor, author of the best-selling *The Practice of Piety* (before 1612), must be added, together with James Ussher, Archbishop of Armagh, Bishops Morton of Durham, Davenant of Salisbury, Prideaux of Worcester, and Bedell of Kilmore;[6] George

[1] James I, *Works* (1616), pp. 308–28. Cf. D. H. Willson, *James VI and I* (1956), p. 82. For James see also pp. 32–4 below.
[2] Ed. N. E. McClure, *The Letters of John Chamberlain* (American Philosophical Soc., 1939), i, p. 284.
[3] P. A. Welsby, *George Abbott: the Unwanted Archbishop* (1962), p. 22. I owe the information about Abbott's will to Dr. N. Tyacke.
[4] Cf. G. Downame, *Two Sermons* (1608), preface.
[5] Op. cit., esp. pp. 168–268.
[6] All these are cited in Nicholas Bernard's *Certain Discourses* (1659), which prints sermons on the subject by Ussher and Bedell (sig. A5–6, pp. 1–20, 61–104, 134–5); cf. R. Mountagu, *Appelo Caesarem* (1625), p. 146; Ussher, *De Christianorum ecclesiarum . . . successione et statu* (1613); compare his posthumous *Judgement* (1659).

Carleton, one of England's representatives at the Synod of Dort: 'the roundhead Bishop of Chichester', as a contemporary called him;[1] Joseph Hall, Bishop of Worcester,[2] and Patrick Forbes, Bishop of Aberdeen.[3] Gabriel Powel, who wrote several pamphlets against deprived Puritan ministers, at least one by the command of some in authority, nevertheless in 1605 produced a large Latin tome, dedicated to the King, in which it was shown that the Pope was Antichrist, with over four hundred pages on the notes of Antichrist, dedicated to Archbishop Bancroft.[4] Another enemy of the separatists was Thomas Drakes, who at Harwich in 1618 or 1619 proclaimed the Pope to be Antichrist.[5]

On the more Puritan wing was Oliver Cromwell's mentor and friend, Thomas Beard, who published *Antichrist the Pope of Rome* in 1625. Beard thought that Luther and printing were together expediting Antichrist's decline.[6] To the best-selling works of Arthur Dent and Lewis Bayly we must add Richard Bernard's *The Isle of Man*, in which 'the babbling Babylonian' who defended 'the old religion' was a 'bloody antichristian adversary'.[7] Other Puritans who agreed that

[1] G. Carleton, *The Madness of Astrologers* (1624), p. 66. The description is from a contemporary manuscript note in the Bodleian copy.

[2] J. Hall, *Works* (Oxford, 1837–9), xii, p. 456. Cf. W. Laud, *Works* (Oxford, 1847–60), iv, pp. 308–9, 312–13, and pp. 34–5 below.

[3] P. Forbes, *An Exquisit Commentarie Upon the Revelation of St. John* (1613), esp. chs. ix, xi.

[4] G. Powel, *Disputationum Theologicarum et Scholasticarum de Antichristo et eius Ecclesia, Libri II* (1605), *passim*. Powel wrote many controversial works, including attacks on religious toleration.

[5] Burrage, op. cit. ii, pp. 143–5.

[6] Beard, op. cit., pp. 181–2.

[7] R. Bernard, *The Isle of Man* (4th ed., 1627), pp. 27–8, 274, 286–7; cf. *The Seaven Golden Candlesticks* (1621); *Looke beyond Luther* (1624); *A Short View of the Praelaticall Church of England* (1641), p. 1.

the Pope was Antichrist were Andrew Willet,[1] John Rainolds,[2] William Symonds in a propaganda sermon before the Virginia Adventurers in 1609;[3] Hugh Broughton, an expert on Biblical chronology, in his *Revelation of the Holy Apocalypse* (1610);[4] Lionel Sharp, defender of Essex, chaplain to Prince Henry, imprisoned in 1614 for opposition activities;[5] William Crashawe, father of the poet;[6] Henoch Clapham, in trouble both with the ecclesiastical authorities and with the College of Physicians;[7] Samuel Hieron;[8] Antony Wotton, Professor at Gresham College;[9] Thomas Taylor, in a sermon preached to the House of Commons in 1624;[10] the renegade Catholic Lewis Owen in 1628.[11] Many commentaries on Thessalonians identified the Man of Sin with the Pope—e.g. those of John Jewell,[12]

[1] A. Willet, *Synopsis Papismi* (3rd ed., 1600), pp. 188–220.

[2] J. Rainolds, *The Discovery of the Manne of Sinne* (1614), posthumously published by William Hinde. Antichrist is not the Bishop of Rome alone but the whole Roman government (p. 8).

[3] W. Symonds, *Virginia* (1609), esp. pp. 14, 53.

[4] Op. cit., esp. sig. F, pp. 95–7, 169.

[5] Leonellus Sharpus Anglus, *Novum Fidei Symbolum* (1612), to which are prefixed three dialogues, *Speculum Papae, Pragmaticus Antichristus*, and *Dogmaticus Antichristus*—300 pages in all. This work was translated in 1623 as *A Looking Glass for the Pope*.

[6] W. Crashawe, *The Jesuites Gospell* (1610), *passim*.

[7] H. Clapham, *Errour on the Right Hand* (1608), pp. 70–6; *A Chronologicall Discourse, touching the Church, Christ, Antichrist . . . etc.* (1609).

[8] S. Hieron, *Sermons* (1624), i, pp. 271, 559–75, 758; ii, p. 318.

[9] A. Wotton, *Runne from Rome* (1624), pp. 7, 78–9. For Wotton see my *Intellectual Origins of the English Revolution* (Oxford, 1965), p. 56.

[10] T. Taylor, *Two Sermons* (1624), Epistle Dedicatory and pp. 4–10, 16; cf. his *Christian Practice*, p. 77, in *Works* (1653); and his posthumous *Christs Victorie over the Dragon* (1633), esp. pp. 693–742. This is an exposition of Revelation 12. See also p. 48 below.

[11] L. Owen, *The Unmasking Of All popish Monks, Friers and Jesuits* (1628), *passim*.   [12] See p. 11 above.

Robert Rollock,[1] William Sclater,[2] William Bradshaw,[3] John Squire,[4] John Mayer.[5] Among the more famous Puritan divines we may list John Carter,[6] William Ames,[7] John Trapp,[8] Thomas Goodwin,[9] John Cotton,[10] Jeremiah Burroughs,[11] and three of the Feoffees for Impropriations—Richard Stock,[12] Richard Sibbes,[13] and William Gouge. The last-named in 1621 got into trouble for publishing Sir Henry Finch's *The Worlds Great Restauration, Or the Calling of the Jewes*. This book assumed that the Pope was Antichrist.[14]

[1] Roberti Rolloci Scoti, *In Utramque Epistolam Pauli ad Thessalonicenses Commentarius* (1601), esp. pp. 282–329.

[2] W. Sclater, *A Briefe Exposition with Notes upon the II Epistle to the Thessalonians* (3rd ed., 1632), esp. i, pp. 96–176; ii, pp. 3–12. First published 1619. Sclater disapproved of attempts—like Napier's—to date the end of the world.

[3] W. Bradshaw, *A Plain and Pithy Exposition of the Second Epistle to the Thessalonians* (1620), pp. 93–128. Published posthumously by Thomas Gataker.

[4] J. Squire, *A Plaine Exposition upon the First part of . . . the second Epistle to the Thessalonians. Wherein it is plainly proved that the Pope is the Antichrist* (1630). Squire was however 'accused of Popish doctrines and ceremonies' in 1641 (*An Answer To a printed Paper Entituled Articles Exhibited in Parliament against Mr. John Squire*, 1641).

[5] J. Mayer, *Ecclesiastica Interpretatio* (1627), esp. pp. 408–10, 421–35. Dedicated to Charles I.

[6] S. Clarke, *The Lives of 32 English Divines* (1677), p. 136.

[7] W. Ames, *English Puritanism* (1641), p. 20.

[8] J. Trapp, *A Commentary or Exposition upon All the Epistles and the Revelation* (1647), pp. 290–4, 543–8; cf. p. 763.

[9] T. Goodwin, *A Sermon of the Fifth Monarchy* (1654), pp. 17, 28; *An Exposition of the Revelation* (1639), in *Works*, iii, pp. 1–205.

[10] J. Cotton, *The Powring out of the Seven Vialls* (1642), *passim*; *An Exposition upon the Thirteenth Chapter of the Revelation* (1655), *passim*.

[11] J. Burroughs, *Sions Joy* (1641), p. 16.

[12] R. Stock, *A Commentary upon the Prophecy of Malachi* (Edinburgh, 1865), p. 166. For the Feoffees, with whom Thomas Taylor was closely associated, see my *Economic Problems of the Church* (Oxford, 1956), esp. pp. 252–70.   [13] R. Sibbes, *Works* (Edinburgh, 1862–4), vii, pp. 517–33.

[14] *Op. cit.*, pp. 54–5, 75. For Gouge see also p. 161 below.

On the opposite theological wing the poet William Alabaster, against whom Beard preached, and whom Oliver Cromwell attacked in his maiden speech in the House of Commons, had nevertheless in 1621 published (at Delft) a treatise *De Bestia Apocalyptica* which argues that the Pope is Antichrist.[1] Nicholas Ferrar, of the Anglican nunnery at Little Gidding, was reported as saying 'that he did as verily believe the Pope to be Antichrist as any article of his faith'.[2] Thomas Jackson also took the idea seriously.[3] It was not the monopoly view of any theological party.

III

The last days, as I have suggested, always presented attractions to mathematicians and chronologists. Indeed, the great chronological studies which are one of the intellectual glories of the late sixteenth and early seventeenth centuries were in large part concerned with dating biblical history and biblical prophecy, not least with the date of Antichrist's coming. John Napier is said to have especially valued his invention of logarithms because it speeded up his calculations of the number of the Beast:[4] he had identified the Pope with Antichrist in his *Plain Discoverie of the Whole Revelation of St. John* (1594). This was dedicated to James VI, with a glance forward to 'that great day, in the which it shall

[1] [W. Alabaster], *Commentarius de Bestia Apocalyptica* (Delphis, 1621), *passim*.

[2] A. Maycock, *Chronicles of Little Gidding* (1954), pp. 41, 50: 'differing therein from Priest Squire' (ibid., p. 52). For Squire see p. 24 above.

[3] T. Jackson, *The Eternal Truth of Scriptures and Christian Belief*, in *Works* (Oxford, 1844), ii, pp. 266, 303–9, 472–4, 501; *A Treatise of the Holy Catholic Faith* (1626), *Works*, xiii, pp. 144–52.

[4] H. R. Trevor-Roper, 'The General Crisis of the Seventeenth Century', in *Religion, the Reformation and Social Change* (1967), p. 47.

please God to call your M. or yours after you, among other reformed princes, to that great and universal reformation and destruction of that antichristian seat and city, Rome'. Napier prophesied 'loud threatenings against the antichristian empire' for 1639.[1] The following fifty or sixty years would see all the exciting events of the last times, ending with the Day of Judgement, either in 1688 (according to Revelation) or in 1700 (according to Daniel). Napier's predictions were reprinted in the early 1640s and received considerable attention.[2] In 1597 a pamphleteer predicted that antichristian Rome would fall in 1666.[3]

Thomas Brightman, in addition to writing two specific refutations of papal theories of Antichrist (*Apocalypsis Apocalypseos*, 1609, and *Antichristum Ponteficiorum monstrum fictitum esse*, 1610), published in 1615 his own interpretation of the Revelation which included a whole scheme of past and future history. There had been a turning point in 1555–8, but for Brightman as for Napier the seventeenth century was to see the climax of human history. 'We wait every day', he wrote, 'while the Antichrist of Rome and the Turk shall be utterly destroyed.' His expectation was that Rome would fall about 1650,

[1] This prophecy was quoted in a sermon preached to the House of Commons in 1641—'and what God hath done from that year and so on, you have eyes and ears to inform yourselves' (Nathanael Homes, *The New World*, 1641, p. 37). See also p. 72 below. Napier was refuted by Henoch Clapham in his *Sommons to Doomes-daie* (Amsterdam, 1595). Cf. *Diary of John Manningham* (ed. J. Bruce, Camden Soc., 1868), p. 128.

[2] [Anon.], *Napiers Narration* (1641), esp. sig. C; cf. sigs. A4ᵛ–Bᵛ, B2ᵛ; [Anon.], *The Bloody Almanack* (1643), esp. p. 4.

[3] T. L[upton?], *Babylon is Fallen* (1597). See also *A Prophecie that hath lyen hid above these 2000 yeares* (1610), which identifies the Pope with Antichrist and predicts his downfall in 1666. This pamphlet was reprinted in 1651 under the title *The Mourners Song*. (The hidden prophecy is Esdras.)

and Antichrist be finally overthrown in 1686.[1] Before 1640 vernacular translations of Brightman had to be smuggled into England from the Netherlands. But the views of 'the bright burning light of our age, Master Thomas Brightman' were studied by the learned, and as soon as the Laudian censorship broke down they circulated widely in translation and in summary. They won a good deal of acceptance from the early 1640s.[2] John Cotton, Thomas Goodwin, John Owen, Thomas Shepard, and John Rogers, among other significant divines, closely followed Brightman.[3] 'Most protestants', said a hostile pamphlet of 1653, accept 'Brightman's strange opinions of Antichrist'.[4] Another influential scholar was Joseph Mede, Fellow of Christ's College when Milton was an undergraduate. Mede studied mathematics as a preparation for divinity. His *Key of the Revelation* had a carefully worked-out chronological

[1] T. Brightman, *The Revelation of St. John Illustrated* (4th ed., 1644), esp. pp. 109–57, 378–81, 520, 566, 612–746, 966–7, 1077.

[2] B. Hubbard, *Sermo Saecularis* (1648), quoted by W. M. Lamont, *Godly Rule* (1969), p. 95; [Anon.], *A Revelation of Mr. Brightmans Revelation, wherein is shewed how all that which Mr. Brightman on the Revelation hath foretold concerning Germany, Scotland and England hath been fulfilled* (in 'the year of fulfilling it, 1641')—a dialogue between a minister and a citizen of London: [Anon.], *Brightmans Predictions and Prophecies* (1641); [Anon.], *Reverend Mr. Brightmans Iudgment or Prophesies what shall befall Germany, Scotland, Holland and . . . England* (1643); *Brightman Redivivus* (1647)—four posthumously published sermons. See also [Anon.], *Six Strange Prophecies* (1642), one being attributed to Brightman; W. Lilly, *A Collection of Ancient and Modern Prophecies* (1645)—also including one attributed to Brightman. Cf. Prynne, *Canterburies Doome*, pp. 277–8, and my 'Newton and his Society', *Texas Quarterly*, x (1967), pp. 41–3. See p. 37 below.

[3] Peter Toon, 'Puritan Eschatology, 1600–1648', *The Evangelical Magazine* (1969), p. 6; J. A. De Jong, *As the Waters Cover the Sea* (Kampen, 1970), p. 26; T. Goodwin, *Works*, iii, pp. 69, 138, 153–7.

[4] E. H[all], *A Scriptural Discourse of the Apostasie and the Antichrist* (1653), p. 79; cf. John Evelyn, *Diary*, 18 June 1690.

scheme from the Waldensians to the fall of the anti-christian papacy. No English version of this work was published under Laud, but a translation was ordered to be printed in 1643 by a committee of the House of Commons. Translated by an M.P., it had a preface by the Prolocutor of the Westminster Assembly of Divines. It could hardly have come out under more official auspices.[1] William Twisse, Prolocutor of the Assembly of Divines, Stephen Marshall, Thomas Goodwin, Jeremiah Burroughs, and William Bridge, among many others, were followers of Mede.[2] He was still being quoted approvingly by bishops in 1689.[3]

Francis Potter, later Fellow of the Royal Society, believed that he had solved the riddle of the number 666, and had proved the Pope to be Antichrist by mathematics[4]—'the greatest mystery that hath been discovered since the beginning of the world', Mede thought.[5] Potter's book still seemed 'mighty ingenious' when another F.R.S., Samuel Pepys, read it in the risky year 1666.[6] John Archer, whose *Personall Reign of Christ upon Earth* also appeared in 1642, enjoyed great influence too. He identified Antichrist with popery, which would be ruined in 1666, the millennium beginning in

[1] J. Mede, *The Apostasy of the Latter Times* (1642) and *The Key of the Revelation* (trans. Richard More, 1643), *passim*. Pub. in Latin, 1627. Ed. J. Worthington, *The Works of . . . Joseph Mede* (1664), i, pp. x, xlviii–li; Mede, *Works* (3rd ed., 1672), esp. pp. xxvi, 647–65, 771, 818, 829, 834–5, 900–6, 916–23.

[2] E. L. Tuveson, *Millennium and Utopia* (Harper Torchbooks, 1964), pp. 78, 87–8; P. Toon, 'Puritan Eschatology, 1600–1648', p. 9; T. Goodwin, *Works*, iii, pp. 103–4, 133–5, 177, 184–7, 193.

[3] Evelyn, *Diary*, 26 April 1689.

[4] F. Potter, *An Interpretation of the Number 666* (1642).

[5] Mede, *Key of the Revelation*, sig. (a2).

[6] S. Pepys, *Diary*, 18 Feb. 1666, 4 and 10 Nov. 1666.

1700. But Archer warned his readers that until 1666 there would be 'sad days'. All princes would 'fall by degrees to tyranny and oppression and enslaving their subjects, that Christ's coming and kingdom may be more welcome to the world'.[1] I should also mention John Henry Alsted's *The Beloved City, Or, The Saints Reign on Earth A Thousand Years*, which was published in English translation in 1643, with dedication to the Mercers' Company. On Alsted's calculation the last four vials were to be poured out between 1625 and 1694, when the millennium would begin. The fall of Antichrist was therefore imminent.[2]

Among philosophical writers of whom posterity thinks more highly, Francis Bacon struck an original note by comparing Aristotle to Antichrist, 'the highest deceiver of all ages', in his *De Augmentis*.[3] Robert Burton the anatomist more conventionally identified Antichrist with the Pope,[4] as did George Hakewill[5] and Lord Brooke.[6] So did Henry More, who believed his ruin was near,[7] and Henry Oldenburg, future Secretary of

[1] Op. cit., esp. pp. 42–53; cf. Toon, 'Puritan Eschatology', p. 10. For Archer, who was a protégé of the Feoffees for Impropriations, see my *Economic Problems of the Church*, p. 260.

[2] Op. cit., esp. pp. 13, 56–62. The Latin original, *Diatribe de mille annis apocalypticis*, was published at Frankfurt in 1627. *The Worlds Proceeding Woes*, published in 1642, was a summary of Alsted's views. John Booker, *A Bloody Irish Almanack* (1646), quoted Alsted (p. 19). For Alsted see also Toon, *Puritans, the Millennium and the Future of Israel*, pp. 42–54.

[3] F. Bacon, *Works* (1857–9), i, p. 549, iv, p. 345; cf. iii, p. 567. Cf. my *Intellectual Origins of the English Revolution*, p. 91.

[4] R. Burton, *The Anatomy of Melancholy* (Everyman ed.), iii, pp. 364–6.

[5] G. Hakewill, *An Apologie or Declaration of the Power and Providence of God* (3rd ed., 1635), pp. 554–6.

[6] Lord Brooke, *A Discourse opening the nature of that Episcopacie which is exercised in England* (1641), in Haller, *Tracts on Liberty*, ii, pp. 94, 97.

[7] See p. 114 below.

the Royal Society, who in 1659 assured Samuel Hartlib
that in England there was more freedom than in France
to say that the Pope was Antichrist.[1] Hartlib and Dury
themselves accepted the identification.[2] When Sir Isaac
Newton was convinced that the Pope was Antichrist,
and devoted a great deal of time and energy to interpreting the Apocalypse,[3] we need not be surprised that
lesser men accepted the identification unquestion-
ingly.

With Newton we have looked far ahead. During the
interregnum, the Scottish general Alexander Leslie[4]
agreed with the English generals Sir William Waller
and Oliver Cromwell that the Pope was Antichrist. The
Lord Protector also believed that Spain was 'described
in Scripture to be papal and antichristian'.[5] Milton
thought that the Pope was Antichrist, the devil's vicar.[6]
The Leveller leaders John Lilburne and Richard Overton ('the kingdom of Antichrist depends on Purgatory')
agreed with Edward Leigh and William Prynne, 'Presbyterian' M.P.s excluded by Pride's Purge, in thinking

[1] Ed. A. R. and M. B. Hall, *The Correspondence of Henry Oldenburg*
(Wisconsin University Press, 1965–   ), i, p. 283.

[2] [S. Hartlib], *Clavis Apocalyptica* (1651), with preface by John Dury,
esp. p. 55; *Apocalypsis Reserata* (bound with the above), esp. pp. 99–101,
128.

[3] F. E. Manuel, *Isaac Newton, Historian* (Cambridge University Press,
1963), pp. 152–5; *A Portrait of Isaac Newton* (Harvard University Press,
1968), pp. 366–70; cf. my 'Newton and his Society', *Texas Quarterly*, x,
pp. 30–51.

[4] Ed. J. G. Fotheringham, *The Diplomatic Correspondence of Jean de
Montereul* (Scottish History Soc., 1888–9), ii, p. 550.

[5] W. C. Abbott, *The Writings and Speeches of Oliver Cromwell* (Yale
University Press, 1937–47), iv, p. 264. For Waller see p. 2 above.

[6] J. Milton, *Works* (Columbia University Press, 1931–40), iii, pp.
54–5; cf. ibid. iii, pp. 5, 27, 77, 116, 121, 269, 324, 352–4, 427, 448; iv,
pp. 18, 22, 28, 84, 131, 220, 305, 337; v, p. 209; vi, pp. 8–10, 175, 249;
vii, p. 429; xvi, p. 315; xvii, p. 395. See also pp. 94, 105 below.

that the Pope was Antichrist.[1] Thomas Fuller, Stephen Marshall,[2] the Presbyterian Thomas Manton[3] and the Westminster Confession of 1643, the Independent Savoy Confession of 1658, the Calvinist Independents John Cotton[4] ('the long night of Antichrist's darkness'), Thomas Goodwin,[5] and John Owen,[6] the Arminian Independent John Goodwin, who thought the real enemy in the Civil War was not the Cavaliers but Antichrist in Rome,[7] Cobbler How ('all men who are true protestants . . . generally believe' Antichrist 'to be the Pope and church of Rome'),[8] the Quakers George Fox, Edward Burrough,[9] and many others, the Baptist John Bunyan[10] and the astrologers William Lilly and John Booker,[11] a sceptic like Francis Osborn[12]—all thought alike on this matter.

The point which I wish to emphasize is that in the

[1] For Lilburne and Prynne see pp. 69–71 below; R. O[verton], *Mans Mortallitie* (Liverpool University Press, 1968), p. 102 (first pub. 1643); E. Leigh, *A Treatise of Religion and Learning* (1656), sig. A5ᵛ.

[2] T. Fuller, *The Best Name on Earth* (1657), in M. Fuller, *Pulpit Sparks* (1886), p. 329; Marshall, *A Peace-Offering to God* (1641), p. 7.

[3] T. Manton, *Smectymnuus Redivivus* (1654), p. 69.

[4] Cotton, *The Powring out of the Seven Vialls* (1642), esp. p. 10; Ziff, *Cotton and the Churches*, p. 72; cf. p. 265.

[5] T. Goodwin, *Works*, i, pp. 471–2, 548; iii, pp. 26–9, 65, 68, 70–5, 120, 157–8, 195–205; *A Sermon of the Fifth Monarchy*, pp. 17, 28.

[6] J. Owen, *Works* (1850–3), iv, p. 243; viii, pp. 24, 180–257, 308; xiv, pp. 547, 555; *Correspondence* (ed. P. Toon, 1970), p. 55.

[7] J. Goodwin, *Anti-Cavalierisme* (1642), p. 31, in Haller, op. cit. ii.

[8] Samuel How, *The Sufficiency of the Spirit's Teaching* (8th ed., 1792), p. 67. First pub. 1639.

[9] George Fox, *Works* (1706), p. 182; E. Burrough, *The Memorable Works of a Son of Thunder and Consolation* (1672), p. 536.

[10] J. Bunyan, *Works* (1860), ii, pp. 49, 76–8.

[11] W. Lilly, *A Prophecy of the White King and Dreadfull Dead-man Explained* (1644), p. 6; J. Booker, *A Bloody Irish Almanack* (1646), p. 42.

[12] F. Osborn, *A Miscellany of Sundry Essays*, p. 51, in *Miscellaneous Works* (1722), i.

century which separates Archbishop Cranmer from
Archbishop Abbott, the old medieval heresy that the
Pope was Antichrist had been almost officially accepted
by the Church of England.[1] As Henry Smith sardonic-
ally put it, 'He who can swear that the Pope is Antichrist and that flesh is good on Fridays is a protestant'.[2]
The 'Homily against . . . Wilful Rebellion' refers to the
'Babylonical Beast of Rome'.[3] The theme was ham-
mered home in 1585 in a semi-official treatise by Thomas
Bilson, later to be a high-flying bishop.[4] Official sermons preached at Paul's Cross reiterated the point,
from Cranmer in 1536 proving the Pope to be Antichrist to the ex-papist Richard Sheldon's recantation
sermon in 1625.[5] The thanksgiving prayer for 5 November in the Book of Common Prayer called on God to
'root out that Babylonish and antichristian sect' of
papists. The Dedication to the Authorized Version
of the Bible congratulated James I for 'writing in defence
of the truth, which hath given such a blow unto the

[1] Cf. W. Prynne, *Canterburies Doome* (1644), pp. 277–8; N. Bernard,
Certain Discourses (1659), pp. 129–57; *The Genuine Remains of That
Learned Prelate, Dr. Thomas Barlow, late Lord Bishop of Lincoln* (1693),
pp. 191–2.

[2] H. Smith, *Sermons*, p. 416.

[3] *Sermons or Homilies* (1802), p. 510; cf. p. 47. Willet cited 'Article 5 of
our English confession' to make the same point (*Synopsis Papismi*, 5th
ed., 1634), p. 255.

[4] T. Bilson, *The True Difference between Christian Subjection, and Un-
christian Rebellion* (1585), sig. Aii, Avi, Aviii, a ii, p. 817. Dedicated to
Queen Elizabeth. For Bilson see W. M. Lamont, 'The Rise and Fall of
Bishop Bilson', *Journal of British Studies*, vii (1966), *passim*, who explains
how extracts from this treatise came to be reprinted in 1641.

[5] M. Maclure, *The Paul's Cross Sermons, 1534–1642* (Toronto University Press, 1958), esp. pp. 25, 185, 244. A Paul's Cross sermon not
mentioned by Maclure is Laurence Deios, *That the Pope is that Antichrist*
(1590), dedicated to Whitgift. Maclure lists that by John Dove in 1594,
Of the Second Coming of Christ and the Disclosing of Antichrist.

Man of Sin'. The 1615 Articles of the Church of Ireland included one declaring the Pope to be 'that Man of Sin'.[1] An official government propagandist, Gabriel Powel, indeed was alleged by Richard Montagu to have said that he was as certain the Pope was Antichrist as that Jesus Christ was the Son of God.[2]

IV

But the mention of Montagu reminds us that there was a reaction. As in so many other matters, it was from the 1590s that we can first see a weakening in what had virtually become an article of faith of the English church. Hooker indeed identified the Pope with the Man of Sin, and Rome with Babylon, but on the Roman church he hedged: 'Antichristianity . . . may nevertheless argue the church wherein Antichrist sitteth to be Christian.' (On this point he professed to be agreeing with Calvin.) In *The Laws of Ecclesiastical Polity* Hooker maliciously pointed out that Polish Socinians described belief in the Trinity as part of antichristian corruption. For them the Pope's triple crown signified the Trinity.[3] Lancelot Andrewes also approached the subject with caution. In his *Responsio ad Apologiam Cardinalis Bellarmini* (1610), even though he is defending James I, he emphasizes (correctly) that the King did not want to press his views on the identification of Antichrist as a matter of faith. Andrewes suggests that Bellarmine's

---

[1] Article 80. Laud succeeded in getting this article revoked in 1634.

[2] Montagu, *Appello Caesarem* (1625), p. 144; Laud, *Works*, iv, p. 309, where the relevant passage from Powel's *De Antichristo* is quoted.

[3] Hooker, *Of the Laws of Ecclesiastical Polity* (Everyman ed.), i, pp. 27, 35, 54; *Certayne Divine Tractates* (1618), pp. 105–6. Nicholas Bernard claimed Hooker among the many English divines who equated the Pope with Antichrist (*Certain Discourses*, p. 135).

arguments do not prove that the Pope is not Antichrist; and though he quotes James, Robert Abbott, and Brightman on the other side and indicates that there are converging signs that the Pope may be Antichrist, nevertheless he leaves the substantive question open, which in the circumstances suggests that he may not have shared the King's opinion.[1]

A change came at the same time as the rise of Arminianism. Arminius himself apparently was sound on the identification of Antichrist.[2] But the idea that failure to make the identification was an Arminian error received strong support when Grotius in 1640 asked a series of questions so sceptical as to make it abundantly clear that he rejected the whole idea.[3] James I, orthodox himself on the subject of Antichrist, became uneasy about the rudeness involved in calling a fellow head of state names,[4] especially when this occurred in a semi-official sermon preached to a popular audience at Paul's Cross.[5] He seems to have advised Joseph Hall in

[1] L. Andrewes, op. cit., pp. 220–37, 273–96; cf. *Tortura Torti* (1609), p. 183. Nevertheless Andrewes was quoted by Joseph Hall, Prynne, and Nicholas Bernard on their side (W. Prynne, *Canterburies Doome*, pp. 275, 278; Bernard, op. cit., pp. 129–31).

[2] N. Bernard, op. cit., pp. 139–41.

[3] [H. Grotius], *Commentatio ad Loca quaedam Novi Testamenti quae de Antichristo agunt, aut agere putantur* (Amsterdam, 1640); *Annotationes in Libros Evangeliorum* (Amsterdam, 1641), pp. 1032–45, appendix, pp. 51–85. Grotius was at once attacked (among others) by Pierre du Moulin (*Hippolyti Frontonis Caracottae, Strigil Adversus Commentationem Authoris Anonymi*, Amsterdam, 1640), and by Samuel Maresius, who altogether devoted nearly 1500 pages to the subject (*Dissertatio de Antichristo*, Amsterdam, 1640; *Concordia Discors et Antichristus Revelatus*, Amsterdam, 1643, 2 vols.).

[4] Sir Thomas Browne shared this objection (*Works*, Bohn ed., ii, pp. 324–6).

[5] Maclure, *The Paul's Cross Sermons, 1534–1642*, p. 244; Laud, *Works*, iv, p. 308. See p. 65 below.

1622 not to call the Pope Antichrist.[1] Antichrist became the subject of a major political controversy at the end of James's reign, when Richard Montagu declared that men were too peremptory in affirming positively that the Pope was Antichrist: 'the church resolveth not'. He believed that the Pope was *an* Antichrist but not *the* Antichrist.[2] It was later alleged that John Cosin, 'like a saucy fellow', changed Montagu's phrase 'Turk . . . as well as the Pope' to 'Turk . . . rather than the Pope'. 'And this you did schismatically and seditiously, to . . . vent your fanatical opinion that the Pope is not the great Antichrist.'[3]

Men may have been lying in wait for Montagu for some time because of his attempt to prove a divine right to tithes.[4] At all events, in 1625 the House of Commons took up his challenge. No less a person than John Pym reported from its committee on religion. The state, Pym said, 'cannot avoid . . . the mischief which groweth' by Montagu's opinions 'concerning the church and the Pope'. Although James I had spent many pages in proving the Pope to be Antichrist, Montagu had the temerity to say he had never heard a convincing argument for it, 'and hereby persuadeth many to incline to Rome'. Mr. Lamont suggests that Montagu's refusal to accept the view that the Pope was Antichrist was 'perhaps his greatest crime in the eyes of his opponents'.[5]

[1] J. Hall, *Works*, xii, p. 455.
[2] Montagu, *A New Gagg for An Old Goose* (1624), pp. 73–5; *Appello Caesarem*, p. 144.
[3] Ed. G. Ornsby, *The Correspondence of John Cosin* (Surtees Soc. 1869), i, p. 196; J. Cosin, *Works* (1843–55), ii, pp. 41–2; Montagu, *A New Gagg for An Old Goose*, p. 75; *Appello Caesarem*, pp. 144–9.
[4] See my *Economic Problems of the Church*, p. 137.
[5] W. Lamont, *Godly Rule*, p. 66.

The Commons were careful 'not to touch on doctrinal points'.[1] But other controversialists were less reticent. George Carleton, British representative at the Synod of Dort;[2] Francis Rous, later lay assessor to the Westminster Assembly, Speaker of the Barebones Parliament, and a Cromwellian peer;[3] John Yates,[4] Henry Burton,[5] and anonymous pamphlets made Antichrist a *cause célèbre*.[6]

At the York House Conference in 1626, the final parting of the ways between the government and the Calvinists, Bishop Buckeridge of Rochester, formerly Laud's tutor, supported Montagu and challenged his brother of Coventry (Morton) to prove that Montagu's doctrine was contrary to that of the Church of England.[7] This remained the Laudian line, proclaimed by John Donne at court in 1627,[8] by Heylyn and Dow in 1637 against Henry Burton,[9] and by the Archbishop himself at his trial. 'No man can challenge me that I

---

[1] Ed. S. R. Gardiner, *Debates in the House of Commons in 1625* (Camden Soc., 1873), pp. 49, 142–4, 179–86.

[2] G. Carleton, *An Examination of those things wherein the Author of the late Appeale holdeth the Doctrines of the Pelagians and Arminians to be the Doctrines of the Church of England* (1626).

[3] F. Rous, *Testis Veritatis. The Doctrine of King James . . ., Of the Church of England, Of the Catholicke Church* (1626); cf. Rous, *A Religious and Worthy Speech in Parliament* (1641), sig. A4ᵛ.

[4] [John Yates], *Ibis ad Caesarem* (1626), esp. Part III, pp. 12–14.

[5] H. Burton, *A Plea to An Appeale* (1626); cf. *The Baiting of the Popes Bull* (1627), introductory verses, sig. § 3, pp. 92–5; *The Seven Vials* (1628); *Truths Triumph over Trent* (1629); *Babel No Bethel* (1629).

[6] [Anon.], *A Second Parallel, together with a Writ of Error Sued against the Appealer* (1626), esp. pp. 37, 144–9.   [7] Cosin, *Works*, ii, p. 42.

[8] John Donne, *Sermons*, ed. G. R. Potter and E. M. Simpson (University of California Press, 1953–62), vii, p. 409.

[9] P. Heylyn, *A Briefe and Moderate Answer to The seditious and scandalous Challenges of Henry Burton* (1637), esp. pp. 114, 126–7; C. Dow, *Innovations Unjustly charged upon the Present Church and State* (1637), p. 5.

hold the Pope not to be Antichrist; it is a great question even among learned protestants whether he be so or not', said Laud; 'the Church of England hath not positively resolved him to be so'.[1] The case against Laud on this point was that his licenser had expunged references to the Pope being Antichrist before allowing books to be published; that the Archbishop himself had in 1634 objected to the phrase 'antichristian yoke' in an appeal for the relief of Palatinate ministers, though the words had been used to describe popery in earlier appeals; that he told Bishop Hall not to affirm positively that the Pope was Antichrist, alleging the command of Charles I, who had fewer Calvinist inhibitions than his father. At his trial in 1645 Laud was denounced as a pander and broker to Antichrist.[2] Antichrist is conspicuously absent from Laud's controversy with Fisher the Jesuit, as he is from Laud's protégé Chillingworth's *The Religion of Protestants* (1637). After Laud's rise to dominance the English church no longer proclaimed the Pope to be Antichrist. No vernacular translation of the seminal works on Revelation and Daniel by Brightman, Mede, Pareus, or Alsted was published in England until after the meeting of the Long Parliament.

It was in this atmosphere that Gilbert Sheldon became 'the first who publicly denied the Pope to be Antichrist in Oxon.', to the horror of John Prideaux, who was examining him for the doctor's degree.[3]

---

[1] W. Prynne, *Canterburies Doome* (1644), pp. 551–2. This point was substantially repeated in the nineteenth century by J. H. Todd, *Six Discourses on the Prophecies relating to Antichrist in the Apocalypse of St. John* (Dublin, 1846), pp. xxii–xxiv.

[2] *Canterburies Doome*, pp. 260–4, 269–79, 541–2, 551–6; J. Rushworth, *Historical Collections* (1680), i, p. 34; Laud, *Works*, iv, pp. 308–13.

[3] Barlow, *Remains* (1693), p. 192.

Another Laudian, the aged Robert Shelford, in 1635 published *A Treatise showing the Antichrist not to be yet come*. Significantly he adopted the medieval idea, repeated by Bellarmine and other Catholic writers, that when Antichrist did come he would be a Jew.[1] In one of the few humorous moments that any writer on this solemn subject allows himself, Shelford reminded his readers that many of the early Fathers had said that Antichrist (like Puritans) hates images. But, added Shelford, images are idols only when worshipped. 'Otherwise our Geneva Bible should maintain idolatry in picturing . . . God in the form of an old man'— exactly as in the window which the Puritan Henry Sherfield had recently demolished at Salisbury.[2] John Cotton may have had Shelford in mind when in 1648 he declared it to be an error to say that Antichrist had not yet come.[3] Archbishop Ussher and others denounced Shelford in the strongest terms: 'rotten stuff'; 'a book neither pious nor learned, written by one wholly savouring of the spirit of Antichrist, and ignorant of the main scope of the Gospel'.[4]

But as Laudian influence grew, significantly fewer books on the subject of Antichrist were published. An exception is a broadside ballad of 1634, *A True and Plaine Genealogy or Pedigree of Antichrist* (deriving him from the Pope); but this may have been published

[1] R. Shelford, *Five Pious and Learned Discourses* (Cambridge, 1635), pp. 229 seq., esp. p. 314. See Appendix I (ii) below.

[2] Shelford, op. cit., pp. 299–300.

[3] Ed. L. Ziff, *John Cotton and the Churches of America* (Harvard, 1968), p. 265.

[4] R. Parr, *Life of . . . Usher* (1686), ii, p. 477; Ussher, *Works* (1847–64), xvi, p. 9. Cf. *The Diary of John Rous* (ed. M. A. E. Green, Camden Soc., 1856), p. 79.

illegally. So rare were such books that Laud claimed the credit of licensing only Daniel Featley's *Clavis Mystica* (1636), 'where he proves the Pope, in his opinion, to be Antichrist'.[1] Joseph Mede at Cambridge in the mid-thirties found that it had suddenly become unfashionable and unpopular to say that the Pope was Antichrist: he felt that he must apologize for his voluminous tomes. His friend William Twisse agreed that Mede should refrain from publishing until better days came.[2] Ussher was sufficiently worried by the trend of events to write to Laud reaffirming his belief that the Pope was Antichrist, despite papist conceits 'that we are . . . every day drawing nigher unto them than other'.[3] It was not until December 1640 that London citizens could subscribe to the Root and Branch Petition complaining of prelates and others who 'plead and maintain that the Pope is not Antichrist'.[4] Next month a clergyman was denounced to Parliament for declaring positively that the Pope was not Antichrist,[5] and the Laudian John Pocklington was attacked for maintaining 'divers wicked, popish and antichristian points, to the great danger and damage of this church and state'.[6] At the same time Robert Baillie discovered that 'many

---

[1] Laud, *Works*, iv, p. 309; Featley, op. cit., p. 808. This was not a fortunate example: Laud forced Featley to omit many anti-Catholic passages.

[2] Mede, *Works* (3rd ed., 1672), pp. xxvi–xxvii, 798, 818, 829, 834–5, 854. [3] Prynne, *Canterburies Doome*, p. 554.

[4] Ed. S. R. Gardiner, *Constitutional Documents of the Puritan Revolution, 1625–1660* (3rd ed., Oxford, 1906), p. 140.

[5] Ed. W. Notestein, *Parliamentary Journal of Sir Simonds D'Ewes* (Yale University Press, 1923), p. 232 (8 Jan. 1641).

[6] [Anon.], *The Petition or Articles exhibited in Parliament against John Pocklington* (1641), p. 3; cf. *An Appeal of the Orthodox Ministers of the Church of England against Richard Montague* (1641).

of the fathers ... did unwittingly bring forth that Anti-christ',[7] so outflanking one line of defence of bishops.

Throughout the period 1530–1640, then, except for a challenge in the last few years, the identification of Pope and Antichrist won very general support in the Church of England. One possible reason for the emer-gence of the noun 'animal' in English at the beginning of the seventeenth century, to replace the hitherto universal 'beast', is that the latter was acquiring too specific a sense as the equivalent of Antichrist. 'Animal' as a noun does not appear in the Authorized Version, based as it is on earlier sixteenth-century translations; but in the decade before 1611 Shakespeare, for instance, was beginning to use 'animal' where the A.V. would have said 'beast'.

But already heretical identifications of Antichrist were coming into prominence: they no doubt helped to cause the Laudian reaction. To these we now turn.

[7] R. Baillie, *The Unlawfulness and Danger of Limited Prelacie* (1641), p. 7.

II

BEFORE 1642:
ANTICHRISTIAN BISHOPS?

A certain oatmeal maker, taking upon him to be a
preacher and therefore imprisoned, was called before
the High Commission, where, keeping on his hat, and
being asked why he did not put it off, he answered he
would never put off his hat to bishops. 'But you will to
Privy Councillors?' said one of them. 'Then as you
are Privy Councillors', quoth he, 'I put off my hat; but
as you are rags of the Beast, lo! I put it on again.'

JOSEPH MEDE to SIR MARTIN STUTEVILLE,
17 April 1630, *Court and Times of Charles I* (ed.
R. F. Williams, 1848), ii, p. 71.

I

WYCLIF had included among the ten signs of Antichrist the exercise of civil jurisdiction and the use of
force.[1] He and his Lollard successors thought that
bishops and archbishops were no less antichristian than
the Pope.[2] This dangerous doctrine flourished in England at the very time King and bishops were reforming
the church. Tyndale declared that 'bishops and priests
that preach not, or that preach ought save God's word,

[1] G. Leff, 'John Wyclif: the Path to Dissent', *Proceedings of the British
Academy*, lii, p. 169; 'Wyclif and Hus: a Doctrinal Comparison', *Bulletin
of the John Rylands Library*, vol. 50 (1968), p. 388.

[2] *The Examination of Lord Cobham* (1413), in *An English Garner* (ed.
E. Arber, 1895–6), vi, p. 128; M. F. Aston, 'Lollards and Sedition',
P. and P., no. 17, p. 30; J. A. F. Thomson, *The Later Lollards* (Oxford
University Press, 1965), p. 65 and *passim*.

are . . . servants of the Beast, whose mark they bear'.
Excommunication is of Antichrist. The section of
his *Obedience of a Christian Man* headed 'Antichrist' is
about church courts, excommunication, ecclesiastical
exactions, and the clergy generally, as well as about
bishops. 'It is impossible to preach Christ', Tyndale
said, 'except thou preach against Antichrist; that is to
say, [those] which with their false doctrine and violence
of sword enforce to quench the true doctrine of Christ.'
When the clergy handed heretics over to the secular
arm, 'the kings are become Antichrist's hangmen'.[1] As
they had been for Wyclif, persecution and failure to
preach are the marks of Antichrist. One can see why
Sir Thomas More referred to Tyndale's 'antichristian
heresies'.[2]

Tyndale held no official position in the English
church and was burnt as a heretic. But these ideas were
ominously repeated in Edward VI's reign by Bishop
Bale. The Beast for him included 'the prelates of Antichrist's church, the two-horned monsters, great-bellied
bishops' and all ecclesiastical officers down to vicars,
including especially officials of church courts: the Reformation had scotched Antichrist, not killed him.[3]
Similarly Hooper, before he reluctantly accepted a
bishopric himself, spoke of the bishops' 'fraud and arti-
fice, by which they promote the kingdom of Antichrist,
especially in the form of the oath'.[4] The Geneva Bible's
marginal notes identified canon law with 'the number
of the name of the Beast', and suggested that ordination

---

[1] Tyndale, *Doctrinal Treatises*, pp. 42–3, 185–6, 232–52.
[2] *O.E.D.*, 'Antichristian'.
[3] Bale, *Select Works*, pp. 420–40, 505, 555.
[4] Robinson, *Original Letters Relative to the English Reformation*, p. 81.

'commemorated the name of the Beast'. Antichrist is still with us. 'His head we have seen in our own memory to have been cut off, and to be cured again.'[1] 'And to be cured again': that was the burden of those who continued to attack Antichrist in England. The Pope had gone, but much of what had been objectionable in popery remained. 'Neque unquam illinc ejectum fuisse papatum', wrote Beza to Bullinger in 1565, 'sed ad regiam majestatem potius translatum.'[2]

That was more outspoken than most Englishmen dared to be, though Anthony Gilbey declared that under the royal supremacy of Henry VIII England had been 'no better than the Romish Antichrist'.[3] Christ's ministers 'go like the servants of Antichrist'. Those who, like Gilbey, wished for further reformation 'show you the right way to throw out Antichrist both head and tail. . . . But they [the bishops], after they have thrown out Antichrist by the head, go about to pull him in again by the tail'.[4] John Cotton thought that though Henry VIII and Elizabeth 'cut off the head of the Beast', they preserved its body in the canons of their Church, and 'an unsafe principle in their hearts'.[5] The phrase 'the tail of Antichrist left behind by the Pope' was often repeated by Thomas Cartwright and other Puritans,[6] which gives point to Whitgift dubbing

[1] Marginal note on Rev. 13: 16–18, 12.

[2] Strype, *Annals of the Reformation* (1824), i, Part II, p. 171.

[3] A. Gilbey, *An Admonition to England and Scotland* (1558), in Claire Cross, *The Royal Supremacy in the Elizabethan Church* (1969), p. 118.

[4] Ed. A. Peel, *The Seconde Parte of a Register* (1915), i, p. 140; [Anon.], *A view of popish abuses yet remaining in the English church* (1646), p. 16—a reprint of mid-sixteenth-century pieces.

[5] P. Miller, *The New England Mind: the Seventeenth Century* (New York, 1939), p. 468.

[6] Whitgift, *Works*, iii, p. 459; ed. W. H. Frere and C. E. Douglas,

Cartwright himself 'the tail of Antichrist' because he stirred up schism. Antichrist, in Whitgift's view, had been working from the earliest days of the Christian church promoting sects and heresies.[1]

It was reasonable for any protestant to see Bloody Mary as Antichrist come to life.[2] But Elizabeth's government was not spared. In 1580 William Fulke thought divers Antichrists were likely to be made Privy Councillors. Antichrist's kingdom seems about to be set up, and no one dares tell the Queen.[3] Anthony Gilbey told Cartwright that the old Beast Popery had been succeeded by 'this second Beast policy, to do all that the other Beast did before'. The change seemed scarcely for the better.[4]

Those who used the symbolism of Antichrist had presumably no consciously evasive purpose in mind. They drew on allegorical habits of mind inherited from the past, reinforced by the availability for all of the Bible in the vernacular. Nevertheless the symbolism of the Beast had its advantages. Its imprecision allowed differing interpretations to be put upon it, either by different people or by the same person in appealing to different groups. Antichrist stood for bad, papal, repressive institutions: exactly which institutions was anybody's choice. This vagueness had security advantages. In the England of 1530–1640 critics of the

---

Puritan Manifestoes (1907), p. 37; Henry Smith, *Sermons*, p. 148; [R. Parker], *A Scholasticall Discourse against Symbolizing with Antichrist in Ceremonies* (1607), p. 136.

[1] Whitgift, *Works*, iii, p. 495; ii, pp. 181–2.

[2] H. F. M. Prescott, *Mary Tudor* (1952), p. 191.

[3] Peel, *The Seconde Parte of a Register*, ii, pp. 62–3.

[4] Ibid. i, pp. 30, 141: References to 'Antichrist's remains', 'the remnants of Antichrist', 'antichristian trash' abound in this work.

hierarchy were in fact attacking the monarchy and the legally established government, as their enemies did not fail to point out. 'The Beast' was a much less specific enemy than 'the system of church government approved by Queen Elizabeth'. The Queen herself could hardly object to denunciations of Antichrist, as long as Antichrist was not too clearly defined. Like sin, everyone was against him.

I do not wish to introduce too much political sophistication into sixteenth- and seventeenth-century theological discussions. Richard Hooker can do it for me. He accused Cartwright and his fellows of using phrases like 'the filthy relics of Antichrist' which were popular with the multitude but whose imprecision made evasion possible when they were pressed for an explanation.[1] When they touch on delicate matters, we should indeed read Puritan sermons and treatises with a care similar to that which Kremlinologists devote to their subject today. Kremlinologists often guess foolishly; but they can sometimes read between the lines, or read what is not said, with effect.[2] In 1637 one of Winthrop's correspondents spoke of not expecting 'protection from God without a mixture of the serpent's wisdom with the dove's innocency'.[3]

When, for instance, Henry Smith complained that 'the tail of Antichrist' had been left behind by the Pope and should be expelled, this was vague enough.[4] But others were more specific about what they thought antichristian in the English church. Edmund Spenser's

[1] Hooker, op. cit. i, p. 372; cf. pp. 384, 412.
[2] Cf. my *Puritanism and Revolution* (1958), p. 260.
[3] C. Bridenbaugh, *Vexed and Troubled Englishmen, 1590–1642* (Oxford, 1968), pp. 305–6.
[4] H. Smith, *Sermons*, p. 148.

earliest published verse was written for a treatise whose
main theme was an attack on the Pope as Antichrist.
But among the blasphemous antichristian institutions
listed we find not only monks and friars but also, quite
casually mentioned, vicars.[1] Knox from Scotland and
Cartwright in England had given, as portions of the
Beast's mark still left in the English Prayer Book, 'cross-
ing in baptism, kneeling at the Lord's table'.[2] Antichrist receives communion kneeling, declared a reply
to episcopal criticisms of the *Admonition to Parliament*.[3]
Robert Parker published (anonymously) in 1607 a
whole treatise arguing that the sign of the cross was 'the
mark of the Beast and Antichrist's ensign', quoting
among others Napier.[4] In the freer days of 1640 Lewis
Hughes reminded Parliament that the sign of the cross
in baptism was the mark of the Beast.[5] Under Elizabeth
William Fulke and others described the surplice as the
'rags of Antichrist'.[6] 'Cap, gown and tippet' were 'antichristian apparel', said the first *Admonition to Parliament*.[7]

[1] John vander Noot, *A Theatre wherein be represented as wel the miseries
& calamities that follow the voluptuous Worldlings* (1569), p. 22 and *passim*.

[2] J. Strype, *Annals of the Reformation*, I, part i, p. 177; G. Gillespie, *A
Dispute against the English-Popish Ceremonies* (1637), Part III, p. 43.

[3] *Certaine Articles collected and taken . . . by the Byshops out of . . . An
Admonition to Parliament, with an Answere to the same*, in Frere and Douglas,
op. cit., p. 140.

[4] [Parker], *A Scholasticall Discourse against Symbolizing with Antichrist in
Ceremonies, especially in the Sign of the Crosse* (1607), esp. pp. 72-3, 76, 108,
136.

[5] [L. Hughes], *Certaine Grievances well worthy the Serious Consideration of
the Right Honourable and High Court of Parliament* (1640), esp. p. 5. Cf.
Richard Drake, *Autobiography*, quoted by A. T. Hart, *The Man in the
Pew* (1966), pp. 135-6.

[6] H. C. Porter, *Reformation and Reaction in Tudor Cambridge* (Cambridge
University Press, 1958), p. 115 (1565); Peel, *The Seconde Parte of a
Register*, i, pp. 68-70 (1571).

[7] Frere and Douglas, op. cit., p. 11.

In 1606 Thomas Whetenhall, esquire, quoted Thomas Becon to the effect that those who love to be distinguished by apparel are chaplains of Antichrist, not ministers of Christ.[1] These apparently trivial conflicts over vestments seemed to many Puritans to be about something very serious indeed.

Anthony Gilbey in 1570 listed a hundred points of popery which deform the English reformation—church courts, vestments, ceremonies, licences, etc. 'These all fill the purse, and were devised of Antichrist to hold his kingdom.'[2] Bishops, deans, and archdeacons, etc., were antichristian, it was argued in a petition to the Parliament of 1587.[3] Both Cartwright and Nicholas Fuller thought church courts derived from Antichrist, that ecclesiastical jurisdiction was 'antichristian'. 'God deliver all Christians out of this antichristian tyranny', the first *Admonition to Parliament* said of church courts.[4] John Rainolds noted 'the want of preaching of God's law' as 'the cause why so many souls among us are not yet delivered from the power of Antichrist.... We accuse Turk and Pope for enforcing men by violence, bands and death to believe their religion, and yet we rather practise man's means than the way God hath appointed'.[5]

---

[1] T. Whetenhall, *A Discourse of the Abuses now in question in the churches of Christ* (1606), pp. 172–85. Whetenhall endowed two London lectureships to the tune of £1,000 (W. K. Jordan, *The Charities of London* (1960), pp. 286, 411).

[2] *A viewe of Antichrist his lawes and ceremonies in our church unreformed* (1570), in *A parte of a register* (1593), pp. 55–72.

[3] Peel, op. cit. ii, p. 209.

[4] Whitgift, *Works*, iii, pp. 265, 279, 459, ii, p. 79; Frere and Douglas, op. cit., p. 34; *The Argument of Nicholas Fuller* (1641), p. 22. Note the date of the reprint.

[5] [J. Rainolds], *The Discovery of the Man of Sinne* (Oxford, 1614), p. 17.

Thomas Taylor in the 1620s very carefully listed the signs of Antichrist, which included excessive emphasis on vestments; persecution—good and godly men condemned for heretics; ambitious and worldly bishops occupying seats of judicature. The application to England was scarcely veiled when he gave, as evidence of 'the open prevailing of Antichrist in many lands', 'infinite increase and boldness of Papists and Recusants, . . . the open increase of . . . Jesuits and priests croaking in corners and streets'. The ideological power of the 'delusions' of Antichrist was greater than his physical force. After fifty pages of this sort of thing Taylor hardly needed to tell his readers that what he said applied especially to England since the reign of Mary.[1] In another work he attacked 'the Roman Antichrist' in terms which suggest that he was thinking of an ecclesiastical authority nearer home: 'Never did the civil authority so much mischief the church in all ages together as the ecclesiastical; never did heathen tyrants and Roman Emperors so much bane the church by the civil sword as the Roman Antichrist by the ecclesiastical.'[2] It is in this spirit that the alliance between Puritans and Erastians was forged.

There was then in the sixteenth century and later a strong tradition which thought that too much of Antichrist remained in the episcopal Anglican church. This view was shared by many of the early Elizabethan bishops, who believed in a doctrine of continuous reformation and not at all in the divine right of epis-

---

[1] T. Taylor, *Christs Victorie over the Dragon* (ed. W. Jennett, 1633), pp. 693–742, 817. Samuel Hieron said persecution was antichristian (*Sermons*, ii, p. 318).

[2] Taylor, *Works* (1653), p. 326; cf. *The Principles of Christian Practice* (1653), p. 77—human traditions are the yokes of Antichrist.

copacy. But gradually 'the responsibilities of office' and resentment at the criticisms of their old comrades in exile drew the dividing lines clearer. The Puritan *Admonition to Parliament* of 1572 said that the church was still governed 'by such canons and customs as by which Antichrist did rule his synagogue'; bishops are given 'titles, livings and offices by Antichrist devised'. The authors denounced 'princes' pleasures, men's devices, popish ceremonies and antichristian rites, in public pulpits defended', and called for the removal of Antichrist 'both head, body and branch'.[1] The condemnation of bishops as antichristian was echoed in the same year by John Field, by the authors of *An Exhortation to the Bishops and their Clergie*, and by Cartwright,[2] by Robert Harvey in 1576,[3] by Edmund Snape in 1590.[4] Gilbey referred to 'this antichristian hierarchy and popish ordering of ministers'.[5] 'Clogs of Antichrist' was Robert Wright's phrase for archbishops and bishops.[6] In 1583 the laity of Norwich petitioned the Queen to remove the government of Antichrist from the church, 'with all his archbishops and also his court-keepers', as his doctrine had already been removed.[7]

The Dedham Classis discussed in 1584 whether bishops' authority was antichristian. Opinions were

[1] Frere and Douglas, op. cit., pp. 12, 19, 34, 37.

[2] P. Collinson, 'John Field and Elizabethan Puritanism', in *Elizabethan Government and Society* (ed. S. T. Bindoff, J. Hurstfield, and C. H. Williams, 1961), p. 137; Frere and Douglas, op. cit., pp. 70–1, 111.

[3] J. Browne, *History of Congregationalism . . . in Norfolk and Suffolk* (1877), p. 22.

[4] Strype, *Life of Whitgift*, ii, p. 8.

[5] *X Solid and Serious Queries Concerning the power of Church Discipline* (1646), p. 16.

[6] Strype, *Annals*, III, part i, p. 178.

[7] Browne, *Congregationalism . . . in Norfolk and Suffolk*, p. 28.

divided; the reason for the majority view that bishops were not antichristian was that their jurisdiction was confirmed by the laws of England.[1] ('Is it therefore not antichristian', was a more radical retort to this argument, 'because that civil laws of earthly princes have confirmed the canon law, and take it now as their own?'[2]) Martin Marprelate summed up the views of many when in 1588 he denounced 'our Lord Bishops', who 'with the rest of that swinish rabble are petty Antichrists, petty popes'. He gave bishops' licensing to preach as a mark of Antichrist.[3] Bancroft quoted Marprelate as saying 'there was never any but antichristian popes and popelings that ever claimed this authority' (that of bishops over the clergy). 'Doth man's allowance or disallowance make a matter antichristian or not antichristian?' Bancroft asked. 'Were they godly bishops which claimed this authority when it was not gainsaid, and are they become antichristian bishops for challenging the same, because some do mislike it?'[4] It was no doubt with reference to the popularity of Marprelate's pamphlets that Izaak Walton much later said that the common people of England in Elizabeth's reign became so fanatic as to believe the bishops to be Antichrist—though he may have been referring to separatists too.[5]

Richard Bancroft did his best to emphasize this point

[1] Ed. R. G. Usher, *The Presbyterian Movement in the Reign of Queen Elizabeth* (Camden Soc., 1905), p. 97; P. Collinson, *The Elizabethan Puritan Movement* (1967), pp. 228, 261.

[2] *Certaine Articles*, in Frere and Douglas, op. cit., p. 145.

[3] M. Marprelate, *The Epistle* (1588), pp. 4–5, 39, 51, and *passim*; *Theses Martinianae* (1589), nos. 60, 79.

[4] R. Bancroft, *A Sermon Preached at Pauls Crosse* (1589), pp. 18–20.

[5] Walton, *Lives* (World's Classics), p. 185.

in his anti-Puritan propaganda. He quoted passages to show that Puritans thought the whole government of the church antichristian, that 'Antichrist reigneth amongst us'. The orders and ceremonies of the church were antichristian, the non-preaching clergy were servants of the Romish Antichrist, wearing his liveries.[1] In an age when every Englishman was automatically a member of the state church, when uniformity in religion was regarded as essential to the unity of the state, it was thus no laughing matter to see Antichrist not safely distant in Rome, but in Canterbury and indeed in every parish in the country. Men who thought the hierarchy of the English church antichristian were at once suspect of disloyalty to the English state. Bancroft and his henchmen cheated in their propaganda by lumping together dissident but conforming Puritans, whose views I have been quoting hitherto, and the Brownists, Barrowists, and Anabaptists whom I am now going to consider. (Indeed, the *Forme of Prayers* printed in English at Geneva in 1561 had denounced anabaptists as well as papists as 'limbs of Antichrist'.[2]) But what was described in the House of Commons in 1643 as 'Bishop Bancroft and the Babylonian faction' prevailed.[3] The hierarchy's propaganda was helped by the abortive revolt of the deranged Hacket and Coppinger in 1591, whose object had been to overthrow Antichrist's kingdom.[4]

[1] R. Bancroft, *Dangerous Positions* (1593), p. 48; ed. A. Peel, *Tracts Attributed to Richard Bancroft* (Cambridge University Press, 1953), pp. 22, 26–7, 56, 167. Cf. *The Seconde Parte of a Register*, i, p. 71.

[2] Quoted by L. Lupton, *A History of the Geneva Bible*, ii (1969), p. 53.

[3] Francis Cheynell, *Sions Memento and Gods Alarum* (1643), p. 30: printed by order.

[4] R. Cosin, *Conspiracy for Pretended Reformation* (1699), pp. 46, 64: first published 1592.

II

In a dialogue published in 1608 Henoch Clapham
makes a separatist say that a conforming Puritan is 'a
limb of Antichrist, and of all the protestants the most
hypocritical'.[1] Let us look for a moment at the separatists. They thought the whole Church of England so
permeated with the relics of Antichrist that it was impossible for the children of God to remain in communion
with it.[2] This had been the view of Richard Fitz's
Privy Church in 1567, whose members also referred to
canon law as 'this secret and disguised Antichrist',
'another Beast'.[3] Separatists in 1586 agreed.[4] 'Chancellors, officials and commissaries' were derived from
Antichrist, said Udall.[5] Giles Wigginton preached 'commonly against Antichrist and all popish prelates and
usurpers'.[6] Many denounced bishops' courts as antichristian.[7] The High Commission was the very throne
of the Beast, declared Barrow.[8] The church's system
of excommunication was denounced as antichristian
by Barrow, by Robert Harrison, by Mrs. Stubbe to
Thomas Cartwright.[9] Thomas Rogers was right to say

[1] H. Clapham, *Errour on the Right Hand* (1608), pp. 1–3, 42.

[2] For an excellent analysis of the way in which the concept of Antichrist led to congregational separatism, see G. F. Nuttall, *Visible Saints*
(Oxford University Press, 1957), pp. 55–61.

[3] Burrage, op. cit. ii, pp. 13, 17.

[4] *The Seconde Parte of a Register*, ii, p. 7.

[5] J. Udall, *A Demonstration of Discipline* (ed. E. Arber, 1880), p. 40.
First published 1588.   [6] *The Seconde Parte of a Register*, ii, p. 247.

[7] Ibid. i, p. 158 (1583); *The Writings of Harrison and Browne*, pp. 32,
37, 87–8; ed. L. H. Carlson, *The Writings of Henry Barrow, 1590–1591*
(1966), p. 319.

[8] *Writings of Henry Barrow, 1587–90* (ed. Carlson, 1962), pp. 458, 468.

[9] Ibid., p. 57; *Writings of Barrow, 1590–1591*, pp. 107, 135; *Writings of
Harrison and Browne*, p. 52; J. Waddington, *Congregational History, 1567–
1700* (1874), p. 19.

that Brownists thought that where their discipline is absent, 'antichristianity doth reign'.[1]

The very names parson and vicar were antichristian, because the holders were not chosen by the people: they were 'the waged servants of Antichrist', 'the excrement of Antichrist'.[2] Barrow was accused of saying that parsonages and vicarages were in name, office, and function as antichristian as bishops and archbishops.[3] He could hardly have expressed himself more strongly than that. Children were baptized into Antichrist in the popish parishes, said Robert Browne; John Robinson agreed that parish assemblies were antichristian.[4] 'The separatists say we are in the midst of Babylon, our assemblies are antichristian', Thomas Taylor complained in 1624.[5] Patronage too was of Antichrist, Udall had said.[6] So were the tithes which maintained parish ministers.[7] In fact the church, in the words of Greenwood in 1590, 'may profess Christianism and Antichristianism, both at a time'.[8] The lordships and great livings of bishops, and the Church of England as a whole, were antichristian, Robert Harrison, Robert Browne and Henry Barrow thought: hence the

---

[1] T. Rogers, *The Faith, Doctrine and Religion of the Church of England* (1681), p. 98. First published 1607. Rogers was Bancroft's chaplain.

[2] *Writings of Harrison and Browne*, pp. 262–3; *Writings of Barrow, 1587–90*, p. 505; *1590–1591*, p. 244; *Cartwrightiana* (ed. Peel and Carlson, 1951), p. 258; Burrage, op. cit. i, p. 328, ii, pp. 67–70.

[3] T. Rogers, op. cit., p. 213; cf. Burrage, op. cit. i, p. 198, ii, pp. 143–5.

[4] *Writings of Harrison and Browne*, p. 256; Robinson, *Of Religious Communion, Private and Publique* (Leyden, 1614), p. 17. Provincial, diocesan, and lordly government was also of Antichrist.

[5] Taylor, *Two Sermons* (1624), p. 16.

[6] Udall, *A Demonstration of Discipline*, pp. 29–30.

[7] J. Waddington, *John Penry* (1858), p. 150.

[8] *O.E.D.*, 'antichristianism'.

necessity of separation.[1] Its worship, laws, ordinances, officers, courts, canons, rites, ceremonies, dispensations, licences, and the authority of bishops and deans—all were antichristian in the eyes of Harrison, Browne, Barrow, Greenwood, and their followers.[2] John Robinson, pastor to the Pilgrim Fathers, thought that 'nothing hath more in former days advanced, nor doth at this day uphold, the throne of Antichrist, than the people's discharging themselves of the care of public affairs in the church, on the one side; and the priests' and prelates' arrogating all to themselves on the other side'.[3]

John Penry in 1593 denounced the ordinances and inventions of Antichrist's kingdom—lord archbishops, deans, archdeacons, chancellors, canons, prebends, priests, deacons, church courts.[4] Not only were these false ecclesiastical offices derived from Antichrist, but so was the manner of calling into them and 'a great part of the works wherein these false officers are employed', as well as 'the livings whereby they are maintained in their offices'.[5] The mingling of civil and church offices was flat antichristianity, Browne agreed; none, he supposed, 'can deny but that Antichrist is come already'. And this kingdom of Antichrist was confirmed by the civil magistrate.[6]

[1] Burrage, op. cit. i, p. 134; *Writings of Harrison and Browne*, pp. 87–8, 523.

[2] Ibid., pp. 52, 206–9, 423, 464–8, 536–7; *Writings of Barrow, 1587–90*, pp. 139, 144–5, 242–3, 286, 339; *1590–1*, pp. 40, 44, 91, 194, 207, 225, 285, 328; Burrage, op. cit. ii, p. 32; cf. p. 101; ed. L. H. Carlson, *The Writings of John Greenwood, 1587–1590* (1962), p. 180.

[3] John Robinson, *Works* (1851), ii, p. 213.

[4] Waddington, *John Penry*, pp. 137, 151.

[5] Ibid., p. 150; cf. *The Notebook of John Penry* (ed. A. Peel, Camden Soc., 1944), pp. 5–6.

[6] *Writings of Harrison and Browne*, pp. 267, 413, 517.

This was the point at which the symbol of Antichrist became politically dangerous. In 1586 Ralph Durden was imprisoned for predicting the downfall of the monarchy in 1589. He had identified the kingdom of England with the Beast of Revelation.[1] When Henry Barrow said the government of the English church was the yoke of Antichrist, the Attorney-General treated this as an attack on the Queen's government.[2] Penry deliberately linked the religious attack with an appeal to national feelings, so closely associated with protestantism. If the ministers of the Church of England take their stand by the law of the land (as the Dedham Classis had argued in the case of bishops), that was itself antichristian, since 'they may by virtue of their office preach only such points as the law of the land doth allow'.[3] They stand 'by virtue of a foreign power'. 'Why should I be delivered unto these Romanists?'[4] Since the Reformation there has been

no alteration at all in the office of the priest, the deacon, the archprelate or bishop, the lord bishop, the archdeacon, the commissary, the chancellor etc.; in the form of calling very little; in the works of book worship, excommunication, suspension, dispensation etc., not much; in the maintenances

[1] J. Strype, *Annals of the Reformation* (1824), III, part i, pp. 693–4; part ii, pp. 479–87.

[2] Barrow, op. cit. i, p. 122; cf. *Cartwrightiana*, p. 260. Barrow denied the accusation, but the references cited at pp. 52–4 above, appear to give him the lie. Cf. a state paper of 1593, probably by Lord-Keeper Puckering, which makes much of this point (Strype, *Annals*, iv, p. 140).

[3] *The Notebook of John Penry*, p. 22; cf. pp. 11–14, 19. 'The dragon and the two Beasts oppugne prophecy' is the Geneva Bible's summary of Revelation 13; the Beast puts down preaching, as Queen Elizabeth had put down prophesying.

[4] *The Notebook of John Penry*, p. 72; cf. Penry, *Three Treatises Concerning Wales* (ed. D. Williams, Cardiff, 1960), p. 78.

nothing at all. Whence it is that we dare not have any society
or fellowship with the assemblies of the land although we
differ from them in no point of the truth established, because the Roman Antichrist and [not] Christ Jesus reigneth
in them by the offices and callings which he hath instituted.

A parallel case would be 'if the Spaniard or any other
enemy of her Majesty . . . did appoint what officers
should attend upon her Majesty, being strangers unto
her, yea sworn servants unto her enemy'.[1]

Penry often repeats that he agrees on all points of
doctrine with the established church. But he cannot use
the unclean vessels of Antichrist. The whole worship
of the state church is performed within the jurisdiction
of the prelacy and priesthood of the kingdom of Antichrist.[2] Commenting on Galatians 3: 23–7 (the law as
schoolmaster to bring us to Christ), Penry makes the
application: 'Before we knew Christ we were kept under
this bondage. But after faith is come we are the sons of
God in Christ, and therefore not subject unto *any of the
ordinances of Antichrist*.'[3] If I understand Penry aright,
the passage I have italicized means that he and others
of the elect are not bound by the ecclesiastical laws of
the land. 'Antichrist', says the Genevan marginal note
to Revelation 13: 8, 'hath not power over the elect'.

Nor was it only canon law and episcopal jurisdiction
that Penry regarded as a survival of the old régime due
for abolition. The preservation of church offices and
livings whets the appetites of Jesuits and seminary
priests for 'Babylonish gold', and keeps 'the Pope and
his sworn subjects in daily hope of replanting the throne
of iniquity again in this land'. 'Whereas if these offices

---

[1] *The Notebook of John Penry*, pp. 81–2.   [2] Ibid., pp. 42–3.
[3] Ibid., p. 9. My italics.

and livings were by public authority once removed and converted to her Majesty's civil uses, . . . there would be no baits to allure them hither, and the home papists would be utterly void of hope to see their expected day.' So the abolition of remunerative ecclesiastical livings is necessary to the safety of the realm.[1] Barrow agreed that war will not cease 'until Antichrist with his army, power and ministry, be wholly cast out of the church'.[2]

For Whitgift the Pope was Antichrist. When Henry Barrow was brought up for trial he professed not to know what to make of the Archbishop. 'He is neither ecclesiastical nor civil; even that second Beast spoken of in the Revelation.'[3] The evil thing was the fusion of the two, in popish fashion. Harrison recalled that from the time of Wyclif onwards the godly had been tormented by persecutors imposing on them the antichristian oath *ex officio*.[4]

III

So far I have been quoting those whom posterity would call congregationalists. But Baptists agreed that the ministers of the Church were antichristian.[5] 'So many lord bishops . . . so many Antichrists', wrote Leonard Busher.[6] Thomas Helwys thought that bishops used the weapons of the Beast—pomp, power, cruelty, imprisonment, silencing and banishing, canons,

[1] Waddington, *John Penry*, pp. 163–4; Burrage, op. cit. ii, p. 85.
[2] Burrage, op. cit. ii, p. 101.
[3] *Writings of Barrow, 1587–1590*, p. 188.
[4] *Writings of Harrison and Browne*, p. 85.
[5] Clapham, *Errour On the Right Hand*, pp. 20–1.
[6] L. Busher, *Religions Peace: Or, A Plea for Liberty of Conscience* (1614), in *Tracts on Liberty of Conscience and Persecution, 1614–61* (ed. E. B. Underhill, Hanserd Knollys Soc., 1846), p. 35.

consistories, etc., offices and officers.[1] 'To sit in the councils of men, to be lawgiver and judge therein, . . . this is Antichrist's practice.'[2] Succession of ministers is 'Antichrist's chief hold',[3] which would appear to mean that any church in which ministers are not elected by the congregation is antichristian. 'What have Antichrist's ministers to do to take God's words in their mouths?' Helwys asked.[4] John Smyth wrote a whole book, *The Character of the Beast* (1609), to demonstrate that the established church was antichristian, and its parish churches 'the assemblies of Antichrist'. Conformists were 'the Antichristians'. (In Helwys's dialogue, *Persecution for Religion Judg'd and Condemn'd*, the Baptist is 'Christian', the Church of England spokesman 'Antichristian'. The latter's opening question is 'why come ye not to church?'[5]) The error of baptizing infants was for Smyth 'a chief part of antichristianism'; 'Antichristians converted ought to be rebaptized'. When 'the practice of antiquity' was quoted against him, Smyth retorted: 'all those churches were antichristian.'[6]

Another Baptist, John Wilkinson, writing in 1619, gave as his main argument for separating from the Church of England that its clergy bore the mark of the Beast. They acquire it when they make the subscription which the bishops demand of them. No one can become a minister unless he will 'submit to their antichristian

[1] T. Helwys, *The Mistery of Iniquity* (1612), p. 16; cf. Burrage, op. cit. i, p. 254.

[2] Helwys, *An Humble Supplication to the Kings Majesty* (1620), in *Tracts on Liberty of Conscience*, p. 230.　　[3] Burrage, op. cit. ii, p. 185.

[4] [T. Helwys], *Persecution for Religion Judg'd and Condemn'd* (1662), p. 41. First published 1615.

[5] Ibid., sig. B[v].

[6] Smyth, op. cit., sig. A2, pp. 30, 47, 53–4; cf. Burrage, op. cit. i, pp. 199, 230, 379; ii, pp. 174–6, 218–20.

rule and government, which they challenge to themselves as being lords over all'. It is a 'trick they have
cunningly devised to bring the land in subjection to their
Antichristian yoke', since 'all persons which receive
these false priests do likewise receive and submit to that
authority which sent them, and also the mark by which
they are sent, as is evident when a priest cometh to take
possession of a parish to which he is by the bishops
appointed . . .'. Doctors and schoolmen are the Beast's
mouth.[1] One of the main works of the Beast is persecution. 'The bishops in forcing men's and women's
consciences', Leonard Busher wrote in 1614, 'do therein
play the Antichrist, as well as the Popes.'[2] 'These
courses of afflicting our bodies for conscience cause',
said Helwys, 'are not of God but of Antichrist.'[3] This
comes from Helwys's *Supplication to James I*. The Baptists appealed to 'kings that have power and authority'
to 'destroy Antichrist's kingdom and cherish Christ's
kingdom'.[4] Busher similarly said that 'antichristian
bishops do draw kings and princes hearts [to persecute]
against their minds'. He too called on kings to 'use their
power and authority against the bloody persecution of
Antichrist and all his bloody bishops and ministers, and
so become nursing fathers to the church of Christ'.[5]

Baptists then rejected the Church of England as
antichristian at least as vehemently as did congregationalists, but they still had some hope of the magistrate,
for whom Brownists had tired of tarrying. Both agreed

[1] Wilkinson, *Exposition of the 13 Chapter of the Revelation* (1619), esp.
pp. 24–5; Burrage, op. cit. i, pp. 371–4.
[2] *Tracts on Liberty of Conscience*, p. 35.
[3] Helwys, *Persecution for Religion Judg'd and Condemn'd*, pp. 50, 74.
[4] *Tracts on Liberty of Conscience*, pp. 127–8.
[5] Ibid., pp. 37, 58; cf. Burrage, op. cit. i, p. 277.

that the whole ministry of the English church bears the mark of the Beast: the agents of the Beast have forced the unregenerate into the church alongside the godly. The elect must separate themselves *both* from the anti-christian ministry *and* from the ungodly multitude who are compelled to participate in Anglican worship. A voluntary gathering of the saints is opposed to the state-compulsive assemblies of Antichrist. It was no doubt this rejection of the national church which led William Harrison to accuse Robert Browne of 'anti-christian pride'.[1]

Before we leave the separatists there is one point to be made, though it is about their critics rather than about separatists. In *The Alchemist* (1610) and *Bartholo-mew Fair* (1614), Ben Jonson has caricatured for all time the farcical extremism attributed to the most radical sectaries, those who had emigrated to the Netherlands in despair of the English church. Antichrist looms large in their dialect. Medieval heretics carried the metaphor of Antichrist as a person to great lengths, Hus, for instance, identifying various institutions and persons as the beard, nose, saliva, lungs, spleen, knees, etc., of Antichrist.[2] Most protestants were less luxuriant in their imagery, but they often spoke of the bishops as limbs of Antichrist, the clergy as his excrement.[3] Bucer (rightly) urged English protestants to attack church courts, 'the nerves and joints of Antichrist', rather than vest-ments, which were mere 'shadows of Antichrist'.[4] The

[1] Burrage, op. cit. i, p. 106.

[2] J. Hus, *Opera* (1524), i, pp. xxxix–xlvi.

[3] e.g. F. Rous, *A Religious and Worthy Speech in Parliament* (1641), sig. A4ᵛ. See also *Cartwrightiana*, p. 258.

[4] Hopf, *Martin Bucer, and the English Reformation*, pp. 135, 158.

preaching oatmeal-maker quoted in the epigraph to this chapter addressed Bishop Neile of Winchester as 'Thou tail of the Beast that sittest at the lower end of the table'. John Bastwick referred to bishops, priests, and deacons as Antichrist's little toes.[1]

So we can appreciate what Jonson was caricaturing when Zeal-of-the-land Busy said that a drum at Bartholomew Fair was 'the broken belly of Antichrist, and thy bellows there are his lungs, and these pipes are his throat, those feathers are his tail, and thy rattles the gnashing of his teeth'. Smithfield was 'the seat of the Beast. . . . Idolatry peepeth out on every side of thee'.[2] In *The Alchemist* Ananias said that Subtle 'bears / The visible mark of the Beast in his forehead', and Tribulation Wholesome asked who could be 'more antichristian than your bell-founders?' But funniest of all, to my mind, is Ananias's greeting in *The Alchemist* of a man clothed in the Spanish fashion: 'Thou lookst like Antichrist in that lewd hat!'[3] Not only funny: also very daring, if we remember how serious a figure Antichrist was, for most Englishmen, in 1610. Yet it also has its social and political point, for Ben Jonson was, if not actually a papist, at least on the most conservative wing of protestantism: he no doubt enjoyed caricaturing the eccentricities of the lower-class lunatic fringe of sectarianism and intended also to discredit the more sober Puritan nonconformists. He succeeded in this sensationally: his stereotype is still applied to respectable seventeenth-century Puritans who would have abhorred Ananias and Zeal-of-the-land no less than did Jonson himself.

[1] See p. 70 below.   [2] Jonson, *Bartholomew Fair*, Act III, sc. i.
[3] Jonson, *The Alchemist*, Act III, sc. i.

The smear was taken over by royalists during the interregnum. Thus Cleveland in 1647 made one zealot call another 'the curled lock of Antichrist',[1] and poems wrongly attributed to Cleveland speak of 'such an Antichrist as pudding pie', and make a Puritan describe a gown as 'the black surplice of the Beast', whose stiffening was by 'ribs from Antichrist's own side'.[2]

IV

By the time we reach the period of Laud's ascendancy there were four distinguishable attitudes among protestant Englishmen towards the Antichrist myth.[3] First and foremost was the almost official doctrine of the Church of England, that the Pope was Antichrist. Second was the moderate Puritan conclusion, that far too much of Antichrist remained in the English church, in the form of political power and persecution of the godly, and of papal forms and ceremonies: further reformation was needed. Third was the separatist viewpoint—the Church of England was so totally antichristian that it was impossible to remain in communion with it. Finally, in reaction to these critical views, there was the Arminian position which questioned whether the Pope was Antichrist at all.

To summarize the argument so far, then. The government of Elizabeth, no less than the governments of medieval emperors, found uses for the doctrine that the Pope was Antichrist. Bucer and Foxe gave ideological respectability to the doctrine of the royal supremacy,

[1] Ed. G. Saintsbury, *Minor Poets of the Caroline Period* (Oxford, 1921), iii, p. 44.
[2] *The Works of Mr. John Cleveland* (1687), pp. 213, 363.
[3] Cf. my *Puritanism and Revolution*, pp. 87–8, where I suggest a similar distinction between attitudes towards the myth of the Norman Yoke.

and their ideas helped to stimulate a protestant patriotism focused on the monarchy. But printing and
protestant preaching ensured that the heretical and
social-revolutionary implications of the doctrine were
always liable to break through. There was indeed a
fundamental ambiguity in the position of the English
church from its inception, illustrated by the change
from Henry VIII's headship of the church to Elizabeth's title of Supreme Governor. Titles like the former,
Jewell told Bullinger in 1559, had been 'so foully
contaminated by Antichrist that they can no longer be
adopted by anyone without impiety'.[1] The ambiguity
was illustrated too by Elizabeth's hostility to protestant
preaching and her hesitations about alliance with the
revolutionary (though protestant) Netherlands against
their legitimate (though papist) sovereign.

The English government had committed schism:
Elizabeth stood under permanent excommunication.
There had been a revolutionary break from the universal church when the Reformation had been exploited
as a pretext for plundering the church and had in the
process become closely associated with a popular
protestant nationalism. So long as England was a
relatively isolated protestant power, on the defensive
against world catholicism, at least one section of Elizabethan and Jacobean governments wished to maintain
close links with continental protestants, embarrassingly
radical though some of them were. Yet for the foreign
protestant churches Antichrist was not merely the Pope.
Martin Marprelate suggested that the authority
claimed by bishops was regarded as antichristian by
most of the (protestant) churches in the world, naming

[1] Ed. H. Robinson, *Zurich Letters* (Parker Soc., 1842–5), i, p. 33.

Switzerland, Scotland, France, Bohemia, the Netherlands, Poland, Denmark, the Palatinate, Saxony,
Swabia.[1] In a Dutch engraving which shows William
the Silent pacifying a Calvinist crowd at Antwerp in
1567, he is denounced as a 'servant of Antichrist'.[2] If
such disrespect could be shown to a revolutionary
leader, what were legitimate sovereigns to expect?
Toleration of such views rightly seemed to conservatives
utterly subversive of a national church as they knew it.
That was one of the reasons why they so fiercely opposed
toleration.

Dr. Collinson has stated the dilemma in classic form,
and described the gradual evolution of Elizabeth's
policy away from ideological foreign commitments in
the greater security of the 1590s: he has shown that
this was inevitably accompanied by a recovery of influence by conservative protestants and crypto-papists
at home.[3] The most obvious example is Bishop Bancroft's manœuvres, with the Queen's full approval, to
split English papists into a Jesuit internationalist wing
and a loyal nationalist party. The success of these
intrigues must have made it very difficult, at least for
those who conducted them, to believe whole-heartedly
that all papists were Antichristians. By 1603 Arthur
Dent was already expressing alarm that popery 'hath
so many friends and upholders, and seemeth to gather
strength and make an head again'.[4]

James I was far more committed than Elizabeth to
the doctrine that the Pope was Antichrist, thanks to his

[1] Marprelate, *The Epistle*, p. 6.
[2] Ed. H. R. Trevor-Roper, *The Age of Expansion: Europe and the World,
1559–1660* (1968), p. 78.
[3] Collinson, *The Elizabethan Puritan Movement*, esp. Parts 4 and 8.
[4] Dent, *The Ruine of Rome*, p. 243. Cf. p. 21 above.

upbringing in a country even less capable than England of standing up to the catholic international. But he faced similar problems after succeeding to the English throne. If England threw her weight decidedly behind an international protestant alliance, this might well encourage hot-headed Calvinist revolutionaries on the Continent, and would certainly strengthen the hands of Puritan Parliaments at home. James hankered after a solidarity of counter-reformation monarchs which would keep rebellious subjects well in their place: it was papal claims to meddle with princes' temporal jurisdiction which he regarded as especially antichristian.[1] When Richard Sheldon, 'a convert from out of Babylon', denounced the Pope as Antichrist too fiercely in a sermon at Paul's Cross, he was severely reprimanded for endangering the government's foreign policy.[2] The Arminian party that appeared in England in the 1620s rejected the international revolutionary Calvinist alliance and had high theories of monarchical absolutism as well as grave doubts about the Pope being Antichrist. James ultimately succumbed, and Charles embraced the new doctrine with enthusiasm.

This produced a crisis of confidence, first in the bishops, then in the monarchy. Apart from separatists, for whom the whole establishment of the English church was antichristian, most Puritans had believed, or pretended to believe, that sharp distinctions were to be drawn between antichristian bishops and godly prince: even Baptists still had hopes of James I—or said they had. For two beleaguered generations national unity

[1] See pp. 20–1 above.
[2] R. Sheldon, *A Sermon Preached at Paules Crosse: Laying open the Beast and his Marks* (1625), *passim*.

focused on the monarchy had been sustained by the belief that the Pope was Antichrist. Bishops and Puritans could agree on this, even separatists did not deny it. In the words of William Ames, 'all deniers that the Pope is Antichrist are secret enemies to the King's supremacy'.[1] John Cosin, we recall, had been charged with sedition as well as schism.[2] The alignment of the royal favourite Buckingham with Montagu's defenders at York House in 1626 had been a traumatic moment: Buckingham was impeached by the House of Commons three months later, and assassinated two years after that. But in the 1630s Charles I himself expressed doubts about the royal supremacy, and took up an attitude towards the papacy which made sense of his patronage of those who denied the Pope to be Antichrist. This rocked traditional certainties and loyalties to the foundation.

One advantage of the symbolism of Antichrist, I suggested,[3] was its vagueness: it could conceal attacks on more than one target. Another advantage, especially in the generation before the Civil War, was that it concealed men's own confusions and shifting opinions as they slowly faced the fact that the King might use his royal supremacy on behalf of Antichrist's party. Cranmer had had to face similar problems when Mary denied the royal supremacy which he had made almost

[1] Ames, *English Puritanism* (1641), p. 20; cf. R. Bernard, *The Isle of Man* (4th ed., 1627), p. 274. This was a point of distinction between separating and non-separating congregationalists. Robert Browne regarded the government of the Church of England, 'confirmed by the civil magistrate', as part of 'the kingdom of Antichrist' (*Writings of Harrison and Browne*, p. 267; cf. pp. 262, 272, 274).

[2] See p. 35 above.

[3] See pp. 44–5 above.

an article of faith. The genuine reluctance to deny his past convictions, which Cranmer ultimately purged by holding his right hand over the flames, should prepare us for vacillations, stops in the mind, rethinking among Englishmen who clung in the 1620s and 1630s to Bucer's belief that the King was to build Christ's kingdom in England. Bucer had had a short way with bishops, few of whom in his view knew about the kingdom of Christ. They were to be subordinated to the King.[1]

Many early Elizabethan bishops would have welcomed further reforms, including a diminution of their own powers; their successors, with Bancroft in the lead, evolved a theory of divine-right episcopacy which inevitably led men to stress continuity with the Roman hierarchy, and made some of them reluctant to condemn all institutions of the Roman church as antichristian.[2] Laud busily severed relations with continental Calvinists and tried to harry Calvinist refugee churches in England into conformity. In the 1630s, in consequence, men lost confidence—first in bishops, then, reluctantly, in the King. In 1639 a sermon by Richard Sibbes, preached under James I on Guy Fawkes Day, was published under the title *The Beasts Dominion over earthly Kings*. Kings had *given up* their kingdoms to Antichrist, Sibbes said. 'Commonly the idol of the people is this king, and . . . they fear him more than they fear God . . . and so they come to this damned religion [popery] by depending upon him.' Sibbes was careful to exempt

---

[1] Bucer, *De Regno Christi*, last chapter; *The Gratulation*, sig. k viii.

[2] For the interesting group of Jacobean and Caroline bishops— Carleton, Downame, Hall—who combined a belief in *jure divino* episcopacy with a conviction that the Pope was Antichrist, see Lamont, op. cit., pp. 52, 64.

'our gracious King' from the accusation: but the cap would fit Charles I considerably better.[1]

Meanwhile chronological studies which placed the fall of Antichrist in the mid seventeenth century helped to shift the emphasis from defensive national unity behind the royal supremacy. The Messianic visions to which the ideas of Bucer and Foxe could so easily give rise seemed on the point of realization. Even if kings were not after all to lead the battle against Antichrist, England was still the chosen nation which would give a lead to Europe—*now*. Only as the Civil War drew to a close did men begin to ask, Who was the nation? King, Lords, and Commons, with the balance of the constitution restored against royal absolutism by the exclusion of bishops from the House of Lords or their total abolition? Or Lords and Commons without the King? Or the Commons alone? When Parliament seemed to fail, who should take its place? The godly? The people? Who are the people?

But this is looking ahead. In the 1630s Laud's innovations convinced a significant number of hitherto conformist Puritans that Antichrist was to be found in England. One copy of an anonymous *Speech against the Judges* (1640) has a contemporary manuscript note adding up VVILL LAUD to 666, adding:

> I am the Beast. Count it who can
> This is the number. I am the man.[2]

[1] Sibbes, *Works*, vii, pp. 517–33.

[2] Messrs. Hofmann & Freeman, *Catalogue No. 21 of English Historical Manuscripts before 1700* (1968), item no. 44; cf. [Anon.], *Mercuries Message* (1641), sig. A.[v] The mathematics of this was challenged by Arise Evans, who thought the total was more correctly 1667 than 666 (*The Bloudy Vision of John Farly* (1653), p. 63). 'The weal publike of England' would add up to 666 in English: so would 'England's idol' in Welsh (ibid., pp.

Antichrist was no longer safely overseas, a problem of foreign policy: though the Laudian clergy who were his agents in England seemed to be only the fifth column of vaster darker forces abroad.[1]

So when in 1629 the Revd. John White published his *General Considerations for planting New England*, and proposed 'to raise a bulwark' in the New World 'against the kingdom of Antichrist which the Jesuits labour to rear up in all quarters of the world',[2] some of his readers may have suspected that in their quarter of the world Antichrist's kingdom was being reared up by Arminians as well as by Jesuits. The House of Commons in the same year voted almost exactly that. Governor Bradford had left England with the Pilgrim Fathers in order to shake off the yoke of antichristian bondage—the officers, courts, canons of the English church.[3] Antichrist was setting up his throne in England.

V

Opposition to Antichrist in England was spotlighted by the famous martyrs of Charles I's reign: Leighton, Prynne, Burton, Bastwick, Lilburne. They were agreed on the antichristian nature of the hierarchy. Bishops, archbishops, chancellors, etc., are assistants to the Pope and so antichristian, declared Alexander Leighton.[4]

61–2). Lady Eleanor Davies also denounced Laud as the Beast (T. Spencer, 'The History of an Unfortunate Lady', *Harvard Studies and Notes in Philology and Literature*, xx, p. 52).

[1] Cf. T. Goodwin, *Works*, iii, pp. 35, 70–1, 107–8, 131, 174, 178–9, 190–1, 195–205.

[2] Quoted in *The Cambridge History of the British Empire*, i, p. 159.

[3] T. Prince, *The New England Chronology*, in Arber's *An English Garner*, ii, p. 348.

[4] [A. Leighton], *An Appeale to the Parliament, or Sions Plea against the Prelacie* (1628), p. 11. Cf. p. x above.

Kneeling at communion was the spawn of Antichrist.[1]
Prynne spoke in 1637 of an antichristian episcopal
tyranny over consciences.[2] Laud might be Antichrist
himself:[3] the identification of Antichrist with the Pope
was only probable, not certain. In 1640 Prynne wanted
to root out the whole antichristian hierarchy.[4] Burton
referred in 1636 to bishops as 'antichristian mushrumps'.[5]
He thought the government of the Church of England
'the perfect image of the papal Beast from horn to hoof',
though by 1641 its destruction appeared imminent.[6]
For Bastwick bishops were the tail of the Beast;[7]
alternatively bishops, priests, and deacons were Antichrist's little toes.[8] If the press were open to them,
Bastwick declared, he and his like would scatter Antichrist's kingdom.[9] In Lilburne's *A Worke of the Beast*
(printed in the year the Beast was wounded, 1638), the
Beast was the antichristian Laudian church. 'Prelates
and their creatures claim an authority and jurisdiction
which is derived from the Pope—i.e. from Antichrist.

[1] J. Rushworth, *Historical Collections* (1680), ii, p. 55.

[2] [Prynne], *A Breviate of the Prelates intollerable usurpations* (1637),
p. 234.   [3] Prynne, *Canterburies Doome*, dedication.

[4] Prynne, *Lord Bishops none of the Lords Bishops* (1640), sig. L2.

[5] *D.N.B.* The form 'mushrumps' seems in the sixteenth and seventeenth centuries to be used especially in the metaphorical sense of 'up-
starts, late or sudden growths' (*O.E.D.*). Clarendon refers to 'that mush-
rump-army, which grew up and perished so soon that the loss of it was
scarce apprehended at Oxford' (*History of the Rebellion* (1888), ii, p. 483).
Cf. Andrew Marvell, *Poems* (ed. H. M. Margoliouth, Oxford University
Press, 1927), p. 162.

[6] Burton, *The Protestant Protested* (1641), sig. B2; cf. *Babel no Bethel*
(1629), sig. ¶3, xx4, xxx2ᵛ, and *passim*; *The Sounding of the Two Last
Trumpets* (1641), *passim*.

[7] Gardiner, *History of England* (1883–4), viii, pp. 227–8.

[8] J. Nalson, *An Impartial Collection* (1682), i, p. 500.

[9] T. Fuller, *Church History of Britain* (1655), iv, p. 155; cf. *Calendar of
Clarendon State Papers*, v (ed. F. J. Routledge, Oxford, 1970), p. 721.

The apostolic succession is antichristian. Ministers 'ruin their own souls while they preach unto the people by virtue of an antichristian and unlawful calling'. Englishmen must reject that antichristian power and slavery, and its laws.[1]

Conscious of this new threat at home, the opposition clung the more desperately to their brethren on the Continent and in Scotland. The Puritan theologian Richard Sibbes rejoiced that Antichrist had been humiliated in the Thirty Years War.[2] Joseph Mede and Thomas Goodwin both thought Spain was Antichrist.[3] Mede indeed discussed, though rather sceptically, converting the American Indians as a blow against Antichrist—yet another argument for colonization.[4]

Closest of all the Calvinist churches to England was the Kirk of Scotland; and as the alliance was cemented in the 1630s between the English and Scottish opponents of Laud, Antichrist became the symbol of their common enemy. Samuel Rutherford in 1637 saw that 'Antichrist stirreth his tail' in Scotland.[5] George Gillespie wanted to remove 'the Babylonian baggage of antichristian ceremonies'.[6] Signatories of the Scottish National Covenant declared their detestation and refusal of 'the usurped authority of the Roman Antichrist',

[1] Lilburne, *A Worke of the Beast*, esp. pp. 17–20, 25–6, 34; *Come Out of Her, My People: or An Answer to the Questions of a Gentlewoman, a Professor in the Antichristian Church of England* (1639); *Innocency and Truth Justified* (1646), p. 14; *A Coppy of a Letter* (?1646), p. 7.

[2] Sibbes, *Works*, iv, p. 389.

[3] Mede, *The Key of the Revelation* (1643), Part II, p. 115; T. Goodwin, *Works*, iii, pp. 103–4.

[4] Mede, *Works*, pp. 799–800, 809, 843–4. Cf. Appendix II.

[5] Ed. A. A. Bonar, *Letters of Samuel Rutherford* (1894), pp. 192, 333.

[6] G. Gillespie, *A Dispute against the English Popish Ceremonies obtruded upon the Church of Scotland* (1637), Part II, p. 28.

whose errors were listed at length.[1] An anonymous English pamphlet on Scotland produced in the
same year was entitled *The Beast is Wounded*. It was
observed that the new Scottish service book of 1638
represented the craft of Antichrist, the Book of Canons
his cruelty, and that the High Commission combined
his craft with his cruelty.[2] Samuel Rutherford in 1638
urged his friends not to welcome Antichrist to Scotland,[3]
and reinforced the spiritual point by adding that 'when
Christ and his Gospel are out of Scotland, dream not
that . . . it will go well with the nobles of the land'.[4]
Yet if the threat was great, so were the expectations.
Brilliana Lady Harley said that 1639 was 'the year in
which many are of the opinion that Antichrist must
begin to fail', Napier having been one of the many.[5]
By November 1639 Rutherford was convinced that 'our
Lord Jesus is on horseback, hunting and pursuing the
Beast'.[6] For three or four years the issues seemed as
clear and simple as that: Christ *versus* Antichrist. But
by 1648 Rutherford (and many others) thought the
most dangerous manifestations of Antichrist were to be
found among those English sectaries who in 1639 had
been whole-hearted allies against the Beast and his
bishops.

The Scottish army in the north of England forced a

[1] Gardiner, *Constitutional Documents of the Puritan Revolution*, p. 125.

[2] J. Aiton, *Life and Times of Alexander Henderson* (Edinburgh, 1836),
p. 222. Cf. R. B[aillie] K., *A Parallel Or Briefe Comparison of the Liturgie
with the Masse-Book . . . taken for the most part word by word out of these Antichristian writs* (1641).

[3] *Letters of Samuel Rutherford*, p. 449.

[4] Ibid., p. 462.

[5] Ed. T. T. Lewis, *Letters of the Lady Brilliana Harley* (Camden Soc.,
1854), p. 41. For Napier see p. 26 above.

[6] *Letters of Samuel Rutherford*, p. 577.

meeting of Parliament in November 1640, and then the day of reckoning had come. The Root and Branch Petition proposed the abolition of bishops as 'members of the Beast', and pointed out that this would bring England into line with other protestant churches.[1] In May 1641 a libel was set up at the entrance to Parliament, denouncing bishops as limbs of Antichrist.[2] The liberated press attacked bishops. 'None but an Antichrist . . . will take upon him to set up altars and to consecrate priests to serve at the altar.'[3] Bishops and the government of the Church of England are antichristian.[4] So are parts of the prayer-book.[5] The etcetera oath in the 1640 canons was 'the curled lock of Antichrist', 'the brand upon the buttock of the Beast'.[6] 'He . . . that commands the least tittle of doctrine or discipline merely *ex imperio voluntatis*, of his own power and authority', is antichristian, said Lord Brooke in 1641. Prelacy is indistinguishable from antichristian popery.[7]

[1] Gardiner, *Constitutional Documents of the Puritan Revolution, 1625–1660*, p. 140.

[2] G. I. Soden, *Godfrey Goodman, Bishop of Gloucester, 1583–1656* (1953), p. 335; cf. [Anon.], *Englands Complaint to Jesus Christ against the Bishops Canons* (1640), sig. C4ᵛ.

[3] [L. Hughes], *Certaine Grievances well worthy the Serious Consideration of . . . Parliament* (1640), pp. 10–11.

[4] [L. Hughes], *Certaine Grievances, or the Errours of the Service Booke* (1641), pp. 28, 32, 40–1; cf. [Anon.], *A Modest Advertisement concerning The present Controversies about Church Government* (1641), pp. 6–7; E. H[all], *A Scriptural Discourse of the Apostasie and the Antichrist* (1653), sig. b4.

[5] [L. Hughes], *Certaine Grievances, or the Popish Errors and Ungodlinesse of so much of the Service Book as is Antichristian* (1642), *passim*.

[6] [Anon.], *The Decoy Duck: Together with the Discovery of The Knot in the Dragons Tayle* (1642), sig. A4–4ᵛ. Sometimes attributed to Henry Walker.

[7] Lord Brooke, *A Discourse opening the Nature of that Episcopacie, which is exercised in England* (1641), esp. pp. 53–9, in Haller, *Tracts on Liberty*, ii.

The bishops had endeavoured 'to build up the kingdom of Antichrist', declared a pamphlet of 1641.[1]
Another answered a defence of the government of the
church on the grounds that it had existed unchanged
since the Reformation by the observation 'then it is the
same which Antichrist had retained so many hundreds
of years'.[2] Michael Quintin called on Charles I to
decide between Christ and Antichrist. The latter had
made the King supreme head of the church, 'as if one
body could have two heads, or two bodies one head'.
Antichrist's supporters were 'apt to breed wars to maintain the truth of their being'. 'Thou committest sin by
a law' in putting men to death for conscience sake, he
told 'the kingdom of Antichrist'.[3] 'The souls, bodies and
estates of Englishmen were trod by the foul feet of the
Roman Antichrist', declared the Scot Robert Baillie.[4]
John Cotton was right to observe in 1642 that the doctrine that bishops were antichristian had risen in the
social scale: 'A great many of the commons of England
and many noble persons do begin to see that episcopacy
is an antichristian frame and form.'[5]

With the fall of the High Commission in 1641,
another pamphleteer wrote: 'the iron teeth of the Beast
were knocked out, and the sting of abused excom-

[1] R. P., *The Bishops Looking-Glasse* (1641), p. 5.

[2] [Anon.], *The Petition for the Prelates Briefly Examined* (1641), pp. 10,
38.

[3] M. Quintin, *A Briefe Treatise containing a full discovery . . . of the
devilish politique state or kingdome of Antichrist* (1641), pp. 10, 17. This
pamphlet had dedications to Parliament and the King, in that order.

[4] R. B[aillie] K., *A Parallel Or Briefe Comparison of the Liturgie with the
Masse-Book . . . taken for the most part word by word out of these Antichristian
writs* (1641), Preface.

[5] J. Cotton, *The Powring out of the Seven Vialls* (1642), 'The fift Viall',
pp. 5, 7.

munications was plucked out of his tail'.[1] John Geree
published a whole treatise entitled *The Down-Fall of
Anti-Christ: or, The Power of Preaching to pull down Popery*,
in which he analysed very sensibly the economic problems of the church, and suggested remedies.[2] Next year
appeared the anonymous *Last Will and Testament of
Superstition, Eldest Daughter to Antichrist*. Even a pamphleteer who disagreed with the sectarian view 'that bishops
are antichristian', yet conceived 'the institution of the
superiority of bishops over presbyters was the first step
by which Antichrist ascended into the throne of universal bishop'.[3] In this atmosphere, anything one disliked tended to become antichristian: choral singing
and the playing of organs in church were the work of
Antichrist, introduced by the Pope in the significant
year 666.[4]

By 1644 Henry Robinson could take it for granted
that episcopacy was antichristian.[5] A year later Lilburne
claimed that 'Parliament and priests acknowledge
the bishops to be antichristian'.[6] The rise of the

[1] R. Culmer, *Cathedrall Newes from Canterbury* (1644), p. 16.

[2] Op. cit. (1641), esp. sig. A4^v–C2^v.

[3] *An answer to Lord George Digbies Apology . . . by Theophilus Geru-
siphilus Philalethes Decius* (1642), pp. 61–2.

[4] H. Burton, *Englands Bondage and Hope of Deliverance* (1641), p. 29;
*Master William Thomas Esq. His Speech in Parliament Iune 1641 Concerning
Deanes, and their Office* (1641), sig. B3. Thomas, otherwise unknown to
fame, had probably heard Burton's sermon, which was preached before
the House of Commons. Not all church music was antichristian, however,
'They be cathedral priests of an antichristian spirit', wrote John Cotton,
'that have scoffed at Puritan ministers, as calling the people to sing one
of Hopkins's jigs, and so hop into the pulpit.' No American church had
'any hand in turning David's Psalms into English songs and tunes'
(Cotton, *Singing of Psalms, A Gospel Ordinance*, 1647, p. 61.)

[5] H. Robinson, *Liberty of Conscience* (1644), pp. 35–6, in Haller, *Tracts
on Liberty*, iii.

[6] Lilburne, *Englands Birthright* (1645), in Haller, op. cit. ii.

congregational way of church government, Thomas
Goodwin said in 1641, and John Cotton in 1648, blocked
the way to the advance of Antichrist. That is why it is persecuted, Goodwin added.[1] John Owen thought prelacy
was antichristian; 'grasping temporal power upon a
spiritual account' was 'the greatest badge of Antichrist'.[2]
Prelaty, wrote Milton, was 'more antichristian than
Antichrist himself'.[3] And this was not merely, as
Edmund Hall suggested in 1653, the view of separatists.[4] A state-church man like Thomas Coleman told
the House of Commons in 1643 that 'the ruin of this
antichristian crew', 'this wicked and most cruel government of the prelacy', its courts and officials, would
never be reversed.[5] 'His noddle brings new Antichrists
to light', Ralph Knevet complained of a sectary:

> The purple Babylonian whore
> Is spoken of no more, . . .
> Our rev'rend mitred priests
> Are now termed Antichrists.[6]

[1] *A Glimpse of Syons Glory* (1641), preface; Ziff, *Cotton and the Churches*,
p. 303. A. S. P. Woodhouse, following Haller, attributed *A Glimpse*
to the Baptist Hanserd Knollys. The best modern view seems to be that
it is by Thomas Goodwin. See J. F. Wilson, 'A Glimpse of Syons Glory',
Church History, xxxi, pp. 66–73; A. R. Dallison, 'The Authorship of
"A Glimpse of Syons Glory" ', in Toon, *Puritans, the Millennium and the
Future of Israel*, pp. 131–6.

[2] Owen, *Works*, viii, pp. 24, 322–3, 386.

[3] Milton, *Works* (Columbia ed.), iii, pp. 158, 212–13, 268–9; cf.
iv, p. 91, v, pp. 158, 209, 250, 305, vii, p. 505.

[4] E. H[all], *A Scriptural Discourse of the Apostasie and the Antichrist* (1653),
sig. b4. Hall gives a very interesting list of reasons for popular hostility
to bishops.

[5] T. Coleman, *The Christians Course and Complaint* (1643), pp. 35–42, 65.
For Coleman, see M. Fixler, *Milton and the Kingdoms of God* (1964),
pp. 119, 129; Lamont, *Godly Rule*, esp. pp. 115–26.

[6] Ed. A. M. Charles, *The Shorter Poems of Ralph Knevet* (Ohio State
University Press, 1966), p. 334.

There is little evidence of popular support for episcopacy at this time.[1] 'The passion of many of the vulgar be such', wrote the conservative Edward Waterhouse in 1653, that they think 'primitive episcopacy' no less antichristian than 'the Roman papal hierarchy'.[2]

So by 1640 we have moved from the Pope as Antichrist—a view held by most Elizabethan and Jacobean bishops—to the bishops themselves as Antichrist; for sectaries the whole hierarchy of the Church of England down to parish ministers was antichristian. 'You call us abominable men, to be hated of all', complained Archbishop Abbott to sectaries caught worshipping in a wood near Newington, 'that we carry the mark of the Beast, that we are his members'.[3] That was in 1632: by 1640 Charles I had destroyed men's confidence in the godly prince as effectively as Laud had destroyed their confidence in bishops. Many conformist Puritans were driven to accept what had hitherto been the separatist position, that bishops were incurably antichristian. The alliance did not last: but it was powerful in the crucial years between 1640 and 1643.

[1] Cf. [Anon.], *A Modest Advertisement, concerning the present Controversies about Church Government* (1641), pp. 6–9: 'to say that episcopacy ... is antichristian is to condemn all Christians as antichristian.' Antichrist is in Rome.

[2] E. Waterhouse, *An humble Apologie for Learning and Learned Men* (1653), pp. 84–5. 'Antichrist was working betimes' was the answer given in the anonymous *Disputation at Winchcombe* (1653) to the argument that bishops existed in the primitive church (pp. 111–12).

[3] Ed. S. R. Gardiner, *Reports of Cases in the Courts of Star Chamber and High Commission* (Camden Soc., 1886), pp. 309–10; cf. Lamont, 'Puritanism as History and Historiography', *P. and P.*, no. 44, p. 144.

III

1640–1660:

ANTICHRIST IN ENGLAND

A great inlet to our late civil wars hath been the mis-
interpretation of the Revelation.

> R. HAYTER, *A Meaning to the Revelation* (1676),
> Epistle Dedicatory, quoted by Lamont, *Godly
> Rule*, p. 21.

Who would not be glad to see Jesus Christ?

> JOHN COOK, *What the Independents Would have*
> (1647), p. 8.

I

WHAT is new after 1640 is the breakdown of obstacles
to and inhibitions in attacking the government as well
as the bishops. Generalized accusations of popery and
Arminianism were thrown at bishops and government
alike; and the peculiar political circumstances of the
early forties, when Parliament needed to win popular
support, led to increasing stress on Antichrist's impending downfall, giving Messianic overtones to what had
previously not necessarily been a revolutionary idea.[1]
Here the imprecision of the word Antichrist helped.
'Arise oh Lord and scatter the Irish rebels!' cried
Edmund Calamy in a sermon before the House of
Commons in December 1641; 'arise oh Lord and confound Antichrist!'[2] The second adjuration was as vague
as the first was precise: many interpretations could be

---

[1] See Lamont, *Godly Rule*, esp. pp. 46–8, 88–96, 118.
[2] E. Calamy, *Englands Looking-Glasse* (1642), p. 10.

put on it. Now is the time to stand up against 'the anti-christian party', said Jeremiah Burroughs in the same year.[1] The second Earl of Essex had been urged in 1599 to put himself on his white horse and follow Jesus Christ in pursuit of the Beast. When he took to horse in 1601 it was not clear whether he was for or against Antichrist, and the godly of London did not follow him. But when his much less romantic son took up arms in 1642, some thought he was John the Baptist, and that Christ would soon follow to destroy Charles.[2] An anonymous pamphlet published in that year was called, simply, *The Camp of Christ and the Camp of Antichrist.*

Use of the phrase 'Antichrist's party' to describe the King's armed supporters at once opened up propagandist possibilities for Parliament similar to those which Elizabeth's government had seen in the equation of Pope and Antichrist. A glimpse of what this must have meant for rank-and-file supporters of Parliament is given by Edward Symmons, a divine who had fled to royalist Herefordshire after being ejected from his Essex living. He is describing a visit which he paid at Easter 1644 to some Parliamentarian prisoners who had been captured at Sir Edward Harley's Brampton Bryan. They told him that they 'took up arms against Antichrist and popery; for', said they, "tis prophesied in the *Revelation*, that the Whore of Babylon shall be destroyed with fire and sword, and what do you know, but this is the time of her ruin, and that we are the men that must help to pull her down?' Mr. Symmons explained

---

[1] J. Burroughs, *Sions Joy. A Sermon of the late Thanksgiving of the Commons house of Parliament* (1641), pp. 23, 57–60.

[2] Ed. I. G. Philip, *Journal of Sir Samuel Luke* (Oxfordshire Record Soc., 1947–53), i, p. 76. See p. 20 above.

to the misguided soldiers that it was the work of kings
to pull down the Whore of Babylon—a theme that we
encountered in Bucer's *De Regno Christi* and which was
still stressed by John Bunyan. They retorted: "'tis said
in the *Revelation*, that the people, the multitude and
nations, should also pull her down'—'but I showed
them they were wrong.' Even more important was a
point of geography on which Mr. Symmons corrected
them: the Whore of Babylon dwells at Rome, not in
England at all. 'They told me that all the true godly
divines in England were of their opinion, that Antichrist was here in England, as well as at Rome, and that
the bishops were Antichrist, and all that did endeavour
to support them.'[1] The tone is different from Milton's
paean in *Animadversions upon the Remonstrants' Defence
against Smectymnuus* (1641), but the assumptions are the
same: 'thy kingdom is now at hand', wrote Milton;
'thou canst vouchsafe to us (though unworthy) as large
a portion of thy spirit as thou pleasest.'[2]

There must have been many encounters all over
England like this one which the refugee divine happened to record. The scene is highly symbolic. Antichrist
has boomeranged against those who located him so
safely in Rome, for kings in God's good time to overthrow. He is here in England, and how do you know
we uneducated troopers are not the men to pull him
down? The next ten years of history are foreshadowed
in that question. With its deep mythological overtones
and its infinite horizons, it reminds us of the more
famous questions soon to be asked in the New Model

[1] Edward Symmons, *Scripture Vindicated* (Oxford, 1644), Preface to the
Readers. I owe this reference to Mr. Lamont's *Godly Rule*. For Bunyan
see pp. 147–8 below.

[2] Milton, *Works* (Columbia ed.), III, part i, p. 148.

Army: 'What were the lords of England but William the Conqueror's colonels? Or the barons but his majors? Or the knights but his captains?'[1] Mr. Symmons thought (after the event) of one retort to the troopers' claim that 'all that did endeavour to support' bishops were antichristian: 'If hierarchy be Antichrist, or monarchy or superiority, then Antichrist is in heaven.'[2] It is a point that ought perhaps to have troubled Milton rather more than it did.

Symmons blamed the popular divine Stephen Marshall for the soldiers' wicked sentiments, referring especially to his sermon *Meroz Cursed*, preached to the House of Commons on 23 February 1642. There is not in fact much about Antichrist in this sermon: Mr. Symmons may have been thinking more of its social than its theological content. (He had occupied a neighbouring Essex parish to Marshall, and had crossed swords with him before being sequestered in March 1643.)[3] In this sermon Marshall says: 'The mighty do frequently oppose the Lord. . . . The Lamb's followers and servants are often the poor and offscouring of the world, when kings and captains, merchants and wise men, . . . give all their strength to the Beast.' What helped to make this sermon notorious is a quite unusual note of savagery: 'If this work be to avenge God's church against Babylon, he is a blessed man that takes and dashes the little ones against the stones.'[4] Marshall was quite aware that he was appealing to the lower orders. In a sermon preached to the Commons two

[1] Ed. M. Sylvester, *Reliquiae Baxterianae* (1696), i, pp. 50–1.

[2] Symmons, op. cit., p. 61.

[3] E. Symmons, *A Loyall Subjects Beliefe Expressed in a Letter to Master Stephen Marshall . . . occasioned by a conference betwixt them* (1643).

[4] Op. cit., pp. 7, 10.

months earlier he had said: 'The *vox populi* is that many
of the nobles, magistrates, knights and gentlemen and
persons of great quality are arrant traitors and rebels
against God, taking part with wicked men and wicked
causes against the truth.'[1] The usual equation of *vox
populi* with *vox dei* can hardly have escaped Marshall or
his audience. In June 1643, again preaching before the
Commons after the exposure of the Army Plot, Marshall
denounced the wrath of God upon 'the antichristian
faction', 'the followers of the Beast', 'this great antichristian enemy'. Throughout Antichrist's reign of
1,260 years, 'Christ always had an army of saints to war
against the Beast'. Now Parliament's victories were
destroying Antichrist.[2]

But Symmons was wrong to put all the blame on
Marshall, unusual as is his conscious appeal to the
lower classes. Many other divines were publicly denouncing the enemy as antichristian. Nathanael Homes,
for instance, in a sermon before the House of Commons
in May 1641, declared after many computations that
'this is the promised time'; Antichrist 'must needs be
utterly thrown down within fifty years hence'. 'For aught
I can see you are the promised people, you are the
Parliament and Parliaments of his majesty's three
kingdoms to be leaders and examples to the Christian
world to pull down that part of Antichrist that is yet
standing.'[3] Homes was more cautious than Marshall
in directing his remarks only to Parliament, not to the
people. So was William Bridge in another sermon to

[1] S. Marshall, *Reformation and Desolation* (1642), p. 45.
[2] S. Marshall, *The Song of Moses* (1643), esp. pp. 7–18, 42–8.
[3] N. Homes, *The New World, or the New Reformed Church* (1641), esp.
pp. 12, 33–7; cf. his *The Resurrection Revealed* (1654), pp. 86–91—Antichrist = the Pope and the Turk.

the House in 1641: 'This Parliament time is a com-
mencement time for good or evil. . . . Down with
Babylon.'[1] Henry Burton in June of the same year told
the Commons of 'the bondage of . . . the hierarchy of
Antichrist', from which England had never escaped
since the Reformation, but whose destruction was now
imminent.[2] Jeremiah Burroughs, again before the
Commons in September, celebrating the peace finally
concluded with Scotland, described it as 'the greatest
blow that ever was given to the antichristian government, . . . God's revenge upon Antichrist'. But he
struck a more apocalyptical note: 'God hath begun a
work that he will never leave till He hath brought it to
perfection. Antichrist shall never prevail again as he
hath done.' 'Time was when God stirred up His servants
to stand against the ways of Antichrist, only to give
testimony to His truth, and to exercise their graces; but
He let Antichrist prevail. . . . But now . . . God intends
to ruin him. . . . All of you therefore who love Jerusalem
take courage in setting yourselves against the antichristian party.' 'God forbid that any of you should
now give in.'[3]

So when John Goodwin in his *Anti-Cavalierisme* (1642)
announced that 'now we know' that Antichrist 'is
about to be destroyed and cast out of the world',
Mr. Allen is absolutely right to say that Goodwin meant
far more by Antichrist than the Pope or the Roman
church[4]—or even, we might add, than bishops. Mr.

[1] W. Bridge, *Babylons Downfall* (1641), pp. 22–3.
[2] Burton, *Englands Bondage and Hope of Deliverance* (1641), pp. 24–5.
Cf. *The Sounding of the Two Last Trumpets* (1641).
[3] Burroughs, *Sions Joy*, esp. pp. 36, 44, 57–61.
[4] J. Goodwin, *Anti-Cavalierisme* (1642), p. 30, in Haller, *Tracts on Liberty*,
ii; J. W. Allen, *English Political Thought, 1603–1660*, i (1938), pp. 475–7.

Allen spoke of 'a vague suggestion of some vast re-
generating change to be brought about by the war. All
the powers of evil, it seems, are to be finally broken.'
But Goodwin was not so vague as that. It is a society
based on subjection and exploitation that he is bidding
Englishmen come out of, of which popery and Laudian-
ism were only one (or two) manifestations. This is what
Goodwin says, ostensibly about the early church, but
the application is obvious:

Had not the spirits and judgments and consciences of
men been as it were cowed and marvellously imbased and
kept under (and so prepared for Antichrist's lure) by
doctrines and tenents excessively advancing the power of
superiors over inferiors, and binding iron yokes and heavy
burdens upon those that were in subjection, doubtless they
would never have bowed down their backs so low as to let
such a Beast go over them, they would never [have] re-
signed up their judgments and consciences into the hand
of such a spiritual tyrant as he. So that you see there was a
special necessity for the letting of Antichrist into the world,
yea and for the continuance of him in his throne, that no
such opinion as this which we speak of, whether truth or
untruth, should be taught and believed; I mean, which
vindicateth and maintaineth the just rights and liberties
and privileges of those that [are] under authority and subjection unto others.

Now that the downfall of Antichrist is drawing near,
it is particularly necessary that God should reveal to his
servants 'the just bounds and limits of authority and
power, and consequently the just and full extent of the
lawful liberties of those that live in subjection'. Antichrist has still swallowed up the secular empire: but
now the attack is turned directly against the political
and social aspects of this power, rather than against the

spiritual Antichrist which sits crowned upon them. Goodwin insisted that men 'of ordinary rank and quality' were to execute God's judgements on the Whore.[1]

The symbolism of Antichrist was, of course, good for morale, as an observer noted in 1645: 'The more our persuasions are that we fight against the Beast, and the nearer we conceive his fall to approach, the stronglier we may conclude that the contrary power shall overcome.'[2] (Remember the Geneva Bible: 'Antichrist hath not power over the elect.') George Wither in 1643 referred to the royalists as 'bands and . . . confederates of Antichrist':

> The Beast to muster up his kings provides . . .
> If this be so . . . how brave a lot
> Have we? . . .
> With what high courage should we march along
> Against this foe? . . .
> Why should we fear to prevail in that fight?[3]

Francis Cheynell told the House of Commons in May 1643: 'It is neither rebellion nor treason to fight for the King, to recover his power out of the hand of the Beast' —'that power which the antichristian faction by force or fraud hath wrested out of the King's hand.' 'Our deliverance . . . from antichristian Babylon . . . will cost blood.' 'The antichristian faction' included many who call themselves protestants, but who 'violently oppose all powerful preaching'.[4] Five months later

---

[1] Goodwin, op. cit., pp. 2–3, 30–1, 49–51.

[2] *Thurloe State Papers* (1742), i, p. 56. Cf. Leighton, p. x above.

[3] Wither, *Campo-Musae* (1643), p. 64, in *Miscellaneous Works* (Spenser Soc. reprint, 1872), first collection.

[4] F. Cheynell, *Sions Memento and Gods Alarm* (1643), sig. A3, pp. 8, 10, 26–7. Printed by order. Cf. Obadiah Sedgwick, *Hamans Vanity* (1643), p. 19. A sermon preached to the House of Commons.

Henry Wilkinson, preaching to the same audience, said that war was waged on Parliament's side against 'the Apocalyptical Beast and all his complices'. 'The old house built up by the faction of Antichrist is leprous.' 'You must expect that the militia of hell and the trained bands of Satan, those that have received the mark of Antichrist, shall be put into a posture of war.'[1] Fortunately, Joseph Caryl assured Parliament in the following year, Christ is come to be captain of the militia.[2] Stephen Marshall, also in 1644, told the House of Commons and the Westminster Assembly of Divines: 'The question in England is, whether Christ or Antichrist shall be lord or king?' 'Away with Antichrist's stuff', he cried, 'root and branch, head and tail, throw it out of the kingdom.'[3]

Three anonymous pamphlets of July and August 1643, *Englands Alarm to War against the Beast*, and its sequels, *Englands Second* and *Third Alarm*, each 'printed in the second year of the Beast's wounding', seem to have been inspired by the City radicals to oppose a compromise peace.[4] 'If we . . . consider the great revolution and turning of things upside down in these our days', the Scot George Gillespie told the House of Commons in March 1644, 'certainly the work is upon the wheel: the Lord hath . . . prepared the instruments of death against Antichrist.' 'The day of vengeance upon

[1] H. Wilkinson, *Babylons Ruine, Jerusalems Rising* (1643), sig. A3, pp. 21, 26; cf. pp. 7–8, 25. Printed by order.

[2] J. Caryl, *The Saints Thankfull Acclamation* (1644), p. 37.

[3] [S. Marshall], *A Sacred Panegyric* (1644), p. 21. Cf. Francis Woodcock, *Christs Warning-piece* (1644), pp. 6–8.

[4] The text contains virtually nothing about Antichrist. Cf. *The Mysterie of Iniquity yet working in the Kingdoms of England, Scotland and Ireland* (1643).

Antichrist is coming, and is not far off.'[1] At the local level, a sermon preached before the Kent Committee in June 1644 declared that any who refused to help Parliament with all his might against 'the fury of antichristian factors and panders is no other than a rebel and traitor against God'. We are in danger of 'losing the Christian religion throughout all the churches of the world if we now be careless and let slip the opportunity put into our hands': it is now or never. The quarrel between Sion and Babylon can be ended only by the sword.[2]

Even a conservative Parliamentarian gentleman like George Smith, who in 1645 thought Parliament intended no religious changes, 'only to purge out the dregs of antichristian doctrines', still believed that 'God proves us now, whether we will follow Christ or Antichrist'. 'God is now about no less work than to set up Jesus Christ on his throne and to pull down Antichrist from his stage.' But 'the devil and his antichristian brood', growing desperate at 'losing their wonted jurisdiction', were stirring up 'their agents of all sorts . . . They have agents in the church and . . . in the commonwealth, . . . learned agents for learned assemblies to trouble religious disputes; military agents, . . . committee agents . . . to breed dissension and to tyrannize'.[3] ('Agents for learned assemblies' presumably referred to the Five Independent Brethren in the

---

[1] G. Gillespie, *A Sermon Preached before the House of Commons*, 27 March 1644, pp. 9, 38. Gillespie thought 1643 had seen the end of the prophetic 1,260 years (pp. 37–8).

[2] Joseph Boden, *An Alarm Beat up in Sion, to War against Babylon* (1644), esp. pp. 13–16, 30–1.

[3] George Smith, Gentleman, *Englands Pressures Or, The Peoples Complaint* (1645), pp. 7, 20.

Westminster Assembly. Already 'antichristian' was becoming a useful term of abuse for anybody one disliked.)

Men looking back after the Civil War was over
recognized that by it 'the antichristian faction hath
been much weakened'.[1] It was Antichristians who were
beaten at Edgehill, Naseby, and elsewhere, said a Bible
commentary.[2] In 1644 Gillespie reminded the Commons that kings 'have before subjected themselves to
Antichrist'.[3] But if the King was of Antichrist's party,
who was to take his place? Prynne and the Long Parliament were heirs to the robust erastianism of Bucer's *De
Regno Christi* in subordinating the church to the secular
power. On the other hand, Bucer never forgot that
kings were themselves subject to the kingdom of Christ,
and godly preachers were expected to do the work
bishops could not be trusted with.[4] Bucer's ambiguities
thus left open the possibility of direct action by the
godly themselves if the secular power failed in its duty.
And if the godly themselves failed? That question was
not asked yet, but meanwhile the democratic possibilities in the apocalyptic interpretation of Antichrist,
at which Stephen Marshall and John Goodwin had
hinted, and whose results Symmons so much deplored,
were being developed.

II

The author of *A Glimpse of Syons Glory* said in 1641
that after Antichrist began to be discovered, it was the

[1] John Maynard, *A Shadow of the Victory of Christ* (1646), p. 10. A
sermon preached before the House of Commons.

[2] John Trapp, *Commentary on the New Testament* (Evansville, Indiana,
1958), pp. 767–8. First pub. 1647.

[3] G. Gillespie, *A Sermon Preached before the Honourable House of Commons*,
p. 8.   [4] Bucer, *De Regno Christi*, Bk. I, ch. i, Bk. II, ch. i.

common people that first came to look for Christ—
contemptible though they might be in the eyes of Antichrist's spirits and the prelacy. He illuminates the process
by which the ideas of their betters were handed down to
a lower social class, and in the process transmuted. 'The
people had a hint of something: down with Antichrist,
down with popery!', though they did not understand
distinctly what they were doing. But they could bring
pressure to bear on Parliament. 'This is the work of the
day, for us to lift up our voice to heaven, that it might
be mighty to bring forth the voice of our Parliament as
a voice of thunder, a terrible voice to the antichristian
party.' In the spirit of Stephen Marshall Goodwin
added: 'Blessed is he that dasheth the brats of Babylon
against the stones.'[1] The failure of the divines assembled
at Westminster to gratify the millenarian hopes of their
lay supporters, especially among the humbler classes,
brought a reaction against clerical claims to leadership
—and a new clerical caution and conservatism.[2]

Fuel was added to the flames by, for instance, the
recantation sermon preached by the ex-priest Thomas
Gage in St. Paul's on 28 August 1642, and published
with dedication to Isaac Penington, Lord Mayor, and
the sheriffs and aldermen of London. Grateful for his
escape from 'the quicksands of antichristian doctrine',
Gage rejoiced that in England men were 'now free
to oppose *all* antichristian doctrine'.[3] But the new

[1] *A Glimpse of Syons Glory*, in A. S. P. Woodhouse, *Puritanism and Liberty*
(1938), pp. 233–5.
[2] This point is stressed by Mr. Lamont, op. cit., esp. pp. 110–12,
125–6.
[3] T. Gage, *The Tyranny of Satan* (1642), Epistle Dedicatory and p. 26.
My italics. Cf. Francis De Neville, *The Christian and Catholike Veritie:
or The Reasons and Manner of the Conversion of Francis de Neville, formerly
Capuchin* (1642), pp. 71–4. Dedicated to Parliament.

freedom was not to the liking of the more conservative supporters of Parliament among the clergy. Sectaries call 'the gravest, ablest and most eminent ministers in the kingdom . . . limbs of Antichrist', Cornelius Burges complained in a sermon before the House of Commons in November 1641, and 'forsake our assemblies as Babylonish and antichristian'.[1] Already such divines were fighting on two fronts. John Brinsley warned his Yarmouth congregation in 1642 against separatists who say our churches 'are antichristian churches, our ministers antichristian ministers, and our worship antichristian worship'.[2] Brownists, Ephraim Pagitt echoed sourly, conclude any action done by our ministers to be antichristian.[3] Decency and order, a disgusted Parliamentarian said when changing sides in 1642, were regarded by the radicals as antichristian.[4]

Experience of the religious changes of the revolution taught Milton that new presbyter was but old priest writ large: it convinced Nathanael Homes and many others that Antichrist could be incarnated in many more forms than the Pope or the bishops.[5] Long ago the Baptist John Smyth had decided that elders were anti-

[1] C. Burges, *Another Sermon preached to the House of Commons* (1641), p. 60.

[2] J. Brinsley, *The Healing of Israels Breaches* (1642), pp. 101–2.

[3] E. Pagitt, *Heresiography* (2nd ed., 1645), pp. 60–1; cf. T. Edwards, *Gangraena* (1646), Part III, p. 38; cf. [Thomas Hall], *The Pulpit Guarded with XX Arguments* (1651), pp. 81–6—six arguments proving our ministry far from antichristianism. Cf. *Memorials of the Civil War* (ed. R. Bell, 1849), i, p. 192.

[4] *A Coppy of A Letter Writ from Sergeant-Major Kirle to a friend in Windsor* (n.d.), reprinted in J. and T. W. Webb, *The Civil War in Herefordshire* (1879), ii, p. 343.

[5] N. Homes, *The Christian Hammerers against the Antichristian Horns* in *Works* (1652), p. 608. Lutherans too, Homes thought, had ceased to hammer the antichristian horns as their founder used to do.

christian.[1] Thomas Edwards's 'Error No. 143' of the
sectaries was that presbyterian government was the
Beast.[2] A broadside which no doubt circulated among
Parliamentarian soldiers like those whom Mr. Symmons met described how

> The crooked Serpent creeps upon the earth,
> An antichristian presbyter by birth.[3]

'Presbyterians worship the Dragon and the Beast',
added Arise Evans later.[4] So the old vocabulary of abuse
came to be directed against a new target. 'Those called
the Presbyterians' were 'decried by all opposition
parties as the antichristian party', grumbled Edmund
Hall: men calculated that there were just 666 words in
the Solemn League and Covenant.[5] As early as 1644 the
Five Dissenting Brethren in the Westminster Assembly
found it necessary to deny that it could ever 'enter into
our hearts to judge' presbyterian government antichristian.[6] But rasher men were not lacking who said
the Assembly was 'an antichristian meeting, which
would erect a presbytery worse than bishops'.[7] Cornelius
Burges and Thomas Edwards both protested against
the view that it was 'antichristian to engage all to unity
and uniformity'.[8] William Dell, on the other hand,

[1] Burrage, op. cit. i, p. 235.

[2] Edwards, *Gangraena* (1646), Part I, pp. 32, 97; Part III, pp. 24,
241–2.

[3] [Anon.], *The Watchmans Warning-peece. Or, Parliament Souldiers Prediction* (n.d.), single sheet.

[4] Arise Evans, *To the Most High and Mighty Prince Charles II, . . . An
Epistle* (1660), p. 42; cf. *The Disputes Between Mr. Crawford and Dr.
Chamberlen* (1652).   [5] E. Hall, *A Scriptural Discourse*, sig. b4ᵛ.

[6] *An Apologeticall Narration* (1644), p. 6, in Haller, op. cit. ii.

[7] Quoted in D. Masson, *Life of John Milton* (1859–94), iii, p. 85.

[8] C. Burges, *The Second Sermon Preached to the House of Commons* (1645),
p. 51; Edwards, *Gangraena*, Part I, p. 212.

flatly declared: 'unity is Christian, uniformity anti-christian'.[1] To oppose the gathering of churches was described as siding with Antichrist in a pamphlet of 1644.[2] Separation from an antichristian church was permissible, Thomas Hill explained to a no doubt sympathetic House of Lords in November 1644; but the argument that justified the protestant reformers of a century earlier was wrongly used by sectaries now.[3]

A pamphlet of 1647 assumed that 'bishops, cross, sur-plices and altar worship and such things . . . are now generally sworn against as antichristian'; but its main theme was that sectaries were 'the Antichrist yet re-maining'.[4] John Goodwin rebuked William Prynne for 'crying down of bishops as antichristian'. How can they be 'more antichristian than any other', since Prynne believed that 'there is no certain government in the world'?[5] 'How doth a heathenish or pagan state differ from an antichristian or parochial state?' John Saltmarsh asked in 1646. 'The people are brethren and saints in Christ's church, but in Antichrist's, parishioners and servants.' This class appeal followed a rejection of 'the antichristian design for reconciliation—to believe as the church or councils, to set up one, as the Pope, for infallibility; to allow that all may be saved in their several ways; to forbid interpretings or disputes; by a compulsive power'.[6] Any national church was neces-

[1] *Several Sermons of William Dell* (1709), p. 64; cf. p. 293. First pub. 1651.

[2] Francis Cornwell, *A Vindication of the Royal Commission of King Jesus . . . against the Antichristian Faction of Pope Innocencies the third* (1644), esp. p. 16.   [3] T. Hill, *The Right Separation Incouraged* (1645), p. 11.

[4] [Anon.], *Hereticks, Sectaries and Schismatickes, Discovered to be the Antichrist yet remaining* (1647), p. 8.

[5] J. Goodwin, *Certaine Briefe Observations* (1645), p. 3.

[6] J. Saltmarsh, *The Smoke in the Temple* (1646), sig. **4–5, p. 23; cf.

sarily antichristian, said Saltmarsh and James Pope in the same year, the latter adding that 'Antichrist hath been in the world this sixteen hundred years'.[1]

There was a strong tradition, going back many centuries, which associated Antichrist with cruelty and persecution of God's people. Obadiah Sedgwick spoke to the House of Commons in June 1643 of 'the antichristian cruelties', meaning those of the royalists.[2] In the free discussion of the 1640s this worked to the deadly disadvantage of those who wanted to preserve a state church, attendance at which should be compulsory, and which was financed by compulsory tithes. Joseph Caryl, preaching to Parliament, Lord Mayor, aldermen, Common Council, and the Assembly of Divines, utilized an old theme to new purposes when he hoped 'we shall never use . . . Antichrist's broom to sweep Christ's house with, or his weapons to fight against errors with'—i.e. that we should not use popish violent suppression of alleged heresy.[3] Intolerance was antichristian, said the Leveller Richard Overton,[4] picking up Caryl's point. Roger Williams thought even Antichristians should be tolerated.[5] Thomas Edwards

his *The Divine Right of Presbyterie* (1646), pp. 2–3, 15. See also E. Rogers, *Some Account of the Life and Opinions of a Fifth-Monarchy Man* (1867), p. 63.

[1] J. Saltmarsh, *Groanes for Liberty* (1646), sig. A2; J. Pope, *The Unveiling of Antichrist* (1646), pp. 1, 9, and *passim*.

[2] O. Sedgwick, *Hamans Vanity* (1643), p. 19.

[3] J. Caryl, *Englands Plus Ultra* (1646), pp. 24–5.

[4] R. Overton, *The Arraignement of Mr. Persecution* (1645), pp. 12, 15, in Haller, op. cit. iii; cf. Pope, op. cit., p. 18; W. Hartley, *The Prerogative Passing-Bell* (1651), Preface to the Reader; T. Collier, *The Pulpit-Guard Routed* (1652), pp. 40, 103–4; E. Rogers, op. cit., p. 121.

[5] R. Williams, *The Bloudy Tenent of Persecution* (1644) (Hanserd Knollys Soc., 1848), pp. 2, 74–5, 83; cf. *Christenings Make Not Christians* (1645), in *The Complete Writings of Roger Williams*, vii (New York, 1963), p. 34.

was referring to many like Overton and Williams when he spoke of heretics who 'make antichristianism to consist in the coercive power of the magistrate in matters of religion'.[1] It would be 'a work worthy a most learned and pious divine', declared a pamphlet of 1646, 'or rather a synod or council, laying all interest and passion aside, to gather and collect all former opinions of the learned concerning Antichrist, and endeavour to give light to the simple and ignorant'.[2]

But many of the simple and ignorant thought they knew. A pamphlet of 1647 said the assumption of infallibility in man was more antichristian than the Pope himself. Usurpation of power over the bodies of the saints in respect of spiritual things, and all persecution, were antichristian.[3] Milton concurred, quoting Dante to the effect that 'the Romish Antichrist' was 'merely bred up by Constantine'. 'All true protestants account the Pope Antichrist for that he assumes to himself this infallibility over both the conscience and the Scripture.' The Presbyterians' aim at a spiritual tyranny was no better than antichristian: persecuting rulers should be accounted antichristian like the Pope. Censorship was popish, deriving from 'the most antichristian council'.[4] 'By the mark of the Beast in the forehead', wrote John Dury, 'I understand the irrationality of obedience of those that subject themselves blindfold in all things.'[5] Praisegod Barebone in 1642, Roger Williams in 1644,

[1] Edwards, *Gangraena*, Part I, p. 26.

[2] [Anon.], *A Vindication of Learning From unjust Aspersions* (1646), p. 14.

[3] [Anon.], *Hereticks, Sectaries and Schismaticks*, pp. 11–17.

[4] Milton, *Works* (Columbia ed.), iii, p. 25, iv, p. 305, vi, pp. 8–10, xviii, p. 252. Cf. Appendix III below.

[5] Abraham von Frankenberg (ed. S. Hartlib), *Clavis Apocalyptica* (1651), Preface by Dury, p. 55.

and William Bartlet in 1647 argued that England was still 'under the defection and apostacy of Antichrist'. 'The whole . . . frame of England's visible church state' had been unsound ever since its liberation 'from antichristian bondage and thraldom' at the Reformation; its ordinances and worship were 'forged in Antichrist's shop'.[1]

Edwards recorded a Baptist who said contending for infant baptism was antichristian, and quoted Samuel Oates as saying: 'Antichrist's way is first to baptize, then to believe and preach.'[2] In 1644 Christopher Blackwood published *The Storming of Antichrist in his two last and strongest Garrisons, Of Compulsion of Conscience and Infants Baptism*. All churches, he argued, have erred for many centuries, since the antichristian apostacy. They now follow Antichrist or human traditions. Parochial churches have been brought in by Antichrist of late days. Congregations should resume 'that power which was committed to the churches, and after cheated away by Antichrist'.[3] Ironically enough, recalling what Symmons was saying this same year, Blackwood's book started as a criticism of a sermon by Stephen Marshall. Henry Denne, future leader of the Leveller regiments

[1] P. B[arebone], *A Discourse tending to prove the Baptism in, or under, the Defection of Antichrist to be the Ordinance of Jesus Christ* (1642); cf. *A Reply to the Frivolous and impertinent Answer of R. B. to the discourse of P. B.* (1643); Williams, *The Bloudy Tenent*, pp. 381–2; W. Bartlet, *A Model of The Primitive Congregational Way* (1647), sig. (b); *Soveraigne Balsome* (1649), sig. A4^v, p. 41. For the conception of apostacy see Erbery, quoted on pp. 128–30 below.

[2] *Gangraena*, Part I, p. 214, Part III, p. 56. Samuel was the father of the more famous Titus Oates.

[3] Op. cit., Part II, pp. 55, 62; Part I, pp. 6–7; cf. *Gangraena*, Part III, p. 98; T. Blake, *Infants Baptisme Freed from Antichristianisme* (1645), a reply to Blackwood.

which revolted in 1649, was also replying to Marshall in his *Antichrist unmasked in Two Treatises* (1645). In the second of these, *The Man of Sin Discovered*, Denne was sceptical about too precise identification of Antichrist. 'Some think the Pope of Rome is Antichrist, some the bishops, some the Turk, etc.' But 'to tie the name of Antichrist to a particular man, or to any particular succession of men, is to confine him unto too narrow a bound. . . . The Pope is a principal member of Antichrist', but 'the great Antichrist' is 'that mystical body of iniquity which opposeth Jesus Christ'. We shall find Antichrist in the temple, in the pulpit, 'at devotion, with great zeal'. 'Not Rome alone, but the pulpits of England also may be discovered to be filled with the Man of Sin.' Denne slily quoted James I to establish that 'a certain note of a fallen church is persecution'.[1]

Thomas Edwards recorded tradesmen who said that 'they are that great Antichrist . . . who deny the general redemption of . . . the whole creation', and he named Henry Denne as one who declared opposition to antinomian errors to be the Man of Sin and the great Antichrist.[2] Denne in return pilloried Edwards's scandalous gossip—'a man in Cheapside, a maid I know not where and a woman in such a lane'—and caricatured his conclusions in words that Oliver Cromwell later echoed: 'Because there are many drunkards (and men of no mean rank) in the City, therefore wine must be banished the city.'[3]

John Saltmarsh was a chaplain and Denne a preacher in the New Model Army, that unique forum or free

---

[1] Denne, *The Man of Sin Discovered* (2nd ed., 1646), pp. 15–19, 27.
[2] *Gangraena*, Part III, p. 10; Part I, p. 26.
[3] *The Man of Sin Discovered*, pp. 21–2, 30.

discussion. So was William Dell, who (like Denne) was
accused of 'contending for perfection and freedom from
all sin in this life'—'antichristian doctrine'.[1] Dell said
the destruction of Antichrist would lead to 'the obtain-
ing of our just rights and freedoms in civil things'.

> This clergy-antichristian power, wherever it is, will still
> sit upon the power of the nation, the power of Antichrist. . . .
> They make the whole kingdom a church, and then require
> a power, authority and jurisdiction in their church-kingdom,
> which the magistrate is not to deal withal, but themselves.
> Whereas we acknowledge the whole power of the kingdom
> to belong to the magistrate, and only give unto Christ the
> power of his own kingdom, which is not of this world but
> spiritual and heavenly.[2]

If the Assembly of Divines should condemn his doctrine,
Dell added, 'they are . . . the last prop of Antichrist in
the kingdom'. 'Christ doth all in his kingdom by the
Word only; but Antichrist doth all things without the
Word by the decrees and consultations of men.'[3] Where
the prelates used to say 'No bishop, no King', now 'their
successors in the kingdom of Antichrist still cry "no
minister, no magistrate" '.[4] The prelatical church and
clergy are the Beast: bishops and presbyters the Beast's
image. The clergy were seducing the magistrates to
Antichrist. To esteem ministers for their human learning, their school divinity, to account their order worthy

---

[1] Rutherford, *A Survey of the Spirituall Antichrist*, pp. 187–8.

[2] W. Dell, *Right Reformation* (1651), a sermon preached to the House
of Commons, 25 Nov. 1646, in *Several Sermons and Discourses* (1709),
p. 118; E. C. Walker, *William Dell* (Cambridge, 1970), p. 116.

[3] Ibid., pp. 121, 143; cf. p. 125. Samuel Rutherford quoted the
phrase about the Assembly of Divines with considerable disapprobation
(*A Survey of the Spirituall Antichrist*, sig. A4).

[4] Dell, *Right Reformation*, in *Sermons*, p. 117.

of worldly maintenance and to give them power to determine and censor doctrine, to allow them any power of jurisdiction or censorship—all these were to receive the mark of the Beast.[1] 'Making the clergy a distinguished sect or order or trade' was an antichristian error. 'I cannot choose but conclude with John Hus, that all the clergy must be quite taken away ere the church of Christ can have any true reformation.'[2] 'For Antichrist could not deceive the world with a company of foolish, weak, ignorant, profane, contemptible persons, but he always hath the greatest, wisest, holiest and most eminent in the visible church for him.' To deny Jesus Christ in his members is as truly antichristian as to deny Jesus Christ in the head.[3] Cromwell supported this attitude when he told the Irish bishops in 1650 that the distinction between clergy and laity was antichristian.[4] It had been 'the doctrine and practice of the antichristian bishops and priests that taught the exposition of Scripture to belong alone to the clergy and not to the laity': so the legal writer William Sheppard put it in 1652.[5]

III

We saw how in the early seventeenth century the international alliance with revolutionary Calvinism ceased to be a necessity for an isolated protestant England and became a matter of choice: and we saw how first James and then more decisively Charles

[1] Dell, *Sermons*, p. 465; cf. pp. 535–40.

[2] Id., *The Stumbling-Stone* (1653), in *Sermons*, pp. 347–8.

[3] Id., *The Tryal of Spirits* (1653), in *Sermons*, pp. 484, 487—a sermon on 1 John 4: 1–6.

[4] Abbott, op. cit. ii, p. 197; Dell, op. cit., pp. 264–5.

[5] W. Sheppard, *The Peoples Priviledge and Duty Guarded* (1652), p. 75.

repudiated this alliance—for a variety of reasons, including finance and the internal social balance in England. Inevitably parties polarized. As the situation in England became more explosive, so there developed a utopian internationalism which carefully studied the time-table of the fall of Antichrist. The popularity of the works of Napier, Brightman, Mede, Archer is evidence of this new interest. Mr. Lamont, who drew attention to the significance of this phenomenon, attributes the new emphasis to the writings of Brightman. I myself would explain the popularity of Napier, Brightman, and other chronologists by the changing political mood. It is the old question of the ultimate priority of ideas or material facts, which some may see as the problem of the chicken and the egg, and all of us will answer in accordance with our own prepossessions.

I would stress the changing international situation, the capitulation of Henry IV to Antichrist in 1593, and the consequent loss of the strongest potential protestant power, followed by Richelieu's defeats of the Huguenots, aided by what Milton later described as Charles I's 'antichristian war against the poor protestants of Rochelle'.[1] At the same time the counter-reformation was slowly advancing in Poland and Hungary, threatening Sweden. Then with catastrophic speed, in the words of Thomas Taylor, Antichrist made 'havoc and waste in the flourishing churches of Bohemia, the Palatinate and other parts of Germany'.[2] Just as suddenly the sensational victories of Gustavus Adolphus saved protestantism in Germany and Scandinavia. John

[1] Milton, *Works* (Columbia ed.), v, p. 153.
[2] T. Taylor, *Christs Victorie over the Dragon* (1633), pp. 721–2, 817. Posthumously published.

Tillinghast in 1654 recalled 'what high expectations were raised' by Gustavus Adolphus: men believed 'that most worthy prince would be the ruin of the antichristian whore'.[1] Soon afterwards, the triumphs of our brethren of Scotland were followed by apparent evidence of the Roman Catholic international at work in the Irish Revolt of 1641. Then the antichristian power broke down in England, freedom of discussion and organization prevailed, separatist churches emerged from underground, new classes entered into political action. Emigration to New England ceased, John Winthrop tells us, because the excitement of the revolution made 'all men to stay in England in expectation of a new world'.[2]

In these circumstances it seems to me all but inevitable that for many the old defensive international alliance against Antichrist should give place to utopian dreams of an aggressive–defensive protestant league against Antichrist in all his forms—Laud, Charles I, the Pope, the Kings of Spain and France. Various signs of political breakdown on the Continent—revolts in Catalonia, Portugal, Naples, the Fronde in France, troubles in the Netherlands, Sicily, the Ukraine[3]— would all advance the conviction that Antichrist's fall was near. Interest in the time-table was increasingly forced upon serious-minded men. To us it may seem that in such chronological studies the resources of scholarship and science were devoted to misguided ends, but this is a familiar enough human habit, not

[1] J. Tillinghast, *Generation-work*, Part III, pp. 68–9; cf. Marshall, *The Song of Moses*, p. 15.
[2] Quoted by Masson, *Life of Milton*, ii, p. 585.
[3] See my *Puritanism and Revolution*, pp. 132–42.

yet extinct: new techniques are applied to the solution of traditional problems without its being seen that the questions have become irrelevant. Ours is the wisdom of hindsight.

When, for instance, Thomas Goodwin in 1639 saw the rise of the congregational churches as a second reformation and fitted this into the time-table, the idea had great consolatory force in those dark days when New England seemed the one focus of hope. But already Goodwin thought old England had a crucial role to play in the struggle against Antichrist: such an approach inevitably gave rise to utopian hopes when Independency enjoyed its sensational triumphs in the England of the forties.[1]

Support from revolutionary utopians of the lower classes was as necessary for the sober leaders of Parliamentary opposition as the international Calvinist alliance had at one time been to the sceptical Elizabeth: in both cases vague denunciations of Antichrist could cover divergent aspirations. But after victory in the Civil War had been won, the incompatibility stood revealed between the aims of those who wanted only to get rid of antichristian bishops in England, and those who saw the fall of Antichrist all over the world as immediately impending. 'When the dog is beat out of the room, where will they lay the stink?' Selden asked pertinently, apropos bishops.[2]

---

[1] T. Goodwin, *Works*, iii, pp. 140, 195–205; P. Toon, 'The Latter-day Glory in English Puritan Thought', *The Gospel Magazine* (July 1969), p. 326.

[2] J. Selden, *Table Talk* (1847), p. 22. Cf. H. White, *Social Criticism in Popular Literature of the Sixteenth Century* (New York, 1944), chs. iii, iv: similar problems arose when the Reformation failed to satisfy the aspirations of religious radicals.

I have already quoted Wither's line, published in 1643, 'The Beast to muster up his kings provides'.[1] The Civil War, Wither thought, showed that the fall of Antichrist (the Pope) was near: it would come not later than 1666.[2] John Cotton envisaged the campaign against antichristian episcopacy being carried 'from our native country to all the Catholic countries round about them, until it come to the very gates of Rome itself'.[3] Stephen Marshall thought Parliament's victories would encourage 'the people of Italy, Germany, France, . . . Denmark, Sweden, Poland, Hungary' to shake off Antichrist's yoke.[4]

As the war progressed, this vision of it as an international crusade gained in strength. A historical account published in 1643 noted how James I ('to dally with Antichrist a little') had corresponded with Cardinal Perron, and how much further Charles I and Laud had carried negotiations with Rome.[5] The Solemn League and Covenant picked up the Scottish National Covenant's reference to the sinister activities of 'Satan and the Roman Antichrist', and prayed for military victories in order to encourage 'the Christian churches groaning under or in danger of the yoke of antichristian tyranny' —i.e. on the Continent.[6] Stephen Marshall in 1644 told the House of Commons and the Westminster Assembly of Divines that the royalists 'have engaged

[1] See p. 85 above.

[2] Wither, *Campo-Musae* (1643), p. 20; cf. Hensley, *The Later Career of George Wither*, p. 68, for other references.

[3] J. Cotton, *The Powring out of the Seven Vialls* (1642), 'The fift Viall', p. 7.

[4] Marshall, *The Song of Moses* (1643), p. 7; cf. Joseph Caryl, *The Saints Thankfull Acclamation* (1644), p. 25.

[5] [Anon.], *The English Pope* (1643), p. 6.

[6] Gardiner, *Constitutional Documents*, pp. 125, 271.

all the antichristian world. . . . You shall see them sending into France, offering offensive and defensive leagues to the antichristian people'.[1] Roger Williams in the same year believed that 'many scriptures concerning the Beast and the Whore' suggested 'that all England and Europe must again submit their fair necks to the Pope's yoke'.[2] John Eachard shared this fear, but drew optimistic conclusions. 'This civil war begun shall last till Rome be burnt and the Jews called.' 'Michael and his angels will fight for you . . . against Antichrist and his instruments.' 'The last persecution of Antichrist which is now come upon all the Christian world in these our days . . . is like to last till the Pope be destroyed.'[3] The astrologer William Lilly in 1644 thought that so long as the army was well paid, and unity among the Parliamentarians was preserved, there was nothing to fear from Antichrist or any other foreign foe.[4]

With the end of civil war, when men naturally were everywhere discussing England's future settlement, apocalyptic overtones sound more clearly. It is important to see this in human terms: the mathematician John Pell, though writing as late as 1655, will help us to understand what it meant. 'Men variously impoverished by the long troubles,' he wrote, 'full of discontents and tried by long expectation of amendment, must needs have great propensions to harken to those that proclaim times of refreshing—a golden age—at

---

[1] [Marshall], *A Sacred Panegyric*, pp. 21, 25. See pp. 81–2, 86 above.

[2] R. Williams, *The Bloudy Tenent*, p. 280. Cf. *The Hireling Ministry None of Christs* (1652), p. 6; and Archer, quoted on p. 29 above.

[3] J. Eachard, *Good Newes for all Christian Souldiers* (1645), sig. A4ᵛ, pp. 1, 3; *The Axe against Sin and Error* (1646), p. 37.

[4] W. Lilly, *A Prophecy of the White King* (1644), p. 6.

hand.'[1] 'It is . . . generally thought by the people of God that the total rooting out of Antichrist draws near', wrote James Pope in 1646. It was therefore a duty to unveil Antichrist in order to root him out.[2] A pamphlet published in 1647 thought that was 'the long-looked-for year that Antichrist shall fall'. It is 'the common talk about London, and so consequently over England, that such a day in such a week the day of doom shall happen'.[3] This may have been due to William Sedgwick, who made the mistake of prophesying the end of the world for fourteen days ahead. He survived to enjoy the name of Doomsday Sedgwick for another fifteen years. But many similar prophetical utterances got into print. In a pamphlet of Jacob Boehme, translated in 1649, 'the Antichrist, the Whore of Babylon, the Beast and False Prophet, in their mystery of iniquity and perverse practices are abundantly described'. A lot of mysterious prophecies followed.[4]

In the Putney Debates in the Army Council (October 1647) Colonel Goffe spoke of the conjunction between Antichrist and 'men in places of power or authority in the world, kings and great men'. Even kings denying the Pope's supremacy—including the King of England —have taken upon themselves papal antichristian authority. The work of Jesus Christ 'in the last days is

[1] Ed. R. Vaughan, *The Protectorate of Oliver Cromwell* (1839), i, p. 156.

[2] Pope, *The Unveiling of Antichrist*, sig. A2.

[3] [Anon.], *Doomes-day* (1647), pp. 4–6. Antichrist was the Pope.

[4] *Mercurius Teutonicus . . . gathered out of the Mysticall Writings of . . . Jacob Behmen* (1649), sig. A2ᵛ. This was the tenth work of Boehme's to be translated into English since 1645; another eleven were to follow by 1656 (S. Hutin, *Les Disciples anglais de Jacob Boehme aux XVIIᵉ et XVIIIᵉ siècles* (Paris, 1960), pp. 38–9). William Erbery quoted Boehme (*The Testimony of William Erbery* (1658), p. 333). Lazarus Seaman possessed two of Boehme's works (see p. 17, n. 5 above).

to destroy this mystery of iniquity'; this must lead to 'great alteration of states'. We must be careful not 'to set up the power which God would not set up again . . . in our compliance with that party which God hath engaged us to destroy'.[1]

'The government of the nations', John Owen told Parliament in April 1649, 'is purely framed for the interest of Antichrist. No kind of government in Europe . . . but that the Beast . . . had a great influence in their constitution or establishment.' Shaking the nations 'shall not stop . . . before the interest of anti-christianity be wholly separated from the power of those nations'. He added that 'the opening, unravelling and revealing of the antichristian interest' was 'the great discovery' of his generation.[2] After hearing this sermon Oliver Cromwell sought Owen's acquaintance, and in the 1650s the latter became almost an official exponent of government policy. Milton, who had taken pains to associate Charles I with Antichrist in *The Tenure of Kings and Magistrates*, has a similar call to a crusade against antichristian monarchy all over Europe in *Eikonoklastes*.[3] 'The present interest of the saints', declared a pamphlet of 1649, is to 'combine together against the antichristian powers of the world'. 'Kings, yea Parliaments also and magistrates' must be put down before Christ's kingdom can be erected.[4]

[1] Woodhouse, op. cit., pp. 39–40.

[2] Owen, *Works*, viii, pp. 264–6, 274. By 1652 Owen was much more cautious (ibid. viii, p. 376); by 1680 he had totally recanted (see p. 146 below). Cf. [Anon.], *Certain Quaeres . . . by way of petition* (1648), pp. 5–7.

[3] Milton, *Works* (Columbia ed.), v, pp. 16, 23–4, 158, 226–7, 306–7; cf. vii, pp. 422–3, xiii, p. 205. For other examples of revolutionary internationalism see my *Puritanism and Revolution*, pp. 123–52 and *God's Englishman* (1970), p. 155.

[4] [Anon.], *The Rule of the Saints* (1649), in Woodhouse, op. cit., pp.

In the spring of 1649 six rank-and-file soldiers of the
New Model Army carried theory into practice. They
entered the parish church of Walton-on-Thames and
symbolically abolished the Sabbath, tithes, ministers,
magistrates, and the Bible. Ministers, they declared,
were 'antichristian, and of no longer use now Christ
himself descends into the hearts of his saints and his
spirit enlighteneth them with revelations'.[1] We do not
know how many troopers in other parts of the country
were making similar demonstrations in the spirit which
Mr. Symmons had detected five years earlier. It may
be significant that Walton-on-Thames is within three
miles of St. George's Hill where in April Gerrard
Winstanley's Diggers started to cultivate the common
fields—also symbolically on a Sunday. The Diggers
too would have abolished tithes, ministers, and magistrates, at least in the hitherto accepted sense of the
terms. Tithes indeed had been denounced as a mark of
the Beast in a pamphlet of 1647,[2] and the Quakers were
often to say the same thing.[3]

It is difficult for us to recapture the importance of
Antichrist in the apocalyptic atmosphere of the late
forties and early fifties, when any change seemed possible. A few examples must suffice. Some argued that
'unequal marriages' were 'antichristian yokes', and
therefore that marriages outside the sect should be

243–5. Cf. William Cooper, *Jerusalem Fatall to her Assailants* (1649),
esp. p. 30: a sermon preached to the House of Commons.

[1] C. Walker, *The History of Independency* (1649), Part II, pp. 152–3.

[2] [Anon.], *The Husbandmans Plea* (1647), p. 3.

[3] e.g. R. F[arnsworth], *Antichrists Man of War* (1655), pp. 13, 48;
G. W[hitehead], *An Unjust Plea Confuted . . . Christs Order Vindicated
against Antichrist* (1659), p. 3. Cf. [Anon.], *Ten Considerable Quaeries concerning Tithes . . . for their total abolition, as Antichristian* (1659).

disallowed.[1] William Cooper urged the House of Commons in August 1649 to 'send all the pack of Babylonish trash' from Ireland back 'to Rome after the Nuncio'.[2] Colonel John Jones hoped in the fifties to pull down the works of Antichrist in Ireland, notably idolatry.[3] Mary Cary, one of the few ladies to write on the subject, thought that 'the King of England was one of those that was of one mind with the Beast'; indeed England had been subjected to Antichrist even in Queen Elizabeth's days. The Civil War in England and the war in Ireland had been made by the Beast. The Parliament's Army had stood up for the defence of the saints against Antichrist, and Charles I's time had expired in 1645. Miss Cary aroused some criticism by precisely dating the resurrection of the two witnesses 4 April 1645, the day the New Model Army marched forth. From that time Jesus Christ 'began to take his kingdom'. But even in 1648 he had only 'begun to bring down the power of the Beast'. She prophesied, however, 'before 20 or 10 or 5 years more shall pass' great spiritual glory and a material utopia on earth for the saints, and a relatively classless society. 'Not only men but women shall prophesy; . . . not only superiors but inferiors; not only those that have university learning but those that have it not, even servants and handmaids.'[4]

[1] Edwards, *Gangraena*, Part II, p. 141. The reference does not seem to be to Milton, who had said the restricting of divorce was the first loosening of Antichrist, and that England's divorce laws still conform to Antichrist's unrighteousness (*Works* (Columbia ed.), iv, p. 220). Edwards mentions only William and Elizabeth Jenny.

[2] W. Cooper, *Jerusalem Fatall to her Assailants*, p. 30.

[3] Quoted by A. H. Dodd, *Studies in Stuart Wales* (Cardiff, 1952), p. 105.

[4] Mary Cary, *A Word in Season* (1647), p. 9; *The Resurrection of the*

As early as 1646 Christopher Feake had denounced monarchy and aristocracy as antichristian—or so Thomas Edwards tells us.[1] Joseph Salmon in 1649 called on the Army to be 'the executioners of that Beast [monarchy] which they had formerly wounded, and whose wound the Parliament had . . . salved over'.[2] The English Army in Scotland on occasion used as its password 'No King but Jesus'.[3] *A Declaration* of this Army in August 1650 looked back to 'the antichristian tyranny that was exercised by the late King and his prelates over the consciences, bodies and estates of the true spiritual church' whose members were 'then by that antichristian crew termed Puritans, sectaries, schismatics, etc.' The godly had prayed the Lord 'that he would arise to destroy Antichrist and to save his people'. They had rejoiced to see the Scots 'appearing against that antichristian power' and supported them. ('Not one sect then durst face the field against the Antichrist,' Rutherford had grimly said.) The Army had helped Parliament 'to bring about . . . the destruction of Antichrist and the deliverance of his church and people'. They had even accepted the Solemn League and Covenant, though some suspected that 'the interests of this world, yea of Antichrist himself' lurked 'under a vizor, as we have since had abundant experience of'.

Witnesses (1648), Epistle Dedicatory, pp. 82–7, 98–9, 153–94; *The Little Horns Doom and Downfall* (1651), pp. 6–7, 118–19, 133, 238, 282, 285–317; cf. [Anon.], *The account audited* (1649), a criticism. Mary Cary's general chronological scheme seems to be that of John Archer, with the conversion of the Jews in 1656, the millennium in 1701 (*The Little Horns Doom*, pp. 207–9). But she has some original features.

[1] Edwards, *Gangraena*, Part I, pp. 147–8.

[2] Salmon, *A Rout, A Rout* (1649), p. 13.

[3] E. Rogers, *Life and Opinions of a Fifth Monarchy Man* (1867), p. 127.

Charles I and his monarchy were one of the ten horns of the Beast.[1]

The Fifth Monarchist William Aspinwall proved Charles Stuart to be the Little Horn and the Beast, and concluded that 'the saints' act in slaying the Beast and taking away his dominion was no rash nor seditious act, but an act of sound judgment, approved of God'. 'The uttermost durance of Antichrist's dominion' would be until 1673.[2] Even the more sober Edward Haughton, in a course of lectures given at Horsham, Sussex, described the Civil War as 'part of the battle you read of in the 16 and 19 chapters of the Revelations'. Charles I was 'the Pope's second', who had 'openly professedly joined interest with the antichristian party'. The century after 1641, he thought, would be more fatal to monarchy in Europe 'than ever any was since this world began'.[3] Bishop Burnet later observed that it was difficult for Oliver Cromwell to accept the throne when it was offered to him in 1657 because men like John Goodwin had long represented monarchy as that great Antichrist which hindered Christ from being set on his throne.[4] This strong association of monarchy with antichristianism by John Goodwin, Milton, Colonel Goffe,

---

[1] *A Declaration of the English Army now in Scotland*, in *Thurloe State Papers*, iii, pp. 136–7; Rutherford, *A Survey of the Spirituall Antichrist*, sig. A4ᵛ.

[2] W. Aspinwall, *A Brief Description of the Fifth Monarchy* (1653), *passim*; *An Explication or Application Of the Seventh Chapter of Daniel* (1654), title-page, sig. A2 and pp. 5–6, 13–17, 25–9. Aspinwall, like the Fifth Monarchy insurrectionist Venner, was a returned New Englander. He expected the name of Parliament to be laid aside no less than that of King.

[3] Haughton, *The Rise, Growth and Fall of Antichrist* (1652), sig. A5ᵛ, pp. 91–6.

[4] G. Burnet, *History of His Own Time* (ed. O. Airy, 1897), i, p. 121. For Goodwin see esp. pp. 83–5 above.

Army leaders, and Levellers helps to explain the eclipse of Antichrist after the Restoration.[1]

Antichrist was thus extended to cover civil government. Parliament itself was called antichristian.[2] The Baptist John Batty, Edwards tells us, had reviled the Lord Mayor of London as 'a limb of Antichrist and a persecutor of the brethren'.[3] A somewhat unbalanced ex-Leveller, George Foster, announced in 1650 that 'all forms and ways of worship, rules and government which is the wisdom of the flesh' were the Beast; and that 'all the powers of flesh, devil and sin that have been set up by king and lords and great men' should be destroyed. Parliament was the Beast with ten horns, as cruel as the King, and would be overthrown 666 days after the execution of Charles I—i.e. at the end of November 1650. Thereby the Leveller martyrs Robert Lockyer and William Thompson would be avenged. Thereafter there would be no power and no law besides God, who would make those that have riches give them to those that have none.[4] The Papacy, Foster added in another pamphlet, would be destroyed in 1654, the Turk two years later.[5] Arise Evans thought the Rump of the Long Parliament had been 'the Beast mentioned in Revelation 13'; its successor, the Barebones Parliament, was the image of the Beast.[6]

[1] See pp. 104–5 above and pp. 146–52 below.

[2] Edwards, *Gangraena*, Part I, p. 39.

[3] Ibid., Part II, pp. 17–18.

[4] George Foster, *The Sounding of the Last Trumpet* (1650), pp. 30–1, 37–9, 46, 50–2.

[5] Foster, *The Pouring Forth of the Seventh and Last Viall Upon All Flesh* (1650), pp. 64–5.

[6] Arise Evans, *A Voice From Heaven to the Common-Wealth of England* (1652), pp. 63, 66–70; *The Bloudy Vision of John Farly* (1653), title-page; cf. pp. 20–1, 51–9.

Johann Hilten, a fifteenth-century prophet popular among protestants, had predicted the end of the world for 1651.[1] John Swan in 1635 noted that some gave 1657 for the date, though he was not himself convinced. Lady Eleanor Davies predicted a repetition of Noah's flood for 1656, since she believed the original deluge was in 1656 B.C.[2] Thomas Goodwin in 1639 thought he was living in the last days. He expected the final climax of Antichrist's power between 1650 and 1656, the millennium in 1700. He was sure that England had a crucial role to play in this great drama. Saints, he thought, 'do now govern the world invisibly'; soon they would 'do it visibly'.[3] William Lilly expected 'the fulness of time' 'near 1700'.[4] William Dell spoke of 'these last of the last times'.[5] Prophecies attributed to Paul Grebner foretold the fall of the Roman Beast in 1666, 'though the carcase of it may lie unburied for thirty years after'. Indeed, 'all Christendom from this year 1650 must expect very sad and woeful days . . . until An. 1698'.[6] 'Before 1650' the Baptist Henry Jessey had made a collection from Revelation, Daniel, and other books of the Bible concerning 'these great changes in the world now at hand'.[7]

[1] M. Reeves, op. cit., p. 234.

[2] J. Swan, *Speculum Mundi* (Cambridge, 1635), p. 19; Spencer, 'The History of an Unfortunate Lady', p. 58.

[3] T. Goodwin, *Works*, iii, pp. 35, 72–5, 120, 157–8, 195–205; cf. *A Sermon of the Fifth Monarchy*, p. 29. Cf. also J. Archer, op. cit., pp. 46–52.

[4] Lilly, *A Prophecy of the White King* (1644), p. 5.

[5] Dell, *Sermons*, p. 471. Antichrist 'is drawing his last breath', Dell still thought in 1667 (Walker, *William Dell*, p. 192).

[6] *A brief Description Of the future History of Europe from Anno 1656 to An. 1710 . . . out of the famous Manuscript of Paul Grebner* (1650), *passim*.

[7] Prefatory note to Mary Cary's *The Little Horns Doom and Downfall* (1651). Jessey placed the slaying of the witnesses before 1654, the conversion of the Jews before 1658 (sig. a4ᵛ–5).

In New England in the 1650s Edward Johnson thought the time of Antichrist's fall had come.[1] Even an old reprobate like Robert Keayne began a fourth great writing-book in which he analysed the prophecies of Daniel, Revelation, and Hosea.[2] In old England in 1651 an acquaintance of Bishop Duppa, who had written a treatise identifying Antichrist, rejected the Bishop's advice to delay publication for a year or two because he was confident the world would not last so long.[3] John Dury observed in 1651 that 'the Beast's rage' was 'greater than ever for the interest of a tyrannical power'. Hartlib thought the prophetical numbers came to an end in 1655.[4] In Sweden and Germany the downfall of the Beast was looked for in 1654 or 1655.[5] Sir Robert Harley on his death-bed in 1656 prayed for 'the ruin of Antichrist, for the churches of God beyond sea, meaning Savoy, Switzerland, Germany'.[6] In his introduction to a sermon which he had preached before the Lord Mayor and the Drapers' Company in 1655, Dr. Robert Gell said in all seriousness 'many place the end of the world' in 1656.[7]

John Rogers too announced in 1653 that doomsday

[1] E. Johnson, *Wonder-Working Providence* (1654), in P. Miller and T. H. Johnson, *The Puritans* (New York, 1938), p. 160.

[2] Ed. B. Bailyn, *The Apologia of Robert Keayne* (New York, 1964), p. 9.

[3] Ed. Sir Gyles Isham, *The Correspondence of Bishop Brian Duppa and Sir Justinian Isham* (Northants. Record Soc., 1955), p. 37.

[4] Ed. Hartlib, *Clavis Apocalyptica* (1651), title-page and Epistolical Discourse by John Dury; cf. Hartlib, *Mysteries made manifest* (1653), title-page, and [Anon.], *The Year of Wonders* (1652), p. 13: 'in August 1655 Rome falleth, and Jesus Christ . . . may reign amongst us.'

[5] Review by Michael Roberts in *Journal of Ecclesiastical History*, vi, pp. 112–15.

[6] Lewis, *Letters of the Lady Brilliana Harley*, pp. xxviii.

[7] R. Gell, *Noahs Flood Returning* (1655), sig. D–D^v. For Gell see also Appendix IV.

was 'drawing nigh'; 'by anno 1656 the flood begins'.
Rome will fall before 1660, and the fifth monarchy will
be visible in all the earth by 1666.[1] 'I doubt not but
there are divers of you who hear me this day', Edward
Haughton told his Sussex congregation in 1652, 'that
shall outlive Rome's ruin.'[2] John Tillinghast in 1654
thought the English Civil War had realized the prophecy
in Revelation 17: 14 of a war 'betwixt the Lamb and
the kings of the earth'. 'This chapter brings us to the
end of the Beast's kingdom.' The second vial began to
be poured out in 1641, when Parliament voted down
bishops as antichristian. But then the kingly office of
Christ was invaded by the 'antichristian lording
discipline' of the Presbyterians. Quoting Napier,
Brightman, and Mede, Tillinghast produced a new
chronological scheme of his own in which 1656 was to
be the decisive year. The millennium would follow in
1701. 'This kingdom of Christ', he was convinced,
'succeeding the kingdom of Antichrist, . . . cannot be a
mere spiritual kingdom.' When Christ said his kingdom
was not of this world, he was speaking (to Pontius
Pilate) of the Roman Empire only. 'This generation
shall not pass', said Tillinghast, 'till all these things be
fulfilled.'[3] Alas, he died himself in 1655, a year too
soon. A bishop like Joseph Hall in 1650,[4] a Presbyterian
divine like Ralph Josselin, an academic philosopher

[1] E. Rogers, *Life and Opinions of a Fifth Monarchy Man*, pp. 76, 83, 95;
cf. p. 163. *The Mourners Song* (1651) taught that Rome would be destroyed in 1666 (Part II).

[2] Haughton, *The Rise, Growth and Fall of Antichrist*, p. 128.

[3] J. Tillinghast, *Generation-work* (1654), Part I, pp. 44–67; Part II,
pp. 18, 50–3, 62–6, 144–60, 263; Part III, pp. 71, 73, 156, 209, 226–49;
Knowledge of the Times (1655), esp. sig. A5ᵛ, pp. 307–9. Cf. *Mr. Tilling-
hasts Eight Last Sermons* (1655), esp. pp. 81, 219, 225.

[4] J. Hall, *Revelation Unrevealed* (1650), in *Works* (1837–9), viii, p. 511.

like Henry More, all thought that 'the ruin of Antichrist is near'.[1] So did the Savoy Declaration of the Independent churches. We cannot over-estimate the effect on public opinion of such widely-held expectations.

The conversion of the Jews was closely connected with Antichrist's fall in the Geneva Bible, in the Presbyterian Larger Catechism, and in the Independents' Savoy Confession—not to mention the prophecies attributed to Paul Grebner.[2] In a sermon of July 1644 Stanley Gower—relying on the calculations of Broughton, Brightman, and Mede—assured the House of Commons that the Jews would be converted in 1650.[3] In 1652 Arise Evans made the strikingly original assertion that Prince Charles was 'the means appointed by God . . . for the conversion of the Jews'.[4] 'Charles Steward', he told the Jewish people four years later, 'is he whom you call your Messiah', under whose banner they would return to Jerusalem. 'All these late transactions in England', he added, 'came to pass only for your sake'[5]—one of the few contemporary interpreta-

[1] A. Macfarlane, *The Family Life of Ralph Josselin* (Cambridge, 1970), pp. 185-9; H. More, *Theological Works* (1708), p. 633.

[2] Toon, *Puritans, the Millennium and the Future of Israel*, pp. 6, 24, 37, 107, 113-25, 137-53; *A brief Description of the future History of Europe . . . out of the famous Manuscript of Paul Grebner, passim*. Cf. *The London Post*, 1 Apr. 1645, quoted in J. Frank, *The Beginnings of the English Newspaper* (Harvard University Press, 1961), p. 93; R. Parker, *The Mystery of the Vialls opened* (1651), p. 14.

[3] S. Gower, *Things Now a-doing* (1644), sig. A3, p. 25, quoted by J. F. Wilson, *Pulpit in Parliament* (Princeton University Press, 1969), p. 211; cf. Trapp, *Commentary*, p. 380.

[4] A. Evans, *A Voice From Heaven*, pp. 11, 70.

[5] Evans, *Light for the Jews* (1656), pp. 11, 20, 39. This was a reply to Menasseh ben Israel's *The Hope of Israel*. There were, of course, many who hoped for the conversion of the Jews without sharing these millenary expectations—e.g. Samuel Hartlib (see *Samuel Hartlib and the Advance-*

tions of the English Revolution which has not yet been taken up by a twentieth-century historian.

In the early fifties John Robins the Ranter had begun to collect an army of 144,000 men to liberate the Holy Land. They trained on bread and water: Robins held ale to be 'the drink of the Beast'. Thomas Tany ('Theaureaujohn') learnt Hebrew preparatory to setting out for Jerusalem 'to call the Jews' in a small boat which he had built for himself. He cried 'Ho for the holy wars in these nations, beginning at France!'—rather a curious sentiment for one who thought 'there is but one truth and that is love'. He also believed that 'all religion is a lie and a cheat, a deceit'. He was drowned on his way to Palestine via Holland.[1] Samuel Hering told the Barebones Parliament to call the Jews to England, 'for their time is near at hand'.[2] The great (and royalist) mathematician, William Oughtred, thought Jesus Christ might appear in person in 1656 to convert the Jews.[3] Mary Cary favoured the same date, though she believed Rome must be destroyed first. John Canne put it back to 1700.[4] These expectations played their part in Cromwell's decision to readmit the Jews to England in 1656.[5]

ment of Learning, ed. C. Webster (Cambridge University Press, 1970), pp. 39, 95, 126, 201).

[1] G. H., *The Declaration of John Robins the false Prophet* (1651), p. 5; [T. Tany], *Hear, O Earth* (1654), single sheet; *Theaureaujohn High Priest to the Jewes His Disputive Challenge to the Universities of Oxford and Cambridge* (1651), p. 3. Cf. my *Puritanism and Revolution*, pp. 141, 316, and references there cited; also Appendix I (ii) below.

[2] J. Nickolls, *Original Letters and Papers of State Addressed to Oliver Cromwell* (1743), p. 100.

[3] Ed. E. S. de Beer, *The Diary of John Evelyn* (Oxford University Press, 1955), iii, p. 158.

[4] Toon, *Puritans, the Millennium and the Future of Israel*, p. 72.

[5] Cf. also Archer, op. cit., p. 72; Hartlib, *Revelation Revealed* (1649);

IV

The most consistent and rational version of the radical and internationalist Antichrist myth is that of Gerrard Winstanley the Digger. He developed the by now familiar argument that anyone attempting to set up the worship of God by human law speaks like the Beast.[1] 'Covetousness or self-love is the Man of Sin.' (Compare Boehme's words, published in English translation in 1649: 'They desire fully to purse up all in covetousness into self, viz. into the antichristian bag.'[2]) Those that do not bear the mark of the Beast, Winstanley declared, neither buy nor sell—for the original reason that the lettering round English coins adds up to 666.[3] The Civil War had not—as hoped—led to Antichrist's overthrow. It was still 'Beast against Beast, covetousness and pride against covetousness and pride'. Antichrist sits 'in the hearts of . . . the powers of the earth'. Kingly government was 'the great Man of Sin' who sanctioned the rule of property; his power 'sets one against another, and so causeth some part of mankind to tread others underfoot and puts them into bondage'. The 'power and government of the Beast' was 'this spirit of monarchy', 'the spirit of subtlety and covetousness, filling the heart of mankind with enmity and ignorance, pride and vainglory, because the strong

Moses Wall, postscript to Manasseh ben Israel's *The Hope of Israel* (1651); P. Toon, 'Puritans and Jews', *The Gospel Magazine* (May 1969), p. 4; G. H. Turnbull, *Hartlib, Dury and Comenius* (Liverpool University Press, 1947), pp. 26, 257, 261–2, 282.

[1] Ed. G. H. Sabine, *The Works of Gerrard Winstanley* (Cornell University Press, 1941), p. 89; cf. pp. 178, 230, and Winstanley, *The Saints Paradice* (n.d., ?1648), sig. C3, C6.

[2] *Mercurius Teutonicus*, p. 45.

[3] Sabine, op. cit., pp. 203, 270.

destroys the weak'. It draws 'the people into the way of buying and selling'. 'That government that gives liberty to the gentry to have all the earth, and shuts out the poor commons, . . . is the government of imaginary, self-seeking Antichrist', and must be rooted out. By the beginning of 1649 Winstanley thought 'the antichristian captivity' was expiring. In a startling development of Foxe's patriotic use of the myth, Winstanley argued that England must be the first to fall off from 'that Beast, kingly property'. 'The age of the Creation is now come to the image of the Beast. . . . We expect this to be the last tyrannical power that shall reign.'[1]

Winstanley also carried the democratic interpretation of the Antichrist myth further than anyone we have yet considered. 'If you would find true majesty indeed, go among the poor and despised ones of the earth,' he wrote; 'for there Christ dwells.' 'Jesus Christ . . . is the head Leveller.' 'The poorest man hath as true a title and just right to the land as the richest man.' Winstanley demonstrated his internationalist sympathies by claiming to write 'for and in behalf of all the poor oppressed people of England and the whole world', and by predicting a communist future when 'this enmity of all lands will cease, and none shall dare to seek dominion over others'.[2]

In their task of repressing the common people, Winstanley thought, government and gentry were aided by the clergy, 'antichristian taskmasters over the common people'. 'The divining doctrine of heaven after death' is 'the language of Antichrist.' But now 'surely light is so broke out that . . . the divinity charmers shall

---

[1] Ibid., pp. 230, 248, 270, 297, 383, 385, 395, 472, 530–2; cf. p. 485.
[2] Ibid., pp. 254, 277, 390, 473.

say, "The people will not hear the voice of our charm-
ing, charm we never so wisely" ', and shall lament the
fall of 'that great city Babylon, that mighty city divinity,
which hath filled the whole earth with her sorcery and
deceived all people, so that the whole world wondered
after this Beast . . . and further as you may read,
Revelation xviii. 10'. Winstanley called on the out-
casts of society to occupy the common lands and form
collective farms. But by 1650 Antichrist was also in the
Army, and the Digger colony was dispersed.[1]

Such views were not peculiar to Winstanley. They
were shared by the anonymous author or authors of
Light Shining in Buckinghamshire and *More Light Shining
in Buckinghamshire*, who thought that 'all our enclosures
and tradings', and landed property, came from taking
the Beast's mark, from royal licences and privileges.
Charles I was 'Antichrist's hackney, and hath his power
from the Beast'—a remark which Dr. Denton reported
to Sir Ralph Verney with some disapprobation.[2]
Kingly power originated both from the Beast and from
the Norman Conquest. The law-courts, lawyers, and
their wicked laws all derived from and continued to
uphold 'the Norman and Beastly power'. Priests who
took tithes were also antichristian.[3] The interesting
fusion of the myth of the Norman Yoke with the myth
of Antichrist was repeated by John Rogers and others.[4]

John Bunyan's description of Antichrist as a gentleman is perhaps a reminiscence of this sort of class idea

[1] Sabine, op. cit., pp. 291, 334, 436, 471, 530, 569–70.

[2] In Sabine, op. cit., pp. 613, 631; F. P. and M. M. Verney, *Memoirs
of the Verney Family* (1892–9), iii, p. 7.

[3] Sabine, op. cit., pp. 636–7.

[4] E. Rogers, op. cit., pp. 82, 95; cf. William Pryor, *The Out-Cries of the
Poor* (1651), pp. 5–14: The Beast protects the rich.

prevalent at the height of the revolution.[1] (We recall too that for Milton Antichrist was 'Mammon's son';[2] for the Ranter Richard Coppin Antichrist's kingdom was 'a kingdom of gain, hire and self-interest',[3] but both he and Milton seem to refer especially to the hireling clergy who buy and sell the word of God.) An anonymous alchemist, Eugenius Eirenaeus Philalethes, was thinking along similar lines when in 1645 he called money 'that prop of the antichristian Beast', and prophesied that 'within a few years' it would be 'dashed in pieces':[4] though in his view this was to be thanks to alchemy, not to the political action on which Winstanley relied.[5] This pamphlet was read with great interest by Isaac Newton, who scribbled marginalia on almost every page of his copy.[6] There is no evidence, however, that the later Master of the Mint ever thought

[1] Bunyan, *Works*, ii, p. 54.   [2] *Works* (Columbia ed.), iii, p. 54.

[3] R. Coppin, *Truths Testimony* (1655), p. 15.

[4] Pierre Borel, in his *Biblioteca Chimica* (Paris, 1654), mentions a prediction by the Englishwoman Maria Rante that 'gold would shortly be commonly made, perhaps by the year 1661' (quoted by A. R. and M. B. Hall, *The Correspondence of Henry Oldenburg*, i, pp. 178–9). This may have been Mary Cary, quoted on p. 107 above, whose married name was Rande. I have not found anything so accurately dated in her writings, but see her account of the millennium in *The Little Horns Doom and Downfall*, pp. 301–2. She expected it in the near future.

[5] *Secrets Reveal'd* (1669), sig. a5, p. 48. There is fortunately no need to go into the vexed question of the authorship of this pamphlet. See G. L. Kittredge, 'Dr. Robert Child, the Remonstrant', *Publications of the Colonial Soc. of Massachusetts*, xxi (1919), pp. 132–3, who asserts that George Stirk was the author; G. H. Turnbull, 'Robert Child' and 'George Stirk, Philosopher by Fire' (ibid., xxxviii); R. S. Wilkinson, 'The Problem of the Identity of Eirenaeus Philalethes', *Ambix*, xii (1964), who suggests John Winthrop, jun. The fact that Stirk was several times imprisoned for debt would suggest that he had not in fact discovered the philosopher's stone.

[6] F. E. Manuel, *A Portrait of Isaac Newton* (Harvard University Press, 1968), pp. 164–5.

money antichristian. The alchemists' hope of creating limitless money was achieved, ironically, by the Bank of England issuing paper money and by other developments of credit in the later seventeenth century.[1]

The hopes of the millenarians were raised again with the meeting of the Barebones assembly in July 1653: they were finally dashed by its dissolution. During its sitting the Baptist John Canne observed that the throne of God had been set up in England when Charles I was condemned: soon it would be 'set up in other kingdoms, as France, Spain, Denmark. . . . As monarchy falls, so falls antichristianism'. Great revolutions, including the sack of Rome, were looked for in 1655, and the antichristian state 'shall be found no more after the year 1660'.[2] John Spittlehouse argued that Charles I had been part of Antichrist.[3] English Antichristians, Canne noted, had disapproved of the dissolution of the Rump of the Long Parliament in April 1653: the job of the Barebones Parliament was to destroy the antichristian kingdom in England—i.e. tithes and a state church whose ministers were not elected by their congregations. The antichristian ministry in Spain, France, England, etc., was all one.[4] Cromwell himself told the Barebones Parliament that its advent manifested this 'to be the day of the power of Christ'.[5]

Four years later Canne was less certain of the future. The rulers of England had proclaimed the destruction

---

[1] Cf. F. Braudel, *Civilisation matérielle et capitalisme* (Paris, 1967), p. 361.

[2] J. Canne, *A Voice From the Temple to the Higher Powers* (1653), pp. 13–14, 16, 19–20, 24–5, 29–31, 36.

[3] J. Spittlehouse, *The First Addresses* (1653), p. 23.

[4] Canne, op. cit., pp. 16–17; *A Second Voyce from the Temple to the Higher Powers* (1653), sig. A2ᵛ, pp. 2, 7, 13.

[5] Abbott, *Writings and Speeches of Oliver Cromwell*, iii, p. 63.

of Antichrist, the approach of Christ's kingdom and the just civil liberties of Englishmen, abolition of antichristian tithes and impropriations. But their actions were the opposite of their words. The enormities of the clergy were even less reformed than in the prelates' times. Foreign policy was aimed at commercial profit, not at the destruction of Babylon. Oliver Cromwell had turned out to be the Little Horn of the Beast: his tyranny would last for three and a half years. Cities and corporations 'do yet stand by the Beast's charters'; London was 'the seat of the second Beast'. Canne denounced woe to lawyers, soldiers, citizens, merchants, gaolers, the rich, and all involved with the Beast.[1]

John Rogers in 1653 had offered to engage with Oliver Cromwell in the quarrel against Antichrist— notably against 'that Babylonian, brazen yoke of tithes'. He soon extended his attack to 'the lawyers, Antichrist's state army', who (like the antichristian clergy) 'have their long tails too, with terrible stings'. But 'the hour of their torment makes haste', and will be here 'by fifty-five next'. After Cromwell had become Lord Protector, Rogers warned him to 'consider how near it is to the end of the Beast's dominion'. Oliver should 'take heed of protecting the carnal, national, antichristian clergy', adjectives which Rogers seems to have regarded as interchangeable. They would seduce Cromwell into Antichrist's cause.[2] 'The great ones', John Tillinghast observed, are 'drawing off from the work'. 'The present work of God is to bring down lofty men.'[3] Rogers soon

---

[1] Canne, *The Time of the End* (1657), sig. A6ᵛ, A8, pp. 58, 84–5, 99–103, 121–2, 130–1; *A Voice from the Temple*, pp. 13, 39.

[2] E. Rogers, op. cit., pp. 53–4, 87–93, 98, 109–10; Toon, *Puritans, the Millennium and the Future of Israel*, p. 71.

[3] J. Tillinghast, *Generation-work* (1654), Part I, sig. A6ᵛ, pp. 103–5,

came to look upon Oliver himself as Antichrist.[1] He
spoke of 'the Beast and his government', and told the
Protector to his face that his Commissioners for Appro-
bation and his national church were antichristian.
Oliver seems to have accepted the unspoken premise
but denied Rogers' conclusion. 'It is not a national
ministry that is now established, nor can you make it
appear they are antichristian. . . . They ordain none.'[2]
Rogers' congregation sang a hymn which declared:

> The saints are marching on;
> The sword is sharp, the arrows swift
> To destroy Babylon;
> Against the kingdom of the Beast
> We witnesses do rise.[3]

John More, a London apprentice or journeyman,
added Cromwell's name and titles up to make 666.[4]

With Thurloe's spies about, prudent men used the
symbolism of Antichrist to avoid being too specific. In
December 1653 Marchamont Nedham reported to the
government on a sermon which Christopher Feake had
preached on Daniel 7. The Little Horn in his account
had the clearly identifiable characteristics of Oliver
Cromwell. ' "I will name nobody", said he, "but he
gave many desperate hints." ' Vavasor Powell followed
and made an even more direct application of the texts.[5]

and *passim.* Cf. [Anon.], *A Declaration of Several of the Churches of Christ*
(1654), in *Trans. Baptist Histor. Soc.,* iii, pp. 129–53.

[1] E. Rogers, op. cit., p. 169; *Thurloe State Papers,* iii, pp. 136, 483–5.
The Fifth-Monarchist poetess Anna Trapnel thought Cromwell was the
Little Horn (L. F. Brown, *Baptists and Fifth-Monarchy Men* (New York,
1911), p. 49). Cf. [Anon.], *A Ground Voice* (1655), pp. 3–6.

[2] E. Rogers, op. cit., pp. 175–6, 213–14; cf. pp. 206, 226, 299–302.

[3] *Thurloe State Papers,* iii, p. 137.

[4] J. More, *A Trumpet Sounded* (1654), *passim.* Cf. p. 68 above.

[5] C. H. Simpkinson, *Thomas Harrison* (1905), pp. 200–3.

Feake had already called Cromwell 'the Man of Sin, the Old Dragon'. In 1657 he described Oliver's state church as 'Antichrist's army'; the Protector's régime was as antichristian as that of Charles I had been.[1] In May 1659 he was still calling on 'the faithful remnant' to unite against the kingdom of the Beast.[2]

The 42 months of the Beast's (i.e. the Protector's) dominion having expired in June 1657, Venner's Fifth Monarchists took up arms to free men 'from violence and oppression and all tyrannical antichristian yokes upon the outward man'. Antichristian tithes would be abolished. Henceforth there should be no tax assessments in time of peace. If war broke out, it should be paid for principally by 'those that are the occasioners thereof, the Beast and false prophet, the wicked, bloody, antichristian magistracy, ministry, lawyers, etc.'[3] This rising and its defeat did much to discredit Fifth-Monarchist versions of the Antichrist myth. The strength of millenarianism lay in the expectation that divine intervention would achieve changes which had proved impossible of attainment by ordinary political means. But hope repeatedly deferred ultimately made the heart sick.

V

As the apocalyptic dreams of the radicals faded in the fifties, controversies revived over the Church of England and its ministers. They were fiercely discussed

[1] *Thurloe State Papers*, i, p. 621, v, pp. 756–9.

[2] Feake, *A Beam of Light* (1659), preface and pp. 58–9, quoted by A. Woolrych in his introduction to vol. vi of Milton's *Complete Prose* (Yale ed.).

[3] W. Medley, *A Standard Set Up* (1657), pp. 19–20, 67. The 'etc.' is ominous.

in 1651 between Thomas Hall, minister of King's Norton, and John Ferriby, minister of Theydon Garnon, Essex, on the one hand, and William Hartley and Thomas Collier on the other. Collier attacked the 'antichristian constituted churches', the 'antichristian anointed forms' of the state church, 'Antichrist's ordination' of its ministers: the dependence of the latter on 'earthly augmentations' was also antichristian. To Hall's argument that the calling of ministers in the English church could not be antichristian because the papists disclaimed them, Collier retorted: 'Your jangling and differing each with other, and reproaching one another, argues not the truth of what you say. . . . Is there but one Antichrist in the world?'[1] 'An antichristian church brings not forth a Christian brood', was the effective retort of a gentleman to this sort of argument, though he too referred firmly to the 'antichristian and prelatical parties'.[2] (Hartley complained that his side 'are branded as Thompson's party, Levellers'. 'The word Leveller is a term of odium cast upon many a person for holding forth of righteous principles.'[3])

Thomas Goodwin declared that the job of the state church in the 1650s was 'the throwing out of every rag, the least dross and defilement that Antichrist or popery

[1] [T. Hall], *The Pulpit Guarded with XX Arguments* (1651), esp. pp. 81–6; W. Hartley, *The Prerogative Passing-Bell* (1651), Preface to the Reader; T. Collier, *The Pulpit-Guard Routed* (1652), esp. pp. 25, 40, 73, 77, 84, 98–104; J. Ferriby, *The Lawfull Preacher* (2nd ed., 1655), p. 41. Cf. John Pendarves, *Arrowes against Babylon* (1656), pp. 4, 10, and *passim*; John Tickell, *Church-Rules Proposed to the Church in Abingdon* (1656), p. 18—a reply to Pendarves.

[2] G. Smith, *Gods Unchangeableness* (1654), sig. A2, p. 41.

[3] Hartley, op. cit., pp. 9–10. Cf. p. 131 below.

brought in or continued in the world'.[1] But it was not easy to agree. William Erbery thought 'the Man of Sin is not manifest in anything more' than in set forms of prayer and long prayers.[2] Samuel Hering wanted the clergy to lay aside writing books against each other, 'for therein sticketh the Antichrist'.[3] John Tickell in 1652, Edward Waterhouse in 1653, and George Hall in 1655 complained of the separatists 'calling us antichristian'.[4] They did indeed. 'The office is antichristian', said Erbery.[5] William Dell spoke of 'the carnal and anti-christian clergy of these nations'.[6] 'Oh poor clergy!' cried the prophetess Anna Trapnel in 1654. 'You have put off the outward badge of Antichrist, and you have retained the inward.'[7] The great Antichrist (bishop and King) has been succeeded by little Antichrists (tithe-priests), said Peter Cornelius [Plockhoy] in 1659.[8]

This line of attack became a Quaker speciality. The Beast is worshipped in the national churches, said one of their pamphlets in 1653.[9] 'The Beast is risen in defence of you,' the Quaker Edward Burrough told

---

[1] Quoted by Peter Toon, 'The Latter-day Glory in English Puritan Thought', *The Gospel Magazine*, July 1969, p. 321.

[2] *The Testimony of William Erbery* (1658), pp. 276–7.

[3] J. Nickolls, *Original Letters*, p. 100.

[4] J. Tickell, *The Bottomless Pit Smoaking in Familisme* (1652), p. 41 (against Abiezer Coppe and the Ranters); Waterhouse, op. cit., p. 85; G. Hall, *Gods Appearing for the Tribe of Levi* (n.d. ?1655), p. 18.

[5] *Minister for Tythes*, in *The Testimony of William Erbery*, p. 200.

[6] Dell, *The Tryal of Spirits . . . The clear Discovery and certain Downfal of the Carnal and Antichristian Clergie of these Nations* (1653).

[7] *The Cry of a Stone, Or a Relation of Something spoke in Whitehall by Anna Trapnel* (1654), p. 69; cf. p. 19. She also told soldiers of the Army that they were 'the Army of the Beast'. Cf. p. 122 above.

[8] Peter Cornelius, *The Way to the Peace and Settlement . . . wherein The liberty of speaking . . . is opposed against Antichrist* (1659), p. 21.

[9] [Samuel Buttivant], *A Brief Discovery Of a threefold estate of Antichrist* (1653), esp. p. 5; R. F[arnsworth], *Light Risen out of Darknes* (1653).

'priests, prophets and teachers of the people' in 1655; priests 'have turned every way according to the changing power of the Beast'.[1] Ministers 'do the work of Antichrist as an hireling', taking Antichrist's wages, said Richard Coppin; though he rejoiced that 'the antichristian law of compelling men to church' was no longer in force.[2] 'Many things are called antichristian which are not so, but are falsely so termed by the separation', complained Nathaniel Stephens in 1656; he instanced the power of magistrates (except where 'it hath no bounds or limits, but he doth all by his will and prerogative in the church of God'), and ordination of ministers. Bishops were antichristian only in so far as they lorded and tyrannized over the church against the people of God. Not all coercion in matters of religion is antichristian: it would not be antichristian to suppress the present sects.[3] Stephens knew what he was talking about. He had been George Fox's parish minister, and had engaged in controversy with Gerrard Winstanley.

William Hickman told Cromwell in November 1650 that 'Antichrist is putting himself into another form, which goes by the name of congregational government by saints. . . . Antichrist begins first to work in the congregational ministry'. Men are using 'the form or shadow of religion for worldly ends'. But 'God hath designed your Excellency to drive Antichrist out of all his forms'.[4] Hickman's point had been made earlier. Roger Williams spoke of 'God's own people, fast asleep

[1] *The Memorable Works of a Son of Thunder*, p. 101.

[2] Coppin, *Truths Testimony* (1655), pp. 15–16, 20, 81.

[3] N. Stephens, *A Plain and Easie Calculation of the Name, Mark and Number of the Name of the Beast* (1656), esp. pp. 247–94.

[4] Nickolls, *Original Letters*, p. 30. Cf. H. Denne quoted on p. 96 above.

in antichristian Delilah's lap'.[1] Joseph Salmon, 'member
of the Army', thought that Antichrist appeared 'in
prayer, in humiliation, in fasting, nay in all outward
ordinances'. 'Thou needest not go far to discover' what
Antichrist is. 'Thou needest not go to Rome, Canterbury or Westminster, but thou mayest find that Antichrist in thee.' 'The spirit of Antichrist . . . is in all of us.'
'Thy heart is that temple of God where this great Whore
sitteth.' The day of judgement will occur, is occurring,
in the heart of each individual: it is the cause 'of all
these commotions that are amongst us'.[2] William Dell
believed that carnal Christians were the true body of
Antichrist. All national churches are more or less the
habitations of Antichrist.[3] 'They who bring in human
power, or the secular arm, into the church of Christ . . .
are true Antichrists.' So also are 'they that bring in
human wisdom, or the learning and philosophy of men
into the church of Christ'.[4] 'The mystery of iniquity is
now become more mysterious and deceiving', because
it prevails under the name of orthodox doctrine, just as
it used to do in the days of Wyclif, Hus, and Luther.
'Christ's church and Antichrist's do often differ very
little or nothing in word or letter.' 'The chief design
of Antichrist is to seduce the elect.' He is indeed chiefly
found 'among those that profess the Christian religion'.[5]

[1] Williams, *The Bloudy Tenent*, p. 83.

[2] Joseph Salmon, *Anti-Christ in Man* (n.d. ? 1647), sig. A2ᵛ, pp. 2, 10,
14 (should be 12), 34, 47–58, 72; cf. p. 16. Mr. J. F. McGregor attributes this pamphlet to Jacob Bauthumley ('The Ranters: 1643–1660',
unpublished, Oxford B.Litt. Thesis, 1969).

[3] Dell, *Sermons*, pp. 184, 186, 535–40.

[4] Id., *A Plain and Necessary Confutation of divers gross and Antichristian
Errors . . . by Mr. Sydrach Simpson* (1654), in *Sermons*, p. 551.

[5] Id., *Sermons*, pp. 466–7, 473–4, 482–3, 492.

'This word godliness', another pamphleteer declared, 'will shortly become the mark of the Beast.'[1]

The most interesting exponent of this approach was William Erbery, a radical who in 1652 had called on Oliver Cromwell to relieve the poor from tithes and lawyers' fees.[2] For him popery was the first Beast, prelacy the second, presbytery the third. The Commonwealth state church was the last Beast or last church-state. He fitted this into the chronology of the prophecies. Prelacy reigned some seventy years, presbytery but three and a half years ('the time of the Beast') by Parliamentary authority; 'Independency is down in a month', 'baptized pastors in one day fly away'.[3] 'When kingdoms came to be Christian, then kingdoms began to be churches; yea, churches came to be kingdoms, and national churches began. Then also Antichrist came to be great.' 'The Beast is the church in her ministers.' 'Antichrist's nest ever was, and is set up to this day, though in a more glorious form, . . . in the Christian church.' Pride, conformity, and cruelty are the characteristics of Antichrist. In 'our own land in these last days', Erbery thought, 'the mystery of iniquity hath been most manifest'. 'Babylon is divided into three parts—prelatical, presbyterian and independent churches.'[4] The faith of all churches was in consequence 'much confused and fleshly, by the spirit of Antichrist ['the traditions and teachings of men'] long prevailing'. It is indeed 'in

[1] Arise Evans, *The Bloudy Vision of John Farly*, p. 60. Evans attributed the remark to the author of *The Grand Politick Informer*.

[2] J. Nickolls, op. cit., pp. 88–9.

[3] *The Testimony of William Erbery*, pp. 336, 80, 136, 148.

[4] Ibid., pp. 268, 198, 78; cf. pp. 88–9, 167, 270–1; Erbery, *Nor Truth nor Error* (1646), sig. A3ᵛ; [Francis Cheynell], *An Account Given to the Parliament by the Ministers sent by them to Oxford* (1647), pp. 35–6.

saints by calling' that 'the apostacy or spirit of Antichrist in the churches' shall be first revealed to the full. 'There shall Antichrist be found at last, as in the disciples of Christ [Judas] appeared first. . . . Our spiritual gifts and graces looked upon and lived in (not looking for our life in God alone) is the Man of Sin.'[1] 'The mystery of Antichrist, the mystery of man, is manifested in every saint, . . . in every particular church.' 'That man is the Beast that counts himself wise, or to have the knowledge of a man.' 'The Beast is the number of a man': but 'God can appear in a Beast'. It is Antichrist who 'denies Christ to be come in our flesh'. But 'the embondaged saints in spiritual Babylon shall attain to the first resurrection and redemption from Antichrist's captivity'.[2]

'Our author was of this mind', his friend the army chaplain and educational reformer John Webster tells us: 'better no ministry than a pretended one. . . . In this darkness he had rather sit down and wait in silence than be beholding to the pretended light and direction of deceivable guides.' (One suspects that John Milton arrived at a similar conclusion towards the end of his life.) 'In my own sense', Erbery himself wrote, 'I did not preach at all. Preaching is for edification, mine was for destruction.' [I poured] 'out a vial full of the wrath of God, even a plague upon all the churches, who say they are in Gospel order, and are not, but do live in Babylon. And there not they only, but all the scattered saints, this day do dwell, and I also with them, waiting

[1] *The Testimony of William Erbery*, pp. 65, 117, 141, 178–9; cf. p. 176; *Nor Truth nor Error*, p. 5, and John Canne, *The Time of the End*, p. 275. On apostacy, see p. 95 above.
[2] *The Testimony of William Erbery*, pp. 13, 16, 33, 269; *Nor Truth nor Error*, pp. 8, 13–15, 18; *Apocrypha* (1652), pp. 6–8.

for deliverance.'[1] There in Babylon we must leave this strange, moving Welshman, who carried one version of the Antichrist myth as far as it could go, and found himself at last with no other message than that. (Erbery was in this typical of many other lost 'Seekers' who might perhaps end as Quakers: his widow was one of James Nayler's admirers.)

In one of his earlier works Erbery announced that 'God appearing in the saints shall punish kings of the earth'. Did he still believe it later, when he asked: 'Is not the state of Holland and Commonwealth of Venice as much for Antichrist as the King of France or Spain?' —with obvious implications for the Commonwealth of England? Nevertheless, he had not lost all his faith in the republic. For in the passage I have just quoted, after placing himself in Babylon, he added: 'I have been ever entire to the interest of this commonwealth.'[2]

So we have moved from Antichrist in Rome, through Antichrist in the bishops or the whole state church, to Antichrist in every man. Against the Antichrist in Rome and his Spanish protagonists the navy was the best defence; Antichrist in the state church could be combated by institutional reform. But if Antichrist was in every man, even in God's saints whom Foxe had seen battling against an external Antichrist through so many centuries, what could be done against him?

VI

Antichrist thus ceased to be exclusively ecclesiastical

---

[1] *Testimony*, pp. 263-5, 337-8; *Nor Truth nor Error*, pp. 1-2, 22. Cf. John Webster, *The Saints Guide* (1654), sig. B[5]: 'The Lord therefore in the tenderness of his mercy give you to see that you are in Babylon.'

[2] *The Testimony of William Erbery*, pp. 40, 186, 338. I have benefited from reading an unpublished article on Erbery by the Revd. B. R. White.

power and could be a symbol for any kind of political power—monarchy, the Lord Mayor of London, Parliament, the rule of the gentry, the protectorate of Oliver Cromwell. In 1659 a pamphleteer denounced the flattering addresses to Richard Cromwell on his succession as emanations of 'the spirit of the Beast and false prophet in the former and present monarchs of this and other nations'.[1] But the reference was still normally to the repressive, persecuting activities of the secular power. When John Goodwin made *A Fresh Discovery of the High Presbyterian Spirit* in 1655, he said: 'a restraint of the press is usually practised where Antichrist hath his throne.'[2] More dramatic extensions of usage were generally the work of radicals: conservatives tended in the fifties to rally to the support of the secular authority—any secular authority—and so to deprecate the use of words like 'antichristian' to describe the government's repressive functions. When Nathanael Homes so labelled persecuting secular powers, Thomas Hall declared that this would be 'good news for Levellers and Fifth Monarchy men'. Proposals for the abolition of 'coercive superiorities' and 'church censures' moved him to exclaim: 'Oh happy Levelling age! oh golden licentious times!'[3]

[1] [Anon.], *A Second Narrative of the Late Parliament* (1659), quoted in A. Woolrych's introduction to Milton's *Complete Prose* (Yale ed.), vi.

[2] Op. cit., p. 49. Cf. Sir Henry Vane, *The Retired Mans Meditations, or the Mysterie and Power of Godliness Shining forth . . . to the unmasking of the Mysterie of Iniquity* (1655), esp. ch. xiv.

[3] T. Hall, *A Treatise against the Millenaries* (n.d., ? after 1657), pp. 4–5, 51; Nathanael Homes, *The Resurrection Revealed* (1654). Cf. W. Hughes's assize sermon, *Magistracy Gods Ministry* (1652), rejoicing that '(through mercy) we are now fairly quit of' the Levellers, and insisting that the Pope is Antichrist (To the Reader, p. 11). Hughes also published *Munster and Abingdon* (1657), a translation of Sleidan's *History of John of*

On the extremist fringe of the sects Antichrist's name seems to have degenerated into a universal term of abuse. Anabaptists, said the poet Ralph Knevet satirically, see new Antichrists everywhere.[1] Archbishop Ussher, who himself was sure the Pope was Antichrist, spoke ironically of men fathering upon Antichrist whatsoever in church matters did not suit with their humours.[2] 'You fix the name of antichristian upon anything,' Cromwell said irritably to John Rogers in 1655—including tithes.[3] Hooker's point that Antichrist had been called the author of the doctrine of the Trinity was repeated in controversy against the Baptists.[4] Ludowick Muggleton, who believed from 1651 that he and another London tailor were the two witnesses foretold in Revelation 11 who would oppose the Beast, denounced his rival John Robins as that last great Antichrist or Man of Sin. His grounds seem inadequate: Robins 'did present his head only to a gentlewoman in her chamber' and 'gave authority to men and women to change wives or husbands', changing his own wife 'for an example'.[5] For Muggleton the Beast was, more generally, 'the spirit or seed of reason', which 'hath the government of this world given into his hands', and

Leyden, with marginal notes and postscript relating to recent disturbances at Abingdon; and *The Man of Sin: Or a Discourse of Popery* (1677). Cf. p. 124 above.

[1] R. Knevet, *Poems*, p. 34.   [2] Ussher, *Works*, vii, p. 45.

[3] E. Rogers, op. cit., p. 213; cf. p. 206.

[4] T. Blake, *Infants Baptisme Freed from Antichristianisme* (1645), To the Impartiall Reader. For Hooker, see p. 33 above.

[5] L. Muggleton, *A Transcendent Spiritual Treatise* (1711), pp. 8, 11–12. First pub. 1651. Cf. Muggleton, *A True Interpretation of the Eleventh Chapter of the Revelation of St. John* (1751), p. 180 (first pub. 1662); *A True Interpretation of All the Chief Texts of the whole Book of the Revelation of St. John* (1665), p. 128; *The Acts of the Witnesses* (1764), p. 48 (first pub. 1699). Muggleton described the Trinity as 'the work Antichrist',

was found, for instance, in the Lord Mayor of London.[1]

Muggleton (and others) later added the Quakers as having the absolute spirit of Antichrist.[2] The Quaker Margaret Fell in her turn called the doctrine of the Ranters 'the Beast which hath seven heads and ten horns'.[3] In 1665 she declared that John Wigan, then sharing a jail with Quakers, was an Antichrist.[4] George Fox, who married Margaret Fell, was accused of preaching that the Scriptures were Antichrist. He denied saying any more than that they which live not in the life and power of the Scriptures, whilst paying lip-service to them, were antichristian.[5] He did think, on the one hand, that the Beast was the first author of hat-honour;[6] on the other, that Fifth Monarchists were servants of the Beast and Whore.[7] It is hardly surprising that conservatives too saw the radicals generally as

[1] Muggleton, *The Eleventh Chapter of the Revelation*, pp. 117, 123, 192; cf. *The Whole Book of the Revelation*, chs. xxxii–xl, esp. p. 129.

[2] Muggleton, *The Acts of the Witnesses*, p. 116.

[3] M. Fell, *A Testimonie of the Touch-Stone* (1656), pp. 24, 36. I owe this reference to the kindness of Mr. J. F. McGregor.

[4] J. W[igan], *Antichrists strongest Hold overturned* (1665), p. 58. Wigan retaliated by declaring that all who should affirm the light in every man to be Christ were themselves Antichrists (ibid., pp. 42, 52).

[5] [Buttivant], *A Brief Discovery Of a threefold estate of Antichrist*, p. 14. In fact Fox thought the Pope was Antichrist (see p. 31 above). For Quakers on Antichrist see also R. F[arnsworth], *Antichrists Man of War* (1655); Thomas Adams, *An Easter-Reckoning, ... shewing the difference of the Ministery of Christ and the Ministery of ... Antichrist* (1656); James Nayler, *The old Serpents voice, or Antichrist discovered* (n.d.); *Antichrist in Man, Christs Enemy* (1656); *An Answer to some Queries put out by one John Pendarves, in a Book, called Arrowes against Babylon* (1656); A. Parker, *A Discovery of Satans Wiles* (1657), p. 14. For Pendarves see p. 124, n. 1 above.

[6] Fox, *The Lambs Officer* (1659), p. 17; cf. *The Vials of the Wrath of God Upon the seat of the Man of Sin* (1655); *The Great Mistery of the Great Whore Unfolded: and Antichrists Kingdom Revealed unto Destruction* (1659), *passim*.

[7] Fox, *Journal* (1902), i, p. 517.

manifestations of Antichrist. 'The Apostle hath plainly prophesied of that sort of antichristian or false prophets now commonly known by the name of Ranters,' Raunce Burthall had written in 1652.[1] The New Englander John Wilson believed Ranters and Quakers were Antichrists.[2] Presbyterian and Independent ministers of Newcastle upon Tyne thought Quakers were papists and antichristian: 'the very distinguishing doctrines and practices of these men are such as are the main principles of that Man of Sin.'[3]

For Humphrey Ellis, for John Hall of Richmond, and for the brothers Thomas and Edmund Hall, republicans were Antichrist.[4] George Smith in 1654 believed Cromwell had been sent by God as 'the instrument of our deliverance from the designs of an antichristian brood', though this brood was probably popish.[5] Robert Weldon said it was blasphemy to maintain that episcopacy was antichristian; on the contrary, it was lower-class revolutionaries who were antichristian. To usurp any part of sacred power was the highest desperate antichristianism: to take it away was the act of the great Antichrist; and regicide 'is that which gives

[1] R. Burthall, *An Old Bridle for a Wilde Asse-Colt* (1652), title-page.

[2] In *Seventeenth-Century American Poetry*, ed. T. Meserole (New York, 1968), pp. 385–6. Written in 1657 or soon after; cf. [Anon.], *The Path of the Just Cleared* (1655), defending Quakers.

[3] *A Further Discovery of that Generation of Men called Quakers* (1654), quoted by R. Howell, *Newcastle upon Tyne and the Puritan Revolution* (1967), p. 257. Cf. Christopher Fowler, *Daemonium Meridianum, Satan at Noon, Or Antichristian Blasphemies* (1655). This is mostly against John Pordage, but at p. 136 the Quakers are also called antichristians.

[4] Humphrey Ellis, *Two Sermons . . . Preached . . . at Winchester* (1647), pp. 50–72; J. Hall, *Of Government and Obedience* (1654), pp. 356–87; T. Hall, *A Treatise against the Millenaries, passim*; E. Hall, *A Scriptural Discourse*, pp. 158–62.

[5] Smith, *Gods Unchangeableness*, p. 29.

him his ultimate perfection'.[1] Walter Rosewell in 1656 quoted John Cotton's warning that 'the loose doctrine of unconscionable liberty of conscience' would prove 'a back door to let in Antichrist', and agreed with it.[2] Even John Owen thought 'grasping temporal power upon a spiritual account' would prove to be 'the greatest badge of Antichrist'.[3] Joseph Sedgwick in 1653 heartily desired 'that encroaching term of Antichrist and antichristian . . . had its unlimited bounds once somewhat fixed by assigning a conception that might tell us wherein the nature of antichristianism consists'. The words had lost all significance by over-use, or survived only as a term of reproach. 'Everything is antichristian in some or other's mouths.'[4]

Gradually social anxiety and a wearied disillusion drove some conservatives to question the whole search for Antichrist. Edmund Hall, who had been a captain in the Parliamentary army during the Civil War before taking orders, and was Thomas Hall's younger brother, wrote in 1653 *A Scriptural Discourse of the Apostasie and the Antichrist*, with the object of vindicating 'the Parliament's cause from the foul aspersion of antichristianism cast upon it'. 'Some make Antichrist a state,' he said, 'some a particular man, a king or a general.' 'Others give out that Antichrist is like the philosophers' stone, much talked on but never seen yet or known.' 'How many learned scholars, both protestants and papists,

---

[1] *Of Antichrist and the End of the World Exhibited in a Collection of severall Passages out of a Tract, Entituled, The Doctrine of the Scriptures concerning the Seate of Dominion* (1651), pp. 24, 123–9, 141–2, 145–7; cf. E. Hall, *A Scriptural Discourse*, sig. c3ᵛ.

[2] W. Rosewell, *The Serpents Subtility Discovered* (1656), sig. A4ᵛ.

[3] Owen, *Works*, viii, p. 386.

[4] Joseph Sedgwick, *Learnings Necessity*, printed with *A Sermon Preached at St. Maries in the University of Cambridge* (1653), p. 39.

set up a Jack-a-lent of their fancy's framing, and then hoot at it for Antichrist?'[1] Hall himself followed up the broad hint of 'a general' by making his own identification of Antichrist pretty clear: not the Pope or bishops, but a deceiver of the people, who talks like a saint, dissembles much virtue in his conversation, makes use of Scripture testimonies, pretends to work miracles, makes 'large promises of promotion to those that adhere unto him, and others he frights into a compliance by the threats of persecution'. Antichrist is a tyrant who feigns holiness; his followers 'are professors of the Gospel of true religion, but hypocritical and temporary professors'. They have 'humbled themselves into the throne, fasted fine clothes upon their backs, self-denyingly wound themselves into all the great and profitable offices. . . . All the heaven they look at is the wealth and greatness and pleasure of the world.' 'Shall I say any more? . . . Reader, I leave thee wisely to comment upon this too too easy text in this present age.'[2]

We may suspect that the application to Cromwell was somewhat light-hearted. But the initial scepticism about Antichrist is typical. Hall just managed to conform in 1660. Richard Baxter just did not. But he too in 1657 was asking whether the Apocalypse had been properly understood. Protestants, he thought, would be well advised not to lay their opposition to popery chiefly on the dark prophecies of the Revelation,

[1] Jack-a-lent = Aunt Sally.

[2] E. H[all], *A Scriptural Discourse*, sig. c3ᵛ, pp. 26, 38, 80, 147–51. Hall makes what I believe is a reference to the royalist story that Cromwell had sold his soul to the devil: 'Some learned men say Antichrist shall be a great magician or sorcerer; to this I could add a strange story, which I received from a person of honour: but to avoid all occasions of offence, I forbear it' (pp. 146–7).

or on the identification of Antichrist.[1] So conservative divines came round to the scepticism which had long ago been formulated by Ben Jonson and repeated by Cleveland and other royalist pamphleteers.[2] Their thought came to move parallel with a strain of academic scepticism illustrated by Robert Burton's citation of those who gave as an example of religious melancholy: 'some foretell strange things *de statu mundi et Antichristi*.'[3] Sir Thomas Browne thought the 'common sign drawn from the revelation of Antichrist is as obscure as any', and like Edmund Hall quoted Paracelsus's reference to Antichrist as 'the philosophers' stone in divinity'. He thought attempts to interpret the number 666 'ridiculous anagrams'.[4] John Selden declared that those who denounced bishops as antichristian were as mad as those who proclaimed their divine right: 'all is as the state pleases.'[5] Thomas Hobbes in *Leviathan* saw no argument that proved the Pope to be Antichrist, and thought that the latter had not yet come[6]—though Hobbes was as much against papal (or any ecclesiastical) authority as anyone. A pamphlet of 1659 ruefully confessed that 'the godly party of this nation, with the state, hath been led forth in a peculiar way of acting against the world and against Antichrist', which had isolated them from their brethren.[7]

One thing which had helped to create this isolation was the attack by some of the radicals on universities

[1] Dr. Williams Library MS., quoted by Lamont, *Godly Rule*, p. 32.

[2] See pp. 60–2 above.

[3] Burton, *Anatomy of Melancholy* (Everyman ed.), iii, p. 312.

[4] Sir T. Browne, *Religio Medici* (1643), in *Works* (Bohn ed.), ii, pp. 367, 392–3.   [5] J. Selden, *Table Talk* (1847), p. 25.

[6] Hobbes, *Leviathan* (Pelican ed.), pp. 580–2.

[7] [Anon.], *The Interest of England in the Protestant Cause* (1659), p. 19.

and classical learning as antichristian. To this there was a long history. Universities had been closely associated with prelatical government of the church, and with social privilege. Tyndale had referred to those who could 'but read a little Latinly', so as to stumble through the neck verse, as 'ready to receive the Beast's mark'.[1] Barrow thought that the universities were the guardians of Antichrist's throne, and Latin the language of the Beast.[2] The latter view Henoch Clapham attributed to the Arian Baptist Legate (who was burnt in 1612), and Ben Jonson to Zeal-of-the-Land Busy.[3] The position gained some intellectual standing by Bacon's attack on Aristotle as antichristian.[4]

The universities had 'lost not a little of the countenance of the state', one of their defenders admitted in 1652, 'for giving too much countenance to . . . doctrines . . . generally suspected of holding intelligence with Antichrist'.[5] Both Oxford and Cambridge were purged of royalists and drones in the 1640s, but the universities still came under fierce onslaught from radicals. University-trained ministers are the Man of Sin, Winstanley thought.[6] Universities and their antichristian tithes, said John Canne, were a nursery 'not of Christ's but of Aristotle's and the state's ministry'.[7] In the

[1] Tyndale, *Expositions*, p. 243. Cf. J. M. Headley, *Luther's View of Church History*, pp. 207–8.

[2] Barrow, op. cit. i, p. 352, ii, p. 221.

[3] Clapham, op. cit., pp. 40–2; Jonson, *Bartholomew Fair*, Act IV, sc. iv.   [4] See p. 29 above.

[5] George Kendall, *A Vindication of the Doctrine Commonly Received in the Reformed Churches* (1653), Dedication to Heads of Cambridge Colleges. The reference is to Arminianism: Kendall is trying to smear Laud and John Goodwin with the same brush.

[6] Sabine, op. cit., p. 240; cf. p. 474.

[7] J. Canne, *The Time of the End*, sig. A4^v–6^v.

controversy between Collier and Thomas Hall in 1651–2, the former declared that it was 'the spirit of Antichrist that seeks out after human helps' like Latin, Greek, and Hebrew, to compensate for lack of the spirit of Christ. 'If Latin be the language of the Beast', Ferriby retorted, Collier used two whole words of it.[1] Henry More attacked those who denounced Galen as Antichrist.[2] Now episcopacy has been destroyed, Edward Waterhouse moaned in 1653, what remains to learning but the universities and tithes?[3] (Any man who at this period begins by praising learning is certain to end by defending tithes.) Nathaniel Stephens believed that 'they who take away human learning do what in them lies to reduce [i.e. restore] the antichristian times'.[4] Richard Farnsworth denounced one of his adversaries as having 'learnt by Antichrist's methodical way in his school'.[5] Richard Coppin was proud to be able to claim that he had not learnt to preach at 'Oxford and Cambridge or the schools of Antichrist'.[6] Erbery thought that 'persecution of the church of Christ sprang up and began from a company of priests by the suggestion

[1] Collier, *The Pulpit-Guard Routed*, p. 25; Ferriby, *The Lawfull Preacher*, p. 53. For Latin as 'the language of the Romish Beast', see also *Mercurius Rhadamanthus* (11–18 July 1653), p. 25, quoted by D. Veall, *The Popular Movement for Law Reform, 1640–1660* (Clarendon Press, 1970), p. 192.

[2] More, *Enthusiasmus Triumphatus* (1656), p. 147.

[3] Waterhouse, *An humble Apologie for Learning*, p. 91. Cf. [Anon.], *A Vindication of Learning From unjust Aspersions* (1646); H. More's letter of 12 March 1649 to William Petty, printed by C. Webster, 'Henry More and Descartes: Some New Sources', *British Journal for the History of Science*, iv, pp. 369–72.

[4] Stephens, *A Plain and Easie Calculation*, p. 269.

[5] R. F., *Antichrists Man of War*, pp. 53, 55; Cf. G. Fox, *The Lambs Officer* (1659), pp. 2–3, 7, 15.

[6] Coppin, *Truths Testimony*, p. 16. Cf. Henry Stubbe's reference to 'antichristian universities', in *A Light Shining out of Darknes* (1659), p. 145.

of university doctors'.[1] In 1656 a Fifth-Monarchist group vowed to execute vengeance upon the universities, among many other institutions.[2]

But the most formidable attack on the antichristian universities and all they stood for came from the Master of Gonville and Caius College, William Dell. To attain knowledge by studies and human learning, and not by inspiration, carried the visible mark of Antichrist.[3] 'One of the grossest errors that ever reigned under Antichrist's kingdom' was 'to affirm that universities are the fountain of the ministers of the gospel.'[4] This belief made universities 'the throne of the Beast in these nations'. 'Academical degrees and ecclesiastical ordination . . . have poured forth into the church whole swarms of false prophets and antichristian ministers.' 'Antichrist and his spirit have remained in their full strength' in Cambridge, notwithstanding their great defeats elsewhere.[5] Dell quoted Hus (or whoever wrote his chapter headings) as calling universities 'the lieutenants of Antichrist'; Luther called them 'stews of Antichrist'.[6] Degrees, Dell thought, were antichristian too.[7] Dell's views not unnaturally upset the dons. On 1 May 1653 Joseph Sedgwick preached a sermon in St. Mary's against him and those who make 'the very foundation of the universities . . . a piece (nay the top) of their imaginary antichristianism'. Sedgwick suggested

---

[1] *The Testimony of William Erbery*, p. 86.

[2] Toon, *Puritans, the Millenium and the Future of Israel*, p. 73.

[3] Dell, *Sermons*, pp. 600, 555; cf. p. 641.

[4] Id., *The Stumbling-Stone*, in *Sermons*, p. 403.

[5] Id., *The Tryal of Spirits*, in *Sermons*, pp. 496, 517, 526.

[6] Id., *A Plain and Necessary Confutation of . . . Mr. Sydrach Simpson*, in *Sermons*, pp. 552–3.

[7] Id., *A Testimony of the Word against Divinity Degrees* (1653), in *Sermons*, pp. 615–27.

that 'the spirit of enthusiasm' was much more anti-christian.[1] And of the Master of Gonville and Caius he asked pertinently: 'Is the university stipend, as paid to a divine, antichristian maintenance? Then under what capacity do Mr. Dell and his associates enjoy their places in Cambridge? . . . With what conscience can any Christian knowingly take the wages of Antichrist? I do not understand much honesty in cheating the Man of Sin of his money.'[2]

Dell's theory has interesting analogies with Winstan-ley's. Both use the word Antichrist to describe every-thing that is catholic in theology and that is associated with the state church in politics. The universities are 'the throne of the Beast' because they produce the ideologists who justify this system. Even if they are themselves good and honest men, university-trained parsons, and incumbents in receipt of tithes, are bound to be corrupted. Artisans and tradesmen must be allowed to preach, in their spare time and from their own inner experience. There is no national solution short of separation of church and state, abolition of tithes, the end of all compulsory authority in religion and of attempting to train a separate clerical caste at universities. There are analogies between these views and those of radical critics of the universities today. Winstanley associated Antichrist with the gentry and with private property in a way that Dell never did, though he too thought covetousness and self-love mostly to blame. But Winstanley would no doubt have

[1] J. Sedgwick, *A Sermon Preached at St. Maries in the University of Cam-bridge* (1653), pp. 11–12.
[2] Sedgwick, *Learnings Necessity to an able Minister of the Gospel* (1653), p. 39 (continuous pagination with the above).

accepted much of Dell's more elaborate analysis of the ideological functions of universities.[1] Both envisaged a future in which the whole educational system should be widely extended, democratized, laicized, and made more scientific.[2] 'The use of human learning in this reformed way' would dissolve the greatest errors of Antichrist, would lead to the fall of the Beast.[3]

VII

The idea that Antichrist is an internal spirit, which Erbery developed so interestingly, runs parallel throughout our period with the doctrine that he is an individual or institution. It starts with Tyndale and Bale, whose concept of Antichrist was the most radical among the English reformers. Antichrist is not an outward thing, wrote Tyndale. 'Antichrist is now, and shall (I doubt not) endure till the world's end.' He has reigned for fifteen hundred years, 'and we not aware'. He can disguise himself as a saint.[4] Bale denied that Antichrist was to be born at the latter end of the world. There is 'one general Antichrist . . . which hath reigned in the church in a manner since the ascension of Christ'.[5] Whitgift too spoke of Antichrist working from the earliest times, though for him Antichrist operated through heretics and sectaries.[6] Henoch Clapham in 1608 attributed to a Familist the statement that Christ and Antichrist were not real persons but fashions of mind;[7]

---

[1] Sabine, op. cit., pp. 238–43, 474–6, 569–70; Dell, *Sermons*, pp. 516–17, 525–38, 554–6.

[2] Sabine, op. cit., pp. 562–6, 577–8; Dell, *Sermons*, pp. 642–8.

[3] Dell, *Sermons*, p. 647; Sabine, op. cit., p. 570.

[4] Tyndale, *Doctrinal Treatises*, p. 42.

[5] Bale, *Select Works*, p. 442.   [6] Whitgift, *Works*, ii, pp. 181–2.

[7] Clapham, op. cit., p. 46.

in 1623 it was reported that Familists said sin was Antichrist come to life when Adam sinned.[1] Thomas Beard devoted a chapter of his *Antichrist the Pope of Rome* to proving that Antichrist was a man, not an abstraction.

This latter idea was extended in the 1640s, like most other ideas. George Wither in 1643 observed that

> While some pursue the Antichrist without them
> An Antichrist ariseth up within them.[2]

John Jubbes in the Putney Debates thought he could not distinguish 'whether the spirit of God lives in me or no, but by mercy, love and peace, and on the contrary whether the spirit of Antichrist lives in me but by envy, malice and war'.[3] Joseph Salmon and Richard Coppin believed the 'carnal spirit . . . working in the natural man . . . is that great Antichrist, that Man of Sin, which exalts and sets up himself in the highest room, in the heart and mind of man'.[4] Gerrard Winstanley wove this Familist doctrine into his new philosophy. The power of darkness is not to be sought at Rome or in a local hell: it is within mankind, indeed in the whole Creation.[5]

The Quakers adopted a similar interpretation. 'Antichrist is in every man', wrote James Nayler in 1656, 'until he be revealed by the light of Christ within.'[6] In the disillusionment of 1659 Edward

---

[1] Edmond Jessop, *A Discovery of the Errors of the English Anabaptists* (1623), pp. 88–9, quoted by Burrage, op. cit., i, p. 212.

[2] Wither, *Campo-Musae*, p. 25.

[3] Woodhouse, *Puritanism and Liberty*, p. 99.

[4] Salmon, *Anti-Christ in Man*, sig. A2ᵛ, pp. 2, 10; Coppin, *Divine Teachings: in Three Parts. Part II, Antichrist in Man* (1653), pp. 28, 99.

[5] Sabine, op. cit., pp. 215–34, 456–7.

[6] Nayler, *Antichrist in Man, Christs Enemy* (1656), p. 2. This was a reply to Joshua Miller's *Antichrist in Man the Quakers Idol* (1655), 'wherein he

Burrough observed that the kingdom of Antichrist had in many things received a mortal wound in England. Yet the oppressive laws of the false church were not rooted out, 'but the rather have seemed to be revived again'. The established ministry was antichristian. After the restoration he declared that Antichrist is not a particular visible person, but an invisible spirit: the Devil in fact, though he often appears to the world as a zealous church-member, a saint. 'The government of Antichrist is in the hearts of men', extends over the governments of many nations, manifesting itself in injustice, idolatry, persecution. All persecutors, and all merely verbal professors of Christ, are Antichrist.[1] In New England around 1661 a discussion about Antichrist and the Pope led a poet to write:

> The whore that rides in us abides,
> A strong Beast is within;
> Able to bear the finest ware,
> There lives the Man of Sin . . .
> Alas, we may, most of us, say
> We're stones of Babel's tower . . .
> If Antichrist be dead within
> We need not fear the Man of Sin.[2]

The Man of Sin 'as God sitteth in the temple of God' (2 Thessalonians 2: 4). Men long interpreted this as referring to the Pope at Rome; then they thought of it as the exercise of civil power in ecclesiastical matters, persecution for conscience sake; but when a Quaker

confesseth Antichrist to be in man, but denies the light of Christ within to be sufficient to reveal him' (Nayler's title-page). See Miller, op. cit., esp. p. 32.

[1] Burrough, op. cit., pp. 584–5, 596, 869–78.

[2] Anonymous poem printed in *Seventeenth-Century American Poetry*, pp. 510–11.

could declare that he was 'a church himself and the temple of the living God',[1] it was easy to see Antichrist sitting in that temple. First in Rome, then in the Church of England: now he was in the heart of every man and woman.

This internalization of Antichrist diluted the radical political doctrine of which Winstanley's had been the most advanced form: it links up with the Quaker pacifism of the later seventeenth century. On the other hand, the depersonalization contains dangerous possibilities for traditional Christianity, as Henoch Clapham and Ephraim Pagitt noted. The Familists, they declared, affirm sin to be Antichrist and righteousness to be Christ, turning Christ and Antichrist into qualities, making Christ a mere fiction or fantasy.[2] The way was open to deism. Meric Casaubon suggested in 1669 that Lord Herbert of Cherbury was trying 'out of the religions of mankind to extract a religion that should need no Christ . . .'.[3] It would also need no Antichrist.

[1] *V.C.H. Oxfordshire*, ii, p. 49; cf. *Anti-Christ in Man*, 'Thy heart is that temple of God where this great Whore sitteth' (p. 10).

[2] See pp. 142–3 above; E. Pagitt, *Heresiography* (5th ed., 1654), p. 86.

[3] *A Letter of Meric Casaubon D.D. &c. to Peter du Moulin D.D.* (Cambridge, 1669), p. 17. My attention was drawn to this passage by Quentin Skinner's 'Thomas Hobbes and the Nature of the early Royal Society', *Historical Journal*, xii (1969), p. 231.

IV

AFTER 1660: ANTICHRIST IN MAN

Take heed of computation. How woefully and
wretchedly have we been mistaken by this!

JOHN OWEN, *The Use of Faith, if Popery should
return upon us* (1680), in *Works*, ix, p. 510.

I

THE Restoration brought back a state church and the
censorship. Henceforth it is very difficult to know how
far the apparent rapid decline in use of the symbolism
of Antichrist is a reality, how far an optical illusion
caused by suppression. It is hardly surprising that
specific association of monarchy with Antichrist, such
as had been made by John Goodwin, Colonel Goffe,
and other Army leaders, by George Foster and other
Levellers, by Gerrard Winstanley and Fifth Monarchists,[1] is no longer heard after 1660. It was safe
enough for a broadsheet to depict Oliver Cromwell
joining the hands of Pride and 'the antichristian
Pontiff of hell', in a marriage whose offspring were
antichristian sectaries.[2] 'We need not go so far as Rome
to look for Antichrist in St. Peter's chair,' the astrologer
John Gadbury jeered in 1664: 'we may find him at
home in the conventicles of our Dippers.' Anabaptists,
like the Man of Sin in Thessalonians, try to get

[1] See pp. 104–5, 109–10, 116–17, 120 above.
[2] [Anon.], *The True Emblem of Antichrist* (n.d., ? after 1660), single
sheet.

proselytes by feigned miracles and prodigies.[1] That was cheap and easy.

A few brave radicals took the risk of publishing attacks on the state church. Cornet Christopher Cheesman, in *An Epistle to Charles the Second, King of England* (1661), declared that 'a forced uniformity in matters of God's worship, and the hireling ministry, are . . . not of Christ but of Antichrist', whether the form be Presbyterian or Episcopalian.[2] In 1664 an anonymous rhyming pamphlet declared that prelates and church courts pleased Antichrist.[3] John Owen believed the popish church-state was antichristian, but now considered Antichrist was a doctrine rather than a person.[4] George Wither, another brave man, denounced Restoration intolerance as 'antichristian tyranny'. He still expected to see the defeat of Antichrist in 1666, or at latest 1700. In the earlier year he urged Charles II to join in alliance with continental protestants against the Beast, to expedite his fall.[5]

But a great deal of rethinking had to be undertaken. John Bunyan, like John Owen, regretted 'the forward-ness of some . . . who have predicted concerning the time of the downfall of Antichrist, to the shame of them and their brethren'.[6] But Antichrist remained, even if

[1] John Gadbury, *A Brief Examination of that Nest of Sedition and Phanatick Forgeries Published by Mr. H. Jessey* (1664), p. 23.

[2] In *Harleian Miscellany* (1744–6), vii, pp. 431, 433.

[3] [Anon.], *Antichrist Unhooded* (1664), sig. B2, p. 6; cf. *Erastus Junior* (1660), by Josiah Webb, 'a serious detester of the dregs of the anti-christian hierarchy'.

[4] Owen, *Works*, iii, p. 63 (1674); xiv, pp. 547–55 (1682).

[5] Wither, *Meditations Upon the Lords Prayer* (1665), p. 180; cf. Hensley, *Later Career of George Wither*, pp. 68, 143.

[6] Bunyan, *Works*, ii, p. 59. For Owen see epigraph to this chapter. Cf. S. Palmer, *The Nonconformist's Memorial* (1775), ii, p. 501.

the time-table for his fall did not. Bunyan among
others continued to speak of penal laws and other
human constraints on worship as being of Antichrist,
including state interference in such matters. Antichrist
—the Pope, and religious persecution of the godly in
any state—must be destroyed. It was the duty of the
magistrate] to defend God's people from Antichrist;
indeed 'Antichrist shall not down but by the hand of
kings'—a reminiscence of earlier Baptist appeals to
James I, and a tribute to the strength of the doctrines
preached in Bucer's *De Regno Christi*. Ever mindful of
the censorship, picking his words with painful care,
Bunyan observed that 'the afflicted church of Christ . . .
hath lain now in the dungeon of Antichrist for above a
thousand years'.[1]

But Antichrist's name was less and less frequently
mentioned, in print at all events. Henry More, who in
1664 published *A Modest Enquiry into the Mystery of
Iniquity*, shows us one reason for this silence. He felt it
necessary to apologize for so 'ignoble, inglorious and
ungenteel' an undertaking. The subject has declined
socially, and now gentlemen are unwilling to 'soil your
pen with the names of Antichrist and antichristianism,
of which the breath of the rude and ignorant vulgar
usually smells as strong as of onions and garlic'. The
lower classes 'have so fouled these words by their
unmannerly mouthing of them without all aim, that
they have made them now unfit to pass the lips of any
civil person'.[2] That might almost be the epitaph on

---

[1] Bunyan, *Works*, i, p. lxxi; ii, pp. 59, 61–2, 73–8; iii, p. 409; cf. i,
p. 237, iii, pp. 227, 521, 524. A preacher at the Presbyterian Morning
Exercise in 1675 took up a similar position (ed. N. Vincent, *The Morning-
Exercise against Popery* (1675), pp. 80–104). See pp. 59, 80 above.

[2] More, op. cit., sig. A3^v.

Antichrist in England. Once second only in importance to Jesus Christ,[1] he had now sunk so low as to be unrespectable as well as iniquitious. It also tells us a lot about the new standards of values in Restoration England. Compare a social sneer on Oliver Cromwell published in 1666:

> A drayman that knows nought but yeast
> Set in a throne like Babylon's red Beast.[2]

More's treatise, on which he had no doubt been working for many years when the subject was more fashionable, lists all the well-worn arguments to prove that Rome rather than the Church of England is Antichrist. He believed that 'the reformed parts of Christendom are the empire of Christ and the real Fifth Monarchy', which 'assuredly began with the Reformation'. Monarchy and episcopacy, Moses and Aaron, had conveniently been restored in England in 1660, the very last year of the Christian and antichristian periods of the church. 'Can there be a more fit fulfilling of the prophecy of the resurrection of the witnesses than this?' Desperate sectaries, therefore, who reject 'a healing and uniting design in the true church of Christ' are 'led by the spirit of Antichrist', and play his game.[3] That could do no harm to the established order. Samuel Lee's *Antichristi Excidium* of 1664 and his *Israel Redux* of 1677 even more conventionally asserted the Pope to be Antichrist. So, perhaps more surprisingly,

---

[1] Cf. John Cotton's reference to Antichrist's rise in the social scale in 1642, p. 74 above. See also p. 2 above.

[2] G. Alsop, *A Character of the Province of Maryland* (1666), quoted in *Seventeenth-Century American Poetry*, p. 450.

[3] More, op. cit., sig. A6, pp. 195–204; *The Apology of Dr. Henry More* (1664—continuous pagination), pp. 563–6.

did the republican Henry Neville in *Plato Redivivus* (1681)[1]—though he uses it in an argument against clerical pretensions. Isaac Newton and Thomas Burnet (*Telluris Theoria Sacra*, 1681) had no doubts of the identification. The ninth Earl of Argyll had nothing to lose when in 1685, just before his execution, he asked the Dean of Edinburgh if he thought the Pope was Antichrist. On receiving an affirmative response the Earl adjured him: 'Be sure you instruct the people so.'[2]

Most frequently in the post-Restoration period we meet with jeers in the Jonson–Cleveland tradition at the routed Puritans.[3] Thus Samuel Butler mocked at Hudibras's reference to bear-baiting as antichristian.[4] Dryden, at the time of the Popish Plot, asked ironically: 'Was there no fear of Antichrist or France?'[5] If opposition continues, in a few years

> Religion, learning, wit would be suppress'd,
> Rags of the Whore, and trappings of the Beast.[6]

There's Antichrist behind to pay for all.[7]

Literary references to Antichrist seem normally ironical henceforwards, and become less frequent. The Popish

[1] Ed. C. Robbins, *Two English Republican Tracts* (Cambridge University Press, 1969), pp. 116, 118.

[2] J. Willcock, *A Scots Earl in Covenanting Times: . . . Archibald, Ninth Earl of Argyll (1629–85)* (Edinburgh, 1907), p. 417.

[3] Cf. [Anon.], *The Cloud opened: Or, The English Hero* (1670), in *Harleian Miscellany*, iv, pp. 143, 154: Presbyterians accused of supporting, for political reasons, an impostor whom under different circumstances they would have denounced as an Antichrist.

[4] Ed. J. Wilders, *Hudibras* (Oxford University Press, 1967), pp. 24, 147–8. The caricature is not too wild, since cruelty was one of Antichrist's marks.

[5] Dryden, Prologue to Nathaniel Lee's *Caesar Borgia* (1679).

[6] Id., Prologue at Oxford to Elkanah Settle's *The Female Prelate* (1680).

[7] Id., Prologue to Thomas Southerne's *The Loyal Brother* (1682).

Plot no doubt helped to deflate Antichrist as a serious concept, though Oldham's lines

> Louder than on Queen Bess's day the rout
> For Antichrist burned in effigy shout[1]

seem to imply that the Beast still retained more popularity than the printed word would suggest. As late as 1682 Richard Steere published *The History of the Babylonish Cabal*. This anti-catholic piece, dedicated to the Earl of Shaftesbury, contains four of the most remarkable lines, from the point of view of prosody, in the whole of English literature. It is Darius reluctantly sentencing Daniel to the lions' den. He sobs:

> Ah Da-Da-Daniel, whom I lo-lo-love
> Thy de-de-death must the-the-thee remove;
> The se-se-sentence I cannot deny,
> Dear Daniel, thou m-m-m-m-must die.[2]

Benjamin Keach (*Antichrist Stormed*) and Hanserd Knollys (*Exposition of the Whole Book of the Revelation*) in 1689 applied the prophecies of the Apocalypse to William's invasion. The year before a pamphlet had traced *The Pedigree of Popery, or the Genealogy of Antichrist* in a very unamusing way;[3] another referred in 1695, not very respectfully, to those who thought all government antichristian.[4] We may believe there were such: but their views were not printed. How far they continued

---

[1] 'The Thirteenth Satire of Juvenal, Imitated' (1682), in *Poems of John Oldham* (1960), p. 174. Elizabeth's accession day, 17 November, was long celebrated, together with 5 November, as a day of anti-catholic demonstrations.

[2] Steere, op. cit., p. 25. I have not seen his *Antichrist Display'd* (1682), mentioned by Mr. H. T. Meserole in *Seventeenth-Century American Poetry*, p. 247.   [3] In *Somers' Tracts*, iv, p. 232.

[4] H. Maurice, *An Impartial Account of Mr. John Mason of Water-Stratford* (1695), p. 1.

to be muttered underground we can only guess. William Blake, who inherited so much of the seventeenth-century revolutionary tradition, described the younger Pitt's censorship in 1798 by saying: 'The Beast and the Whore rule without control.'[1]

As for the Church of England, it was natural that it should continue the retreat, begun by the Laudians, from the traditional view that the Pope was Antichrist. Weldon during the interregnum said that the identification had been a case of misplaced zeal.[2] The very influential Henry Hammond denied that the Pope was Antichrist, suggesting Simon Magus instead.[3] Griffith Williams, Bishop of Ossory from 1641 to 1672, announced in 1660 that Antichrist was neither Pope nor Turk but the Westminster Assembly of Divines. The number 666 might refer either to Oliver Cromwell or to the Long Parliament.[4] John Bramhall, Laud's protégé, for his Doctorate of Divinity in 1630 had defended the thesis that the papacy was the cause of all greater controversies in the Christian world. But in 1649 he observed, 'It were worth the enquiring whether the marks of Antichrist do not agree as eminently to the Assembly General of Scotland as either to the Pope or to the Turk'.[5] The protestants 'have defined nothing

[1] Blake, *Poetry and Prose* (Nonesuch ed., 1927), p. 949; cf. pp. 731–3, 764–6: 'the outward ceremony is Antichrist.' Cf. A. L. Morton, *The Matter of Britain* (1966), pp. 83–121, and p. 164 below.

[2] *Of Antichrist and the End of the World . . . in a Collection of Severall Passages, out of a Tract* (by R. Weldon) (1651), p. 110. For Weldon see A. G. Matthews, *Walker Revised* (Oxford, 1948), p. 247.

[3] H. Hammond, *Dissertationes Quatuor* (1651), pp. 1–51, and *De Antichristo; A Paraphrase and Annotations Upon all the Books of the New Testament* (1653), pp. 715, 718, 875–6.

[4] Williams, *The Great Antichrist Revealed* (1660), *passim*.

[5] J. Bramhall, *A Fair Warning to take Heed of the Scottish Discipline* (1649), in *Works* (1842–5), iii, p. 287.

concerning Antichrist; howbeit some particular persons have delivered their private opinions with confidence'. The Pope may be an Antichrist, 'yet it doth not follow that every bishop under his jurisdiction is formally antichristian'.[1] Bramhall paraphrased Laud: 'I dare not swear that the Pope is that great Antichrist, but I dare swear that I never had any design to bring Popery into England.'[2] So far from episcopacy being 'an antichristian innovation and a rag of Popery', it was 'the most gross schism' to make such an accusation.[3]

Bramhall, who died in 1663, was one of the most powerful figures among the royalist exiles and in the restored Church of England. Gilbert Sheldon, Archbishop of Canterbury from 1663 to 1677, was the man who had scandalized Oxford Calvinists before the Civil War by publicly maintaining that the Pope was not Antichrist. His view now prevailed. Almost the last seventeenth-century bishop to denounce the Pope as Antichrist was John Owen's former tutor, Thomas Barlow, appointed to the see of Lincoln in 1675 against Sheldon's opposition.[4] Henry Jones, who preached a *Sermon of Antichrist* in 1676, was only an Irish bishop,

[1] Bramhall, *Protestants Ordination Defended*, in *Works*, v, pp. 256–8 (written 1644–54, pub. posthumously in 1676). Cf. *Works*, ii, p. 582.

[2] Id., *Vindication of Himself and the Episcopal Clergy from the Presbyterian Charge of Popery as it is managed by Mr. Baxter in his Treatise of the Grotian Religion*, in *Works*, iii, p. 520 (written 1659–60, pub. posthumously in 1672). For Laud see pp. 36–7 above.

[3] Bramhall, *Replication* to the Bishop of Chalcedon, in *Works*, ii, p. 71.

[4] T. Barlow, *Brutum Fulmen* (1681), esp. pp. 152–213; *Letter to the Earl of Anglesey* (1684), in *The Genuine Remains of That Learned Prelate Dr. Thomas Barlow* (1693), pp. 190–201; cf. p. 228. Barlow explicitly rejected the views of Grotius and Hammond (*Brutum Fulmen*, p. 173). He had written in favour of limited toleration for Jews under the Protectorate (Barlow, *Several Miscellaneous . . . Cases of Conscience* (1692)).

who had been Scoutmaster-General to the English army in Ireland under the Commonwealth and later was a supporter of Shaftesbury. He was consciously setting himself against the prevailing trend in maintaining that the Pope was Antichrist, and had in fact nothing new to say on the subject.[1] In 1655 the astrologer William Lilly had predicted that long before 1663 the opinion that the Pope was Antichrist would be exploded out of both universities.[2] For once he proved to be right. It is interesting that the tide was running so clearly in that direction as early as 1655. Here too we are at the end of a story.

II

In attempting to draw conclusions, my problems are first to explain the rapid, kaleidoscopic evolution of the content of the Antichrist myth, culminating in the 1640s and 1650s; and secondly to explain its no less rapid disappearance after 1660. In the sixteenth and early seventeenth centuries the conviction that the Pope was Antichrist helped to strengthen defensive sentiments of national solidarity focused on the monarchy: Antichrist was in Rome, the safest protection against his machinations was Drake and the navy. Then more men came to stress the conviction, originally confined to a few sectaries, that Antichrist was in England, was the bishops, perhaps the whole national church, and was protected by the antichristian royalist party. The dramatic happenings of the early forties transformed the battle against Antichrist from defensive to offensive, rousing utopian hopes, especially in the

[1] Op. cit., sig. B3.
[2] W. Lilly, *The Astrological Judgments* (1655), sig. A4^v.

classes hitherto excluded from politics. The disappoint-
ment of these hopes, the social decline of interest in
locating Antichrist, the dangers of Fifth-Monarchist
revolution against him, led the respectable to abandon
the search for him altogether, and led disillusioned
sectaries to place him within the human heart rather
than in ecclesiastical or political institutions. *What*
happened is clear enough. But *why* did it happen?

The prominence of Antichrist and the end of the
world are normally associated with social and political
crisis—in the fourteenth century, in the age of the
Reformation, and in the English Revolution. In
seventeenth-century Russia, shaken by Cossack revolt
and religious schism, Patriarch Nikon and Tsar Alexis
were denounced as precursors of Antichrist, who was
expected in 1666. Peter the Great was thought to be
Antichrist himself. Antichrist reappeared before and
during the Russian Revolution: Old Believers attacked
Lenin as Antichrist. The latter is not unknown in
twentieth-century Africa.[1] The identification of the
enemy as Antichrist produced a black–white simplifica-
tion which was excellent for morale. ('The more our
persuasions are that we fight against the Beast, and the
nearer we conceive his fall to approach, the stronglier
we may conclude that the contrary power shall
overcome.')[2] The symbol of Antichrist had the further
advantage that it would cover a multitude of different
enemies.

[1] See Appendix I below. One of the few modern theologians to write
seriously about Antichrist was Paul Schutz, who published *Der Antichrist* in Nazi Germany in 1933 (repr. 1949, and in part in his *Gesammelte
Werke*, 1963). Cf. the opening sentence of Tolstoy's *War and Peace*.

[2] See p. 85 above. Cf. Wadstein, op. cit., pp. 154–8, on Antichrist
and crisis.

Protestant reformers inherited two traditions: first, that the Pope was Antichrist, secondly that the whole ecclesiastical structure was antichristian. There was no necessary contradiction between these two traditions so long as the English church was papal. But after the Reformation an attempt was made to isolate the identification of the Pope with Antichrist. The printing press and the protestant emphasis on preaching helped to broadcast this rapidly. Sixteenth-century governments in England gladly accepted the identification, and it was given a historical dimension by Foxe's *Acts and Monuments*. Inevitably the hierarchy shied away from the more radical interpretations which can also be found in Foxe's work. So long as national unity survived, the godly prince was its focus against the dangers from antichristian Pope and Spain. The dividing of the ways first appears towards the turn of the century, with the decline of the foreign danger and therefore of enforced unity. Sects began to denounce the state church as antichristian; bishops retorted by proclaiming the divine right of episcopacy. James I succumbed to the necessities of foreign policy, and played down the doctrine which he had earlier proclaimed, that the Pope is Antichrist. Arminians began in the 1620s to question the identification on theoretical grounds, since they were anxious to stress the apostolic succession, and they, like the government, feared the increasingly subversive tendency of attacks on the church as totally antichristian. It was men of Presbyterian leanings—Napier, Brightman—who began to introduce a time-table for the fall of Antichrist in the near future.

The emergence in the seventeenth century of

doctrines of the divine right of kings and of bishops provoked fundamental questions. For the opposite of antichristian rule is not royal or episcopal government, but the rule of Christ. If king or bishops claim a divine right to rule against Christ and his people, this shows that they are antichristian. One aspect of the seventeenth-century nostalgia for the reign of Good Queen Bess was that the Queen was believed to have subordinated bishops to the civil power: it was worth tarrying for such a magistrate. But Charles I accepted the divine right of episcopacy, and so seemed to many to align himself with Antichrist.

So the allegedly pro-papist bishops and government, and the royalists generally in the Civil War, became 'the antichristian party'. The collapse of hierarchy and government led to freedom of organization and propaganda for the separatist sects, who used it to denounce *all* ecclesiastical power. Victory in the Civil War raised millenary expectations which were disappointed by the Westminster Assembly of Divines and by a rapid succession of governments. Presbyterians too persecuted the godly: any state church came to be denounced as antichristian. Many sectaries, all thinking they monopolized the rule of Christ, condemned not only the state church but all rival sects as antichristian: some republicans saw the institution of monarchy as antichristian. The instant revolution of the Fifth Monarchists combined the two in something very like a theory of anarchism. Winstanley carried the attack over from monarchy to the gentry and the property system in general. Conservatives, who wanted only Parliamentary control over a state church, not its dissolution, still less a democratic republic or dictatorship of the godly, rallied to any attempt to restore discipline and order. Faced with Vavasor Powell's question, would the Lord 'have Oliver Cromwell or Jesus Christ to rule over us?', they finally decided that God was against godly rule, and opted first for the Protectorate of Cromwell, then for the consensus of Charles II's restoration. King and bishops came back to drive Antichrist out of politics. For once the revolutionary decades had shown how very radical the quest for Antichrist could become, conservatives began to draw back from the attempt to identify him at all. Radical protestants continually postponed the date of Antichrist's fall, finally abandoning the time-table altogether, and with it the hope of realizing Christ's rule by a change of institutions. They came more and more to think of Antichrist as a spirit rather than as a person. From both wings, for very different reasons, interest in him seems to have lapsed, swiftly and almost finally. After 1660 the Church of England dropped the identification of Pope and Antichrist. The sects accepted that Christ's kingdom was not of this world, and so ultimately ceased to look for an antichristian enemy in this world either.

The practice of occasional conformity by conservative dissenters demonstrated that they did not think the Anglican church antichristian; the defeated sects asked only for the right to coexist in a pluralism of religious communities. The erastian scepticism of a Selden or a Hobbes militated against *any* ecclesiastical power. Scientific rationalism and expediency were posed against enthusiasm. In thirty years of tight censorship after 1660, political uses of the myth of Antichrist virtually disappear. And indeed: bishops as restored in

1660 had lost most of the lordly, antichristian characteristics denounced in 1640–1. 'The iron teeth of the
Beast' were not restored, and 'the sting of abused
excommunication' never recovered its former venom,
even for the lower classes.[1] Persecution of sectaries was
conducted by the gentry in Parliament and as J.P.s, not
by the church. The fact that the quest for Antichrist
turned out to be a blind alley, and the disillusion which
resulted, must have had a great deal to do with the
collapse of revolutionary fervour after 1660. Too many
eggs had been put into that basket.

Antichrist was not seriously used against James II.
When bishops opposed a popish king, where indeed
was Antichrist? All that remained, on the surface at
least, was a continuing tradition among conservative
dissenters that the Pope was Antichrist. But the date of
his fall had continually to be postponed. The 1690s
came and went; Jurieu's date of 1710–15 also passed.[2]
Samuel Lee in 1677 predicted that the ruin of Antichrist would be amply manifest around 1736, and that
the millennium would come in 1811.[3] Antichrist disappeared into the nonconformist underworld, ultimately
into the world of cranks. Aleister Crowley, who in the
twentieth century saw himself as the Great Beast, was
born of parents who were Plymouth Brethren: it was
his mother who first recognized him for what he was.[4]

[1] See pp. 74–5 above. Cf. my *Society and Puritanism*, pp. 353, 374–81.

[2] G. H. Dodge, *The Political Theory of the Huguenots of the Dispersion*
(Columbia University Press, 1947), pp. 35–8.

[3] S. L[ee], *Israel Redux*, pp. 111–22; cf. *Antichristi Excidium* (1664), sig. b7,
pp. 183–93. Under William III Bishop William Lloyd still expected
the conversion of the Jews and the fall of Antichrist in the near future
(Evelyn, *Diary*, 26 April 1689, 13 April and 18 June 1690, 16 April 1699).

[4] John Symonds, *The Great Beast: the Life of Aleister Crowley* (Panther
ed., 1952), pp. 8–11.

What we are discussing here is a great revolution in thought, which we feebly call the separation of religion from politics. It is associated with (or contemporaneous with) the decline of belief in witches and hell, with the rise of religious toleration, with a rapid spreading of Arminianism at the expense of Calvinist theories of an oligarchy of the elect, with a decline in the authority of the Bible, with the emergence of rationalism and deism. But the mechanics of this intellectual mutation have been insufficiently examined. The obviousness of the conclusion, once arrived at, has prevented us from appreciating the difficulties of the journey. It was not merely that all men suddenly became wiser. *Tantum religio potuit suadere malorum* was an old adage. We must probe deeper than the sufferings which religion caused in these centuries to explain the cessation of wars of religion, and ultimately of persecution and witch-burning. It is connected, of course, with the seventeenth-century scientific revolution, in which—as Sir Herbert Butterfield expressed the same problem—mankind 'put on a different kind of thinking-cap'.[1] All I can hope to do by this case study is to throw a little light on the larger problem. But first I should like to make one or two simpler points.

III

One important aspect of the Antichrist myth is its contribution to the Englishman's sense of history. Bale saw the protestant reformation prophesied in Revelation.[2] The time-tables worked out by Napier, Bright-

[1] H. Butterfield, *The Origins of Modern Science, 1300–1800* (1949), p. 1; cf. Lamont, *Godly Rule*, pp. 174–6.

[2] Bale, *The Two Churches*, in *Select Works*.

man, and others were convincing because they were based on an agreed interpretation of history for which Foxe's great work had laid the basis. (Nor was the idea of a time-table new: Joachim of Flora and his followers had one, focusing on the year 1260; Servetus thought 1565 the crucial year; Melanchthon prophesied the fall of Antichrist for 1588.)[1]

Foxe, Bale, and others drew on Joachim, and William Perkins quoted him to show that the Pope was Antichrist.[2] John Penry, Henry Barrow, and William Gouge looked back to Wyclif's struggle against 'the thick dark cloud of antichristianism'.[3] Dell cited Wyclif, Hus, and Luther; John Rogers quoted Hus.[4] Stephen Marshall and Richard Byfield gave their Parliamentary congregations a great deal of post-Reformation European history.[5] Protestants never tired of quoting Pope Gregory I's denunciation in 595 of John, Patriarch of Constantinople, as a forerunner of Antichrist because he had aspired to be a universal priest and only chief bishop.[6] The Waldenses and other heretical predecessors were frequently referred to as authorities.[7] Even

[1] M. Reeves, op. cit., esp. pp. 43–54, 234, 303, 486, 502; Garret Mattingly, *The Defeat of the Spanish Armada* (1959), p. 159.

[2] Reeves, op. cit., pp. 107–8, 489.

[3] Waddington, *John Penry*, p. 149; for Barrow see pp. 52–5 above; W. Gouge, *The Progress of Divine Providence* (1645), pp. 32, 35: a sermon preached before the House of Lords.

[4] See pp. 98, 127, 140 above; E. Rogers, op. cit., p. 82.

[5] Marshall, *The Song of Moses*, esp. pp. 15–22; Byfield, *Zions Answer to the Nations Ambassadors* (1645), pp. 29–30: a sermon preached to the House of Commons.

[6] Foxe, op. cit., i, p. 340; Francis Dillingham, *A Disswasive from Poperie* (1599), p. 6; Bramhall, *Works*, i, pp. 32, 253; ii, p. 134; v, p. 252.

[7] John Mayer, *Ecclesiastica Interpretatio* (1627), p. 428; T. Goodwin, *Works*, iii, pp. 81, 87–8; J. Owen, *Works*, viii, p. 263; Durham, *A Commentarie Upon the Book of Revelation* (1658), pp. 501–4.

Bramhall cited the Waldensian view that the Pope was Antichrist, though naturally unfavourably.[1] The medieval controversies between Pope and Emperor enabled the Geneva Bible, Foxe, and John Cotton to quote Dante and Petrarch in support of the view that the Pope was Antichrist;[2] Duplessis-Mornay, John Mayer, Abbott, Bedell, and Milton quoted Petrarch alone.[3] The Levellers were to make much of the heretic succession in their propaganda; so did a Baptist like Praisegod Barebone, so did John Bunyan.[4] The heretic tradition was valuable precisely because of its ambiguities. Before the Reformation Antichrist could be either the Pope or the whole established clergy. After the Reformation there were two alternative interpretations, one conservative, the other revolutionary: but it was often to the advantage of radicals to blur them.

Protestantism, with its concentration on the Pope, shed many of the popular legends which had accreted round the figure of Antichrist. Foxe quoted Walter Brute, tried for heresy in 1392, not only to this effect but also as criticizing some of the applications of Scripture to Antichrist. Brute queried the identification of the Second Beast in Revelation 13 with Antichrist, and the

[1] Bramhall, *Works*, i, p. 451; Barlow, *Brutum Fulmen*, pp. 170–2, 210–12.

[2] Geneva Bible, note on Revelation 14: 6; Foxe, op. cit. ii, pp. 706–8; F. A. Yates, 'Queen Elizabeth as Astrea', *Journal of the Warburg and Courtauld Institutes*, x, pp. 43–6; P. Miller, *The New England Mind: the Seventeenth Century*, pp. 467–8.

[3] Mornay, *A Notable Treatise of the Church*, sig. Uiiii; J. Mayer, *Ecclesiastica Interpretatio*, p. 428; ed. N. Bernard, *Certain Discourses* (1659), p. 123— a sermon by Bedell in 1634; G. Abbott, *The Perpetuall Visibilitie . . . of the True Church* (1624), p. 81; Milton, *Complete Works* (Columbia ed.), iii, p. 27. Cf. p. 16 above.

[4] *A Reply to the Frivolous and impertinent Answer of R. B. to the Discourse of P. B.* (1643); Bunyan, *Works*, iii, p. 429.

relevance to him of many of the prophecies of Daniel: but he had no doubt that the Pope was Antichrist.[1] This foreshadows a stricter protestant biblical scholarship, which gave the equation of Antichrist with the papacy an apparently scientific basis as well as a long pedigree. In time such biblical criticism was to contribute to the drift towards scepticism, and so to the disappearance of Antichrist;[2] but this was far ahead.

Antichrist contributed to the sense of history in yet another way. The time-tables of Napier, Brightman, Mede, Archer put the rule of Christ on earth in the near future. This gave a utopian perspective for political action.[3] At the same time men like Bacon and Hakewill were beginning to defend the Moderns against the Ancients in the great controversy which runs through the seventeenth century. Both millenarians and the protagonists of the Moderns contributed to a theory of historical progress, as against traditional cyclical theories, or theories which put the golden age in the past.

One example of such a myth is the Norman Yoke, which I discussed some years ago. There are parallels between this myth and that of Antichrist. Here too a theory used by the respectable Parliamentarians (the King has invaded the liberties of freeborn Englishmen: we must restore the ancient Anglo-Saxon constitution and common law) was transformed by lower-class revolutionaries into its opposite (our very laws were

[1] Foxe, op. cit. iii, p. 63.

[2] D. C. Allen, *The Legend of Noah* (Urbana University Press, 1963). ch. iii; D. Bush, *Science and English Poetry* (Oxford University Press, 1967), p. 59.

[3] Lamont, *Godly Rule*, draws attention to this point. Cf. E. L. Tuveson, *Millennium and Utopia* (New York, 1949), pp. 79 seq.

made by our conquerors, all existing laws must be abolished). The free Anglo-Saxons, however, survived the Restoration, and were used again by eighteenth- and nineteenth-century radicals, even if in a muted form.[1] But Antichrist died in 1660, at least as an intellectually respectable theory. I asked myself Why?

The first answer is that he did not in fact die then. M. Vereté tells me that there was a revival of interest in Antichrist from about 1760 onwards.[2] A print of 1762 depicted Lord Bute as the Beast.[3] This interest was intensified by the French Revolution. A tract of 1809 republished a pamphlet of 1701, which prophesied that Antichrist would be exceedingly weakened, though not destroyed, between the years 1794 and 1848.[4] These years, from the French Convention to the proclamation of the Roman Republic, were in fact bad years for the papacy. A pamphlet of 1795, *Antichrist in the French Convention*, saw the end of the 1,260 years coming in 1796, with the Second Beast rising in France against papal power.[5] Many English millenarians proclaimed

[1] See my *Puritanism and Revolution*, pp. 50–122. The sleeping kings whom I discuss on pp. 55–6 were expected to rise and lead armies of the faithful against Antichrist.

[2] See p. 165, n. 1 below.

[3] Ed. F. G. Stephens, *Catalogue of Prints and Drawings in the British Museum, Division I, Political and Personal Satires*, iv, no. 3983. I owe this reference to the kindness of Professor Herbert M. Atherton of Yale.

[4] R. Fleming, *An Extraordinary Discourse on the Rise and Fall of the Papacy* (1809), pp. 18, 46, 54. The millennium would start in A.D. 2000.

[5] Op. cit., esp. pp. 13, 23, 30. *The French Revolution Foreseen in 1639* (1796) reprints extracts from Thomas Goodwin's *Exposition of the Revelation*. John Owen's sermon quoted on p. 105 above was reprinted in 1793, 1794, and 1861 (Toon, *Puritans*, p. 30). Cf. also the prophecies of Richard Brothers and others in the 1790s, quoted by E. Thompson, *The Making of the Working Class* (Penguin ed.), pp. 127–9.

that the French Revolution had ushered in the latter days: the fall of the papacy, the destruction of the Turkish Empire, and the return of the Jews were eagerly expected. The overthrow of the Papal States and Napoleon's Egyptian campaign lent themselves to interpretation in this context.[1] So similar circumstances of revolutionary crisis led to a revival of the ideas of the 1640s. There was also, parallel to the Saxonism of some nineteenth-century radicals, a new emphasis on the identification of the Pope with Antichrist among evangelicals alarmed by the popish tendencies of the Oxford Movement. Newman discussed this with becoming seriousness in Tract 83, and he and J. H. Todd fought over again the great battles of the seventeenth century.[2]

Still, as a serious popular political force it must be admitted that Antichrist lacked the staying-power of the free Anglo-Saxons. This can largely be attributed

[1] I owe these points to M. Vereté's 'The Idea of the Restoration of the Jews in English Protestant Thought, 1790–1840', in *Zion*, xxxiii, pp. 145–79. The article is in Hebrew, but there is an English summary. I have also benefited greatly from discussion of the subject with M. Vereté. For a list (incomplete) of identifications of the Man of Sin, see W. Bornemann, *Die Thessalonicherbriefe, ein kritisch-exegetischer Kommentar über das Neue Testament* (Göttingen, 2nd ed., 1894), pp. 400–59, 538–708.

[2] J. H. Newman, *The Patristical Idea of Antichrist* (1835), in *Discussions and Arguments on Various Subjects* (1872), esp. pp. 55–70; *The Protestant Idea of Antichrist* (1840), in *Essays Critical and Historical* (1872), ii, esp. pp. 158–73; J. H. Todd, *Discourses on the Prophecies relating to Antichrist in the Writings of Daniel and St. Paul* (Dublin, 1840), *passim*; *Six Discourses on the Prophecies relating to Antichrist in the Apocalypse of St. John* (Dublin, 1846), *passim*. Cf. R. W. Church, *The Oxford Movement* (1891), i, pp. 46–8; R. W. Hunt, 'Newman's Notes on Dean Church's Oxford Movement', *Bodleian Library Record*, viii, pp. 136–7; cf. B. Jowett, *Excursus on the Man of Sin*, in his commentary on *The Epistles of St. Paul to the Thessalonians, Galatians, Romans* (2nd ed., 1859), i, pp. 178–94.

to general changes in the political climate between the seventeenth and nineteenth centuries. Neither Pope nor bishops were significant political enemies by the time radicalism revived in the later eighteenth century. The Norman Yoke was a class as well as a patriotic theory: the aristocracy was Norman. Antichrist, as we have seen, could be put to the use of class politics; but his main role had been to identify a foreign enemy and his fifth column in England. In the nineteenth century he is the Pope and little else.

I thought at one time of arguing that personification of the enemy is especially characteristic of a pre-industrial civilization, just as Mao Tse-tung derived the Stalin cult from the peasantry's need for a father image.[1] One thinks of the appeal from the king's evil councillors to the king himself, which betrayed the rebels of 1381, 1536, and 1549, and was still operative in the 1640s. One thinks of our Lord Jesus on horseback in Scotland in 1639, hunting and pursuing the Beast. One thinks of Oliver Cromwell's effigy lying in state, and being visited, like Lenin's, by large crowds of simple people. One thinks of the Duke of Monmouth, the improbable leader of the last peasant revolt in England, the last of this country's sleeping heroes. Many of the commentators on Antichrist are very anxious to *prove* that he was a person, not simply an abstract quality, as he became after our period: this annihilated his *political* significance. But this explanation will not go very far. Many later societies, including our own, found it necessary to personify the enemy, whether as Boney, as Kaiser Bill, or as Adolf Hitler.

[1] Quoted by Rudolf Schlesinger, 'Marxist Theory and the New Programme of the Soviet Communist Party', *Science and Society*, xxvi, p. 147.

IV

The main importance of Antichrist, after all, is in theology. To this we must now turn.

When I discussed Antichrist with a group at the University of East Anglia, and tried to suggest some reasons for his rise and fall in sixteenth- and seventeenth-century England, a member of the audience reminded us that Antichrist's prominence in these centuries is paralleled and caused by the prominence of Christ in theology. This simple point is obvious once it is made, though I had missed it. These are the great centuries of justification by faith in Christ alone, succeeding a period in which salvation had been obtained through the ceremonies and sacraments of the church, succeeded by a period in which works, morality, were to be re-emphasized as against justifying faith alone. Historically the belief in Antichrist was strongest amongst those protestants who most strongly emphasized justification by faith and were most hostile to the ecclesiastical establishment and its ceremonies; it survived after 1660 among the less intellectual salvationist nonconformist sects. For the classical protestant reformers Christ was our only king and priest. Christ and his people, the elect, are aligned against the rest, against Antichrist and his synagogue. Those most conscious of Antichrist held a predestinarian theology, including a belief that the elect minority could be assured of their salvation.

The perseverance of the elect, the impossibility of falling from grace, was proclaimed in the *Homilies* of the Church of England, in countless Puritan catechisms, by John Penry as well as in Whitgift's Lambeth Articles.[1]

---

[1] *Homilies*, p. 317. One of the catechisms of which this is true was bound

Hobbes thought the doctrine appealed especially to the urban middle class.[1] Assurance of election was 'a mighty and powerful preservative against Antichrist's apostasy', declared William Bradshaw in a posthumous treatise published by Thomas Gataker.[2] The crucial texts about Antichrist in John's Epistles were also held to be among the crucial texts about predestination. 'The Jesuit is troubled at this place,' said one commentator of 1 John 2: 18 ff., 'making so plainly for the perseverance of the elect.'[3] The two are linked.

But if men could be assured of their own salvation, could they not be sure about the status of other men and women? Were not the elect visible, to be identified on earth? This question of the possibility of identifying the godly remnant split the Calvinist movement. The sects (and the churches of New England) held that the godly should organize themselves voluntarily in their own churches, utterly distinct from the antichristian institutions of the English church: the hierarchy began by having doubts about the visibility of the elect[4] and ended in scepticism about the predestinarian theology as a whole, and about Antichrist. The first theoretical questioning of the identification of the Pope with Antichrist came from Arminians who also questioned the predestinarian theology. Both were discussed at the

up with many sixteenth-century Bibles (Strype, *Annals*, iii, p. 239). For Penry's confession of faith, see Burrage, op. cit. ii, p. 81.

[1] Hobbes, *Behemoth*, in *English Works* (1839–45), vi, pp. 194–5.

[2] W. Bradshaw, *A Plain and Pithy Exposition of the Second Epistle to the Thessalonians* (1620), pp. 136–40. Cf. my *Puritanism and Revolution*, pp. 248–9—John Preston; and Sibbes, *Works*, vi, pp. 388–9, 479–83.

[3] J. Mayer, *Ecclesiastica Interpretatio, or The Expositions upon the Different and Doubtful Passages* [of the Epistles and Revelation] (1627), p. 193. Cf. J. Owen, *The Doctrine of the Saints Perseverance* (1654), in *Works*, xi.

[4] Cf. Latimer, p. 10 above.

crucial York House Conference in 1626. In the long run they stood or fell together.

The revolutionary decades saw the brief flourishing and the equally rapid collapse of revolutionary Calvinism in England. Its logic and its contradictions come out fully only in circumstances of revolutionary crisis. The doctrine that Christ alone rules over the elect, that Antichrist has no power over them,[1] is ultimately a doctrine of anarchy: the individual (or the congregation) is subordinate to no earthly authority, but only to the holy spirit within. This built-in anarchy of protestantism, and especially of the doctrines of assurance of grace, of the visibility of the elect, so closely associated with the belief in Antichrist, revealed itself in England once 'the antichristian party' had been overthrown. One could indeed argue that one of the advantages of the symbol of Antichrist, in the 1640s as in the 1530s, was to conceal divergences: men could agree in calling the Pope or Laud Antichrist whilst having very different views about what Christ wanted.

In the 1640s and 1650s somebody could see every government, nay every rival sect, as antichristian. The higher and more utopian the standards of the godly, the less attainable on earth, the more frightening to the ruling class (e.g. the attack on the antichristian universities). Hobbes's diagnosis of the society in which he lived as self-destructively competitive unless controlled by a sovereign authority came to be accepted by the soberer of his contemporaries.[2] (Hobbes's state of nature drew so powerfully on Calvinist doctrines of the

[1] See pp. 56, 85 above.
[2] Though Bishop Duppa called Hobbes's political theory antichristian (Routledge, *Calendar of Clarendon State Papers*, v, p. 641).

sinfulness of natural man that it was widely acceptable once godly rule had been tried and found wanting.) Winstanley's diagnosis—that the rule of the men of property was antichristian—was a logical alternative, and it was a diagnosis towards which much of radical protestantism had tended, with its emphasis on the poor and humble as Christ's chosen people.[1] But Winstanley's theory ran up against the facts of social life in England, inevitably dominated by the gentry, the ignorance of the masses of the population, and the impossibility of organizing them politically. Even in the New Model Army, the only focus of organization for the lower classes, the generals managed to keep control out of the hands of political radicals. The Leveller leaders themselves rejected Winstanley's communism.

Emphasis on Antichrist has its advantage in time of acute crisis because of the simple Manicheanism of the doctrine: the world is divided into black and white, Christian and Antichristian. What seems to us the more sophisticated view, which sees good and evil, Christ and Antichrist, in every man, appears to gain popular acceptance only when the crisis is over.[2] Winstanley was about the only significant thinker to suggest that Antichrist might be both internal and external, the rule of the propertied *and* the spirit of covetousness within each of us. He had grasped what appears to

[1] Cf. Marshall, Thomas and John Goodwin, cited on pp. 81, 83–5, 88–9 above. Also Perkins and others quoted in my *Society and Puritanism*, pp. 259–97.

[2] I am speaking here of the level to which the Quakers and other sectaries appealed. The poets' conception of man's 'double heart' spoke for the sophisticated at a rather earlier date, as they became conscious of deep divisions in their society (see my *Puritanism and Revolution*, pp. 341–2, *Reformation to Industrial Revolution*, p. 161).

moderns the essential point, that the external battles themselves related to the internal contradictions.[1] But this insight was not followed up: the internalization of Antichrist among the later seventeenth-century sectaries is associated with an abandonment of political goals.

The institutional changes following the end of civil war failed to bring utopia: Cromwell was denounced as Antichrist no less than Charles I. Some radicals turned to the violent methods of the Fifth Monarchists in order to achieve what a more peaceful approach had failed to gain. Others came to think that the continuing omnipresence of evil must be due to the fact that Antichrist had been wrongly located. The kingdom of Antichrist, like the kingdom of heaven, was within each individual. This was parallel to the theological universalism, the proclamation of Christ within every man, that the Quakers took over from earlier religious radicals. Thus the Arminianism of the right, of Montagu, Sheldon, and the Laudians—associated with clericalism and a sacramental theology—was complemented by an Arminianism of the left, a reaction against the oligarchy of the elect and towards a democratization of salvation, together with a revival of interest in justifying works, in morality.

So men no longer saw two armies lined up, Christ's elect against the synagogue of Antichrist, 'the antichristian party': the Holy War is conducted inside each believer. So long as the elect were a minority, their rule on earth was impossible without divine intervention, without violence. Once salvation is open to all, once Christ and Antichrist are in all men, the

[1] But cf. Eugenius Eirenaeus Philalethes, William Dell, and Milton's intriguing reference to Antichrist as 'Mammon's son' (p. 119 above).

problem changes its pattern. Revolutionary Calvinist theology was replaced by a new emphasis on works, on morality; this led to the segregation of the spiritual, the separation of church and state, the end of millenary dreams of the rule of the elect, to that pacifism and withdrawal from politics after the Restoration of which the Quakers are the most obvious example. Erbery accepted the fact that he lived in Babylon, and waited for deliverance. The glorious utopian hopes had all ended in nothing. If Antichrist was in everyone, in the elect as well as in the antichristian party, he was no longer a political target. He disappeared from practical politics. If he is in every man, he is indistinguishable from Satan, from the general force of evil. Christ in every man perhaps has a role to play *vis-à-vis* God, but if Antichrist ceases to be a person, he ceases to exist. Whether the decline of predestinarian theology caused the fall of Antichrist, or the end of belief in Antichrist expedited the decline of predestinarian theology, or whether some third cause must be found for both effects—these are questions I cannot now try to answer.

Meanwhile, at the opposite pole, the propertied Parliamentarians were scared back to acceptance of episcopacy. The weakness and political ineffectiveness of the alleged popish fifth column had been revealed during the Civil War; it was a paper tiger.[1] The Thirty Years War in Europe had ended without an antichristian alliance against England resulting; indeed, the Pope had ceased to be a figure of any significance in international affairs. Calling the Pope Antichrist had

[1] See Robin Clifton, 'An Examination of the fear of Catholics and of Catholic plots in England, 1637 to 1645, with principal reference to central sources' (unpub. Oxford D.Phil. thesis, 1967).

helped to build up a *defensive* patriotism under Elizabeth. But the extraordinary manifestation of English strength under the Republic and Protectorate, when first the Dutch, then the French and Spaniards, were successfully browbeaten, made it clear that England was no longer on the defensive in international affairs. The motives for an international crusade against Antichrist vanished just at the moment when it might have become a political possibility.

Antichrist lost his *raison d'être* as commercial rivalries between protestant powers cut across the division of Europe into two religious camps. 'Is not the state of Holland and Commonwealth of Venice as much for Antichrist as the King of France or Spain?' Erbery had asked.[1] One Dutch retort is found in a print of 1656, which showed Oliver Cromwell as Antichrist, riding a seven-headed Beast.[2] Here too, if Antichrist was everywhere, he was nowhere. In the 1620s the denial that the Pope was Antichrist had gone together with rejection of the international Calvinist foreign policy, with a *penchant* for counter-reformation absolutism. But after 1660 absolutism was as unacceptable to those who mattered in England as was a protestant crusade. Some of the last vocal defenders of the view that the Pope was Antichrist were those who were trying in the 1660s to revive the idea of an international protestant alliance.[3] The danger to sober propertied protestants now came not from Antichrist in Rome or his fifth column in England, nor from antichristian bishops, but from the indiscipline of the lower classes, too often encouraged by sectarian willingness to denounce as

[1] See p. 130 above.
[2] *Kort Beworp vande dry Tighenwoordighe Aenmerkens-Weerdige Wonderheden des Wereldte* (1656). [3] See pp. 147, 149–50 above.

antichristian what their betters regarded as the most essential institutions of society: even a state church and the rule of the gentry.

Looking back, we may perhaps see a new depth in Marx's dictum that 'the English Republic under Cromwell shipwrecked in Ireland'.[1] For at many stages in our story Ireland was vital. The Revolt of 1641 confirmed men's belief that an international antichristian conspiracy against England existed, in which at least Henrietta Maria, if not the King, was involved. The revelation of Charles's Irish intrigues after Naseby finally completed his ruin. From 1647 to 1649 desperate efforts were made to divert the energies of the rank and file of the New Model Army from internal English politics to the reconquest of Ireland. Ultimately, under Cromwell's leadership, they succeeded. It is difficult not to believe that part of the motive force behind the Irish campaign was the revolutionary utopian millenarianism which we have been considering. The regiments in Ireland remained the most radical in the English army. The campaign there was conducted with a savagery such as Stephen Marshall had recommended to those fighting against Antichrist.[2]

Yet in retrospect the Cromwellian conquest of Ireland looks less like a religious crusade than the first of those colonial wars which were to occupy England for the next two and a half centuries. It was followed by the Navigation Act, proclaiming the existence of the British Empire as a single economic unit, enforced by the first Anglo-Dutch War. John Owen, who had

[1] K. Marx, Letter to Dr. L. Kugelmann, 29 Nov. 1869.
[2] See p. 81 above.

observed the Man of Sin in Ireland in 1649, in 1652
thought the protestant Netherlands had joined the antichristian interest when they went to war with England.[1]
If we can believe Henry Stubbe twenty years after the
event, the Barebones Parliament declared that 'Antichrist the Man of Sin could never be destroyed in Italy
whilst the Dutch retained any considerable strength in
the United Provinces'.[2] It was more plausible to see
Antichrist at work among Irish papists than in the Calvinist Netherlands; yet the fact that the radical regiments were persuaded—contrary to the advice of some
Levellers[3]—to go hunting for Antichrist in Irish bogs
certainly contributed to the shipwrecking of their cause
in England. A remote consequence is that Northern
Ireland is one of the few places in the world where
Antichrist is still alive today.

Against this wholly black mark for Antichrist we may
perhaps set the relative absence of anti-semitism in
England. One explanation for this is the absence of
Jews from England between 1290 and 1656. Another is
that protestants rejected the medieval theory retained
by sixteenth- and seventeenth-century catholic theologians—that Antichrist had not yet come and that when
he did come he would be a Jew. We can see how easily
the association of Jews with the tortures and atrocities
expected to characterize Antichrist's future period of
rule could lend itself to anti-semitic overtones—not only

[1] Owen, *Works*, ix, pp. 216, 401, 505; viii, pp. 235, 382.
[2] H. Stubbe, *A Further Justification* (1673), quoted by C. R. Boxer,
'Some Second Thoughts on the Third Anglo-Dutch War, 1672–1674',
T.R.H.S., 5th ser., vol. 19, p. 80. Cf. John Canne's warning, quoted on
p. 121 above. Cf. also my *Puritanism and Revolution*, p. 326, and references
there cited.
[3] *Puritanism and Revolution*, p. 142, and references there quoted.

in Roman Catholic countries, and not only in the seventeenth century. The most notorious of all anti-semitic forgeries, *The Protocols of Zion*, was originally published in Russia in the revolutionary year 1905, in a volume entitled *Antichrist as an Imminent Political Possibility*.[1] In revolutionary England, on the contrary, where Antichrist was believed already to have come, the conversion of the Jews seemed an essential pre-liminary to the next items on the agenda—the fall of Antichrist and the millennium. This could be expedited either by invading the Holy Land with John Robins and Theaureaujohn[2] or more prosaically by admitting the Jews to Christian England, as Cromwell did.

So I wish to relate the rise and fall of Antichrist to the evolution of the fundamental doctrines of protestantism as well as to the development of the crisis of the sixteenth and seventeenth centuries. Which is another way of saying that the evolution of the theology must also be related to the economic and social history of these centuries.

The Antichrist myth goes back to the beginnings of Christianity, if not further. But its essential content also looks forward. I have barely hinted at modern analogies, and this is no place to develop them. The reader interested in the comparative history of revolutionary ideologies should find much in my story that is worth pondering. Joseph Caryl, for instance, warned the House of Commons, as early as April 1642, 'we are short-breathed and short-sighted, and so very apt to antedate the promises in regard of their accomplishment'.[3] He might—with slight changes in idiom

---

[1] See Appendix I (ii) below.   [2] See p. 115 above.

[3] J. Caryl, *The Workes of Ephesus explained in a Sermon before the Honourable House of Commons* (1642), pp. 24–5.

—have been any socialist speaking of Marx's forecasts at any time during the present century. Marx too had his 'vulgar Fifth Monarchists', his impatient Venners: though so far Marx has lasted better than Brightman and Mede. 'Men fight and lose the battle', William Morris wrote, 'and the thing that they fought for comes in spite of their defeat, and when it comes, turns out not to be what they meant, and other men have to fight for what they meant under another name.'[1] Under other names Antichrist has outlived even the memory of those who so earnestly laboured to date his final overthrow.

Finally, I am conscious that I lay myself open to the charge of having stated a pseudo-problem: of having over-emphasized the contortions of a group of clerical intellectuals and lower-class sectaries; of having made more of Antichrist than he warrants. But when we recall the near unanimity of the Elizabethan Church of England; the vigour of Pym's report on Montagu from the House of Commons's Committee on Religion; Mr. Symmons's soldiers, John Goodwin, Gerrard Winstanley, William Dell, and William Erbery; Ireland and anti-semitism, I do not think so. In one sense we have been exploring a trivial blind alley in human thought: but at all points it trembles on the edge of major intellectual issues. Above all, I hope I may have made good the point with which I started, that history is not an exclusively rational process; or if it is, then history's reason must include much which seems irrational to the historian, too obsessed perhaps by the standards of rationality fashionable in his own age and society.

[1] W. Morris, *A Dream of John Ball*, in *Selected Writings* (Nonesuch ed.), p. 214.

APPENDIX I

OTHER ANTICHRISTS

(i) *Roman Catholic views*

I HAVE confined my attention to protestant commentators on Antichrist. Naturally things seemed very different to Catholics. Nicholas Sanders, for instance, thought that to set the temporal power above the Pope, as Henry VIII did, was the very mark and badge of Antichrist, whose coming the Reformation demonstrated.[1] Cardinal Allen agreed that Elizabeth's supremacy was antichristian.[2] But apart from such polemics, and they were many, catholics mostly argued that Antichrist had not yet come. A dangerous radical like Thomas Campanella looked forward to a golden age in the form of a world republic under a regenerated church after the ruin of Antichrist.[3] In general the widespread adoption by respectable protestant scholars of the view that the Pope was Antichrist led Roman Catholic interpreters to lay new emphasis on Antichrist as a Jew—men of great erudition like Ribeira and Alcassar, Bellarmine and Malvenda.[4]

(ii) *A Jew*

In medieval tradition Antichrist was to be a Jew, born in Babylon of the tribe of Dan. He will reign in Israel, rebuild the temple at Jerusalem, and persuade the Jews that he is the Messiah. He will also succeed in deceiving many

[1] N. Sanders, *The Rocke of the Churche* (Louvain, 1567), pp. 517, 824, quoted by F. A. Yates, 'Queen Elizabeth as Astrea', *Journal of the Warburg and Courtauld Institutes*, x (1947), pp. 76–7.

[2] W. Allen, *An Admonition to the Nobility and People of England and Ireland* (1588).

[3] M. Reeves, op. cit., p. 451, quoting Campanella's *Atheismus Triumphatus* (Rome, 1631).   [4] Bousset, op. cit., pp. 131–2.

Christians, though two witnesses will defend the faithful against him until Antichrist slays them. Three and a half years of terrible persecution will follow, until God finally destroys him on Mount Olivet. The millennium will then begin. This mythical biography, attributing many monstrous attributes to Antichrist, seems to have derived from Jewish and apocryphal Christian sources. Hippolytus (writing *c.* A.D. 202) and St. Cyril of Jerusalem (315–86) accept it, and it seems to have enjoyed a good deal of popularity. The legend was summed up by the tenth-century French monk Adso, and taken over by orthodox scholastics like Thomas Aquinas and Albertus Magnus.[1] The identification of the Pope with Antichrist by medieval heretics led to the assumption that Babylon must be Rome, where Joachim of Flora thought Antichrist had already been born.[2]

To combat the papal Antichrist of the heretics, Roman Catholic scholars re-emphasized that the future Antichrist would be a Jew. This version lent itself to anti-semitic overtones, from the fifteenth century, when Messianic expectations among crypto-Jews in Spain were interpreted by the Inquisition as relating to the coming of Antichrist,[3] to *The Protocols of Zion* in 1905. In this last instance, true to type, Antichrist reappeared in a revolutionary crisis.[4] In most

---

[1] The *Epistola Adsonis . . . de Ortu et tempore Antichristi* is printed in Ernst Sacher, *Sibyllinische Texte und Forschungen* (Halle, 1898), pp. 97–107, and in translation in J. Wright, *The Play of Antichrist* (Toronto, 1967), pp. 101–10. Cf. H. Preuss, *Die Vorstellung vom Antichrist im späteren Mittelalter* (Leipzig, 1906), pp. 11–17; Ernst Wadstein, *Die eschatologishe Ideengruppe Antichrist-Weltsabbat-Weltende und Weltgericht* (Leipzig, 1896), pp. 80–158; Joshua Trachtenberg, *The Devil and the Jews* (Yale University Press, 1943), pp. 34, 40; N. Cohn, *The Pursuit of the Millennium* (1957), pp. 58–63, 71–2, 385–6; M. Reeves, op. cit., *passim*; ed. H. Th. Musler, *Der Antichrist und die fünfzehn Zeichen* (Munich, 2 vols., 1970). The Jewish Antichrist was Armilus, thought by some to be a corruption of Romulus.

[2] Wadstein, op. cit., p. 83; Preuss, op. cit., p. 17.

[3] Trachtenberg, op. cit., p. 32.

[4] John S. Curtiss, *An Appraisal of the Protocols of Zion* (Columbia University Press, 1942), esp. pp. 2, 29–31, 66–7.

protestant versions, on the other hand, despite occasional references to 'Antichrist and his synagogue', the Jews play a much less sinister role: their conversion indeed is the prelude to the fall of Antichrist and to the millennium. Brightman had given 1695 as the date for the conversion of the Jews, but Mede and Archer brought it back to 1650–6.[1] Mary Cary, Henry Jessey, John Tillinghast, and Thomas Goodwin, among a host of others, expected it in 1655–8 or by 1666 at the latest.[2] Much controversial protestant energy was therefore spent in proving that Antichrist could not be a Jew, and that he had already come.[3] Only Shelford in 1635 seriously suggested that Antichrist would be a Jew;[4] and Prynne, in an unpleasant pamphlet aimed at preventing the readmission of the Jews, called them deceivers and Antichrists, referring to their 'Jewish antichristian rites and superstitions'. But this was an incidental argument among many others which he brought forward against their readmission.[5]

Commentators have noticed topical references to the conversion of the Jews in Henry Vaughan's poem 'The

[1] Brightman, *A most Comfortable Exposition of . . . Daniel*, in *The Revelation of St. John Illustrated*, esp. pp. 967–8; Mede, *Remaines* (1650), p. 33; Archer, *The Personall Reign of Christ*, p. 48. See p. 108 above.

[2] M. Cary, *The Little Horns Doom and Downfall*, sig. a5, pp. 139–68, 207; Tillinghast, *Generation-work*, Part I, pp. 44–67; Part II, pp. 62–6; Part III, pp. 226–49; T. Goodwin, *Works*, iii, pp. 62–3, 72–5, 157, 195–205. Samuel Hering in 1653 thought 'the Jews' . . . time is near at hand' (ed. J. Nickolls, *Original Letters* (1743), p. 99). Cf. [Anon.], *A Narrative of the Proceedings of a great Council of Jewes . . . on the Twelfth of October, 1650* (1655), in *Harleian Miscellany*, i, esp. p. 375; Owen, *Works*, viii, pp. 374–88. See also pp. 114–15 above.

[3] See, for instance, Brightman, op. cit., pp. 621–40; [Anon.], *A Second Parallel, together with A Writ of Error Sued against the Appealer* (1626), p. 37—one of the pamphlets against Richard Montagu; G. Wither, *Vaticinia Poetica* (1666), in *Miscellaneous Works* (Spenser Soc., 1879), iv, pp. 15–18. Cf. Nicolas Vignier, *L'Antéchrist romain opposé à l'antéchrist juif du cardinal Bellarmine . . . et autres* (1604); Fridericus Balduinus, *Diatribe Theologica de Antichristo* (1615), p. 79.   [4] See p. 38 above.

[5] W. Prynne, *A Short Demurrer to the Jewes* (2nd ed., 1656), pp. 73, 115, 126.

Jews' (*Silex Scintillans*, 1655) and in Cowley's preface to his *Poems* (1656). But they have, I think, missed an overtone of wit in Marvell's lines in 'To His Coy Mistress':

> And you should if you please refuse
> Till the conversion of the Jews.

For most readers the conversion of the Jews might seem as far in the future as Noah's flood was in the past (1656 B.C. was the conventional date); but others expected it in A.D. 1656.[1] The poet's 'vegetable love', growing 'vaster than empires, and more slow', might be overtaken by the end of all empires. The lady might be getting a bad bargain. The fantastic outrageousness of the joke would not be out of keeping with the hyperbole of the first twenty lines of the poem; and Marvell was certainly capable of the ambiguity.

(iii) *The Turk*

In Mediterranean countries the idea that the Turk was Antichrist naturally had some popularity. In England the Turk was less of a menace, but Aylmer and Foxe were prepared to add him to the Pope as Antichrist,[2] and many followed them.[3] But others denied this status to the Turk, since he was not a Christian.[4] Richard Montagu proposed the Turk rather than the Pope as Antichrist.[5] This thesis may have been given fresh currency by a Balliol man, Christopher Angelos, a Greek who had suffered at the hands

[1] See p. 111 above.

[2] John Aylmer, *An Harborowe for Faithful and trewe Subjectes*, sig. Q; Foxe, op. cit. iv, pp. 97–109.

[3] Nathanael Homes, *The Resurrection Revealed* (1654), pp. 86–91; *Writings of Browne and Harrison*, pp. 523–4.

[4] J. Rainolds, *The Discovery of the Manne of Sinne* (1614), p. 14; J. Mede, *The Apostasy of the Latter Times* (2nd ed., 1644), pp. 46–53; J. Durham, *Commentarie Upon the Book of the Revelation* (1638), p. 572. Luther at one point in his *Table Talk* said the head of Antichrist was the Pope and the Turk together. But on another occasion Luther excluded the Turk. He never excluded the Pope (*Table Talk* (1652), pp. 298–9, 312, 325–6).

[5] Montagu, *A New Gagg for an Old Goose*, p. 75; *Appello Caesarem*, pp. 144–9. See pp. 35–6 above.

of the Turks and had it revealed to him in a vision that
Mahomet was Antichrist.[1] 'I cannot blame the poor Greek
for thinking so', said the English translator of Alsted, who
knew Christopher Angelos, 'considering the horrid tyranny
and slavery his countrymen live under, being vassals to the
Great Turk. . . . I rather wonder that there should be found
among us learned men who are abettors of this opinion.'[2]

By contrast, Antichrist figures in Islamic millenarian
doctrines,[3] and reappears in twentieth-century revolutionary versions of them. The identification of European colon-
izers with Djadjdjal (Antichrist) was, in the discreet words
of an English government report of 1927, 'potentially the
most important factor in arousing the ignorant and credu-
lous African Mohammedan to fanaticism and unrest'.[4]

[1] Christophori Angeli Graeci, *De Apostasia Ecclesiae, et de Homine
Peccati, Scilicet Antichristo* (1624), pp. 10–11, 22.

[2] J. H. Alsted, *The Beloved City* (trans. by William Burton, 1643), p. 73,
translator's marginal note. Cf. [Anon.], *A Vindication of Learning From unjust
Aspersions* (1646), pp. 13–14: the Turks as Antichrist.

[3] Marshall G. S. Hodgson, 'A Note on the Millennium in Islam', in
Millennial Dreams in Action, ed. S. L. Thrupp, Comparative Studies in
Society and History, Supplement II (The Hague, 1962), p. 218.

[4] G. F. F. Tomlinson and G. J. Letham, *History of Islamic Political
Propaganda in Nigeria* (1927), i, pp. 10, 62; ii, p. 12. I owe this reference
to the kindness of Mr. Thomas Hodgkin.

APPENDIX II

ANTICHRIST IN AMERICA

THERE is no doubt a lot more to be said about Antichrist in seventeenth-century America, but I am not the person to say it. Here are a few suggestions, over and above those to be found in the body of this book. The founders of the Massachusetts Bay Company intended to erect in New England 'a bulwark against the kingdom of Antichrist'.[1] John Cotton's dangerous disciple Mrs. Sarah Hutchinson concluded that papists could not be Antichrists, since they did not deny that Christ was come in the flesh. After puzzling for some time whether Antichrist could be the Turk only, she had it revealed to her that the ministers of the Church of England were Antichrists, because they did not preach the new covenant.[2] Many referred to England as Babylon.[3] John Eliot, the Apostle to the Indians, and Cotton himself identified Rome with Antichrist; Cotton thought that there was no hope of converting the American Indians until Antichrist was ruined.[4] In 1652 he favourably contrasted the congregational system of government with either the

[1] Cotton Mather, *Magnalia Christi Americana* (Hartford, 1855), i, p. 69, quoted by J. A. De Jong, *As the Waters Cover the Sea* (Kampen, 1970), p. 31.

[2] C. F. Adams, *Three Episodes of Massachusetts History* (Cambridge, Mass., 1892), i, p. 500.

[3] R. C. Simmons, 'Richard Sadler's Account of the Massachusetts Churches', *The New England Quarterly*, xlii, pp. 416–17.

[4] De Jong, op. cit., p. 74; J. Cotton, *The Way of the Congregational Churches Cleared* (1648), in *John Cotton and the Churches of America* (ed. L. Ziff, Harvard University Press, 1968), pp. 274, 276. Cf. Cotton, *The Churches Resurrection, or the Opening of the Fift and sixt verses of the 20 Chapter of the Revelation* (1642) and *The Powring out of the Seven vials: or, An Exposition of the Sixteenth Chapter of the Revelation* (1645).

international Roman church or a national church, each of which

> . . . seems to me to be too near akin
> Unto the kingdom of the Man of Sin:
> In frame and state and constitution
> Like to the first Beast in the Revelation.[1]

The prelates had been the forlorn hope of Antichrist's army, Edward Johnson declared in 1654; the people of New England were the forlorn hope of Christ's army.[2] Like Cotton, he called on the Lord to increase the congregational churches and 'down headlong cast all antichristian power', as well as (this too was 1654) unmasking

> . . . those men that lie in corners lurking
> Whose damned doctrine daily seats advance.[3]

But an unknown R. B. a few years earlier had complained of the intolerance which meant that 'Old England's saints are banished out of New'. 'The Man of Sin's the same' in both countries.[4] A poem of 1681 anxiously asked:

> Shall Antichrist his wound now heal
> By trampling down the common-weal?[5]

Increase Mather became a chiliast some time after 1660, noting that 'but few papists have been chiliasts'.[6]

---

[1] In *Seventeenth-Century American Poetry*, p. 382.

[2] E. Johnson, *Wonder-Working Providence of Sions Saviour . . . in New England* (1654), in *The Puritans*, ed. Miller and Johnson, pp. 160–2.

[3] *Seventeenth-Century American Poetry*, p. 155.

[4] Ibid., p. 395.

[5] Ibid., p. 444. Cf. also pp. 38, 69, 75, 112, 144 above.

[6] P. Miller, *The New England Mind: From Colony to Province* (Harvard, 1953), p. 87. Increase's son Cotton called Louis XIV Antichrist.

APPENDIX III

THE POETS AND ANTICHRIST

SPENSER was associated as a schoolboy with John vander Noot's *Theatre*, whose main object was to denounce the Pope as Antichrist.[1] Spenser himself referred to Rome as that

> great seven-headed Beast,
> That made all nations vassals of her pride.[2]

In *The Faerie Queene* Duessa rode on 'a dreadful Beast with sevenfold head', which the Red Cross Knight ultimately killed.[3] It has been suggested that Spenser's Archimago was intended to be Antichrist; and there is also the Beast in Book V, Cantos x and xi.[4] Apart possibly from Ariel's 'You are three men of sin' in *The Tempest* (III. iii), Shakespeare never refers to the legend. Joshua Sylvester, translating the French Huguenot Du Bartas, naturally identified the Pope with Antichrist. But he also inserted a passage of his own in which he called on 'Ministers of Christ' to 'cease civil wars, war all on Antichrist', whose 'subtle agents' are taking advantage of controversies between protestants to 'sow tares of treason'.[5] George Wither, whom I have frequently quoted, proclaimed the Pope to be Antichrist as early as 1612, in a poem on Prince Henry's death: he still believed this fifty

[1] See pp. 45–6 above.

[2] 'The Ruines of Time', in *Works* (Globe ed.), p. 490; cf. 'Visions of Bellay', ibid., p. 539.

[3] *The Faerie Queene*, Book I, canto vii, stanzas 16–18; canto viii, stanza 6; canto xi, *passim*.

[4] J. W. Bennett, *The Evolution of the Faerie Queene* (Chicago, 1942); J. E. Hankins, 'Spenser and the Revelation of St. John', *P.M.L.A.*, lx, pp. 364–81.

[5] J. Sylvester, *The Complete Works* (ed. A. B. Grosart, 1880), i, pp. 48, 122, 209; ii, p. 16.

years later.[1] Phineas Fletcher thought in 1627 it was time
for the Lord to rise against 'that cursed Beast', 'thy cursed
foe that pro-Christ trophies rears', as he had done in 1588
against the Spanish Armada.[2] George Goodwin also makes
the equation in his Latin elegies, translated into English
satires by John Vicars in 1624.[3]

John Donne has it too, perhaps not entirely seriously, in
Ignatius His Conclave. In his elegy on Mistress Boulstred he
referred to 'all the four monarchies and Antichrist'.[4] George
Herbert was more serious:

> As new and old Rome did one empire twist,
> So both together are one Antichrist.[5]

Milton, whose prose references to the Pope as Antichrist
I have frequently cited, makes no direct mention of the topic
in his English poems. It has, however, been argued that
Satan in *Paradise Regained* would be recognized by contemporaries as representing both Antichrist and prelacy,
foisting worldly distinction upon the church, tempting it to
traffic with supersition, money, secular power.[6] I have tried
to indicate on pp. 150–1 above the decline of poetic as of
other interest in Antichrist after 1660.

---

[1] Wither, *Prince Henries Obsequies* (1612); *Hallelujah* (1857), p. 202—
a hymn for the Fifth of November, first published 1641. Cf. Hensley, *The
Later Career of George Wither*, pp. 68–70. See also pp. 85, 143, 147 above.

[2] P. Fletcher, *The Locusts or Apollyonists* (1627), in *The Poetical Works
of Giles and Phineas Fletcher* (ed. F. S. Boas, Cambridge University Press,
1908), i, pp. 183–5.

[3] G. Goodwin, *Babels Balm* (1624), pp. 4, 20, 101.

[4] J. Donne, *Complete Poetry and Selected Prose* (Nonesuch ed.), pp. 365–6,
407, 244.

[5] G. Herbert, 'The Church Militant'. For William Alabaster, Barnabe
Googe, and Ben Johnson, see pp. 17, 25, 60–1 above.

[6] Howard Schulz, 'Christ and Antichrist in *Paradise Regained*', *P.M.L.A.*,
lxvii, pp. 790–808. Milton mentions the antichristian Pope in his Latin
poem, 'In Salmasii Hundredam' (*Complete Poems and Selected Prose*,
Nonesuch ed., p. 529).

APPENDIX IV

ANTICHRIST AND ASTROLOGY

As one might expect, astrology was linked with Antichrist in the minds of some commentators. Bishop Carleton thought all sound early Christian writers opposed astrology until 'antichristian corruption came in'.[1] John Chamber in 1601 compared magistrates who failed to prosecute astrologers with 'Romish antichristian caterpillars'.[2] A pamplet published in 1649 said that astrology was 'the very knowledge of good and evil'. 'As it were by eating of the forbidden tree, or by whoring with the creatures', man 'maketh his soul the Babylonian Whore sitting upon the Beast'. The remedy was to theologize astrology.[3] Robert Gell preached two sermons to the Society of Astrologers in 1649 and 1650, whose object was to show the harmlessness and indeed the usefulness to Christianity of astrology.[4] An opponent thought that God before the Gospel, and again in the state of Antichrist, 'used the ministry of the elect angels to direct the starry powers'. Only in the millennium will

[1] G. C[arleton], *The Madness of Astrologers* (1624), p. 66. Written against Sir Christopher Heydon 'nearly twenty years ago' and now published by T. V[icars].

[2] Sir Christopher Heydon, Knight, *A Defence of Iudiciall Astrologie, In Answer to a Treatise lately published by M. Iohn Chamber* (1603), p. 489. I have not found the relevant passage in Chamber's *Astronomiae Encomium* (1601).

[3] V. Weigelius, *Astrologie Theologized* (1649), pp. 1, 36, 39–41.

[4] R. Gell, *Stella Nova, A New Starre leading Wisemen unto Christ* (1649); *A Sermon Touching Gods Government of the World by Angels* (1650). Gell was a Fellow of Christ's College when Milton was an undergraduate, and almost certainly married the poet to his third wife in 1663 (W. R. Parker, *Milton, A Biography* (Oxford University Press, 1968), i, pp. 26, 583). For Gell see p. 112 above.

God cease to 'act by starry powers to deceive the nations', when 'the doctrine of Antichrist shall cease, . . . the learning professed in academies of Aristotle, etc.'[1] The associations of astrology and alchemy with Antichrist might be worth investigating further.[2]

[1] John Brayne, *Astrologie Proved to be the old Doctrine of Demons* (1653), title-page.

[2] For alchemy see p. 119 above.

INDEX

PRINTED IN GREAT BRITAIN
AT THE UNIVERSITY PRESS, OXFORD
BY VIVIAN RIDLER
PRINTER TO THE UNIVERSITY

GLASSBORO STATE COLLEGE